TEXAS

From Spindletop Through
World War II

TEXAS
From Spindletop Through World War II

A Sequel Volume to
TEXAS: FROM THE FRONTIER TO SPINDLETOP

JAMES L. HALEY

St. Martin's Press
New York

976.4
Hal

ISBN 0-312-09401-9

First Edition: June 1993
10 9 8 7 6 5 4 3 2 1

To Greg, for his
encouragement, and to
Wallis, for his nagging.

Contents

Acknowledgments

IN preparing this book I have had the pleasure of working with several old comrades, and also that of making the acquaintance of several new ones. The list of my greatest debts:

At the Archives of the Big Bend in Fort Davis, Melleta Bell and Karen Green; at the Admiral Nimitz Museum State Historic Park in Fredericksburg, Paula Ussery; at the Austin History Center of the Austin Public Library, Molly Brown, Tim Wilder, Grace McIvoy, Mary Jo Cooper; at the Center for American History at the University of Texas in Austin, Trudy Croes, Bill Richter, Fred Burchsted and John Slate; at the Battleship Texas State Historic Monument, Margarita Marders; at the Baylor University Texas Collection in Waco, Ellen Brown and Kent Keeth; at the Dallas Public Library in Dallas, Gerald Schroeder and Jimm Foster; at the Daughters of the Republic of Texas Research Library at the Alamo in San Antonio, Ann Fears Crawford and Martha Utterback; at the Fayette Heritage Museum and Archives in LaGrange, Kathy Carter; at the *Houston Post* in Houston, Leanne Reidy; at the Humanities Research Center of the University of Texas in Austin, Andrea Inselmann and Nick Lerman; at the Kilgore College Rangerette Museum in Kilgore, Archie Whitfield; at the Moody Texas Ranger Library, Janice A. Reece; at the Panhandle-Plains Museum in Canyon, Claire Kuehn; at the Red River Historical Museum in Sherman, Laura McLemore and Ed Meza; at the Rosenberg Library in Galveston, Margaret Schlanky; at the Spindletop Museum in Beaumont, Christy Marino; at the Steen Library Special Collections of Stephen F. Austin University in Nacogdoches, Linda Nicklas; at the Texas A&M Library Special Colletions in College Station, Charles Schultz; at the Texas Christian University Library Special Collections in Fort Worth, Roger Rainwaters; at the Texas Parks and Wildlife Department in Austin, Barry Hutchison; at the Texas State Archives in Austin, Mike Green, Donaly Brice, Jean Carefoot and John Anderson; at the Texas Tech University Special Collection in Lubbock, Jim Matthews; at the United States Naval Institute in Annapolis, Maryland, Dot Sappington; at the University of Texas at Arlington Library Special Collections, Betsy Hudon; and at the University of Texas Institute of Texan Cultures in San Antonio, Diane Bruce and Tom Shelton.

Preface

IN the nearly seven years since the first appearance of my book *Texas: From the Frontier to Spindletop* (so retitled by the present publisher), to which this is a sequel, I have been enormously gratified, but not really surprised, at the response of Texas readers to a largely pictorial treatment of our history. In some forty-five Texas cities, I have met scholars, teachers, buffs, mavens, and aficionados who have more than substantiated the claims I made to the original publisher about what the avidity of their interest would be like. However, for the casual student of Texas history, interest often fades with the frontier.

Undeniably, those eras of Austin's and the other impresarios' colonies, the Republic, the Confederacy, the cattle kingdom, and the Texas Rangers, do retain the most luster and remain the focus of most history books. In T. R. Fehrenbach's excellent *Lone Star*, which is perhaps the most widely read general history of the state, the period from Moses Austin to the end of the century occupies five hundred pages; that covering the twentieth century, only eighty-six. In the more deliberatively time-balanced standard school textbook, Rupert Richardson's *The Lone Star State*, the frontier story occupies 260 pages; the twentieth century, just over 100. And I guess that is as it should be, but in a way it is unfortunate, because the history of Texas in the twentieth century has gotten a bum rap. It does not become less interesting. On the contrary, it becomes more complex, and provides a greater variety of ways for a greater diversity of people to make a mark on a wider range of issues and topics.

That has admittedly made this a more difficult book to stitch together than the first one. With the Texas story just beginning and with so few people on such a vast stage, it was possible to tell the story almost chronologically. In the twentieth century, so much has occurred simultaneously that it has been all but impossible to cover the period in one stroke. But certain principles and patterns do emerge, and they do much to make a case for a book such as this.

For one thing, it is only by looking into the twentieth century that one can see what sort of fruit was borne by all those frontier seeds. Texas did not even elect its first native-born governor until 1890, and in looking at him or at the last governor treated here, Coke Stevenson, the Texas stamp on their personalities is unmistakable. For a second thing, Texas did not cease to be a land of opportunity with the close of the open range. Certainly the new days focused on areas not foreseen by the frontier era—fighting liquor instead of Indians, for instance—but the personalities involved, whether true heroes and role models, or the continuing political parade of goobs, dandies, and blowhards, are no less oversized than earlier Texas history would lead one to believe they should be. Frank Hamer was no less a Texas Ranger than Leander McNelly or John B. Jones just because he drove a Ford as well as riding a horse. Jesse Jones was no less an empire builder than Richard King because he was in business instead of in cattle.

And, while society has undergone tremendous changes in the twentieth century, the history, if anything, becomes richer, for it was only as the frontier closed that other arenas opened in which those who were relegated to secondary roles on the frontier—women and minorities, particularly—could begin to show themselves as equal bearers of the Texas heritage.

A New Texas

HOMER ON THE RANGE. The moment at which the frontier era ended is defined differently by different people. The first time cowpunchers dismounted for a game of baseball, however, is surely a contender.

By the opening of the twentieth century, the economic changes that had begun with the close of the frontier, and which had accelerated during the progressive administrations of the 1890s, assumed dramatic proportions. Texas's economy had once been almost entirely agricultural and pastoral: cotton and cattle. By 1901, however, industry comprised a full third of all production. Railroad interests, though they complained loudly of Governor Hogg's regulatory commission, prospered to the point that, by 1904, Texas had more miles of track than any other state.

Eighty-three percent of the population was still rural in 1900. And although industry claimed that growing share of the economy, it employed less than 2 percent of the work force—and even then, much of that was still agriculture-related. The top three industries were lumber, cottonseed milling, and flour milling.

San Antonio was the largest city, with 53,000 people. Houston was only a shade larger than Dallas—45,000 to 43,000; Galveston was falling behind, with 38,000, and Fort Worth had 27,000.

Heedless of both calendar and statistics, the frontier had ways of its own to say good-bye. In 1897, five years after the notorious Dalton gang was decimated in Kansas, its last stragglers were overhauled and rubbed out in Menard County by a posse led by Sheriff John L. Jones. "Black Jack" Ketchum, one of the last of the free-ranging outlaws to terrorize west Texas, was hung in Clayton in April 1901. Defiant to the last, he uttered, "I'll be in Hell before you start breakfast. Let her rip!" His words were more prophetic than he intended, for, by a quirk, the noose snapped his head from his body. These were not the only ones who had to be helped across the Great Divide: A retired John Wesley Hardin was gunned down—from behind—in El Paso in 1895; there were no mourners at his funeral.

The hardiest of Texas's revolutionary figures, those who had moved with Austin and Milam and Travis, departed almost in a body—so to speak—to meet their maker. John Duval, the last survivor of Fannin's army, exited quietly in 1897. Bigfoot Wallace went in 1899, and Noah Smithwick, the blacksmith who repaired the Gonzales cannon, followed in 1901. The most tenacious of them, William Zuber, was the last survivor of the victorious San Jacinto army when he went to join his friends in September of 1913. And those who were children during the glory of Texas independence were not far behind. Dilue Rose, whose graphic reminiscences of the aftermath of San Jacinto thrilled a generation who never saw what she saw, was three weeks short of eighty-nine when she passed away at Eagle Lake in April of 1914.

Even once gone, some of the old-timers rose and beckoned. In 1901, a couple of young cowboys in the sand dunes of Ward County made camp at Willow Springs, a pool of good water below Flag Point, which was well known in frontier days as a Comanche lookout. One built a fire; the other, Arthur Hayes, noticed that the shifting dunes had, as they often did, exposed some artifacts. When they finished digging, they had uncovered the charred remains of a forty-wagon train—implements, bone fragments, ox yokes, a bedstead. They had camped in an open V, a sign that they were utterly surprised by Indian attack. Probably eastbound, this might have been the train that disappeared after passing through Yuma in 1873; if it was the Yuma train, the Comanche raiders must have been dizzy with the amount of booty from their four hundred victims. What the Indians could not carry away, Arthur Hayes used twenty-eight years later to open a museum in the nearby town of Monahans.

Aside from loading the past into glass display cases, modern times had ways of their own to announce their presence. On October 5, 1899, railroad baron Ned Green, the bloated, one-legged debauchee who was the son of the infamous "Witch of Wall Street," chugged and flivvered from Dallas to Terrell at a scandalous six miles per

A living link with the revolution, the last five survivors of the army of San Jacinto meet for a final reunion. ALFONSO STEELE (*standing at right*) enlisted with Louisiana volunteers in November 1835, was caught up throughout the war, and was wounded at San Jacinto. WILLIAM ZUBER (*standing and holding up the flag at left*) was only fifteen at San Jacinto, and, as part of the camp guard, was left out of the fight, a fact that did not deter him from leaving to posterity a somewhat lurid reminiscence of his war experiences.

The people who witnessed history were not the only Texas artifacts to pass from the scene in the early 1900s. The VERAMENDI PALACE, where Jim Bowie and Sam Houston were received into San Antonio society, was a shell of its former self when it was torn down in 1902.

hour in the first horseless carriage Texans had ever seen. The frontier reeled before such an onslaught of technology. The first telephone in the tiny high-plains village of Lubbock jingled only three years later.

Institutions died. In May of 1900, a Texas court ruled, on a technicality, that enlisted men of the Frontier Battalion of Texas Rangers had no power to make arrests, a function they had not only performed for a quarter of a century but that had secured the frontier for civilized people. It was a citified ruling that would have been unthinkable only a few years before.

Roles changed. In 1901, Dr. Mollie Wright Armstrong became the first of her sex to be licensed as an optometrist in Texas (she was the second in the nation) and in a sixty-year career rose to the pinnacle of respect and influence in her profession. And perceptions abroad began to change. Europe once regarded Texas as the home strictly of yahoos and gunslingers, but longtime Denison resident Thomas Munson, member of the American Academy of Science, grew bowed with honors as perhaps the world's foremost authority on wine grapes. The French government bestowed on him its Legion of Honor, for rescuing its wine industry from certain ruin at the hand of a devastating phylloxera infestation. Munson's solution was to graft their delicate

For several years after their introduction, the appearance of an automobile turned enough heads that they were used as a popular advertising medium.

Gallic varieties onto hardy Texas Mustang roots. The French, who during the Texas Republic once recalled their chargé d'affaires in protest of his getting beaten up by an Austin tavern keeper, must have thought the world had stood on its head.

Of frontier characters who survived colorful adventures, none made trade on them with greater relish than HERMAN LEHMANN of Loyal Valley. Captured by Apaches at the age of ten in 1870, he later took up residence with, fought alongside, and ultimately surrendered with Quahadi Comanches. Recognized as a white captive, he was returned to his family in May of 1878.

His readjustment was slow, and never really complete. In his later years, he scandalized family and neighbors with his disruption of religious gatherings and his keeping of Apache traditions, such as his disgusted refusal to eat pork. He was a staple celebrity at old-timers' reunions, and he is shown here with former Ranger Captain JIM GILLETTE, whom he had fought in wilder days. By contrast, white women who survived Indian captivity usually buried the experience as far in their past as they could. For them, captivity among Plains Indians usually meant rape and sexual bondage, and polite society still judged that they should have committed suicide before submitting to being ravished by savages.

The Melting Pot Cools

Foreigners in Texas did not assimilate readily, and often settled in towns of their own that retained strongly ethnic flavors—Alsatians in Castroville, Czechs in West, Poles in Panna Maria, and so on.

THOSE French, however, would have been only partly correct: For though much was changing in Texas, much was still the same, as their own immigrants around Castroville could have told them. One reason that populism, for instance, survived in Texas as long as it did was that its people had become perhaps the most parochial in the United States. Partly this was due to the vast geography: Nowhere else in the country could you be more rural than in Texas. More importantly, it was a result of stagnant demographics.

During independence, Texas had been a nation of immigrants, and an impresariolike policy continued after statehood. Texas became a haven for British, Irish, French, Germans, Czechs, Swedes, Norwegians, Poles, Italians, Slavs of all kinds, stateless Jews—every possible Western nationality contributed to Texas's ethnic mix.

As might be expected in such isolated and strongly self-identified communities, the visits of itinerant photographers (such as the outfit depicted on the frontispiece of this book) were eagerly awaited. Families who wanted their picture taken sometimes allowed nothing to stand in their way. In the case of the Swedish family *(above)* that settled in the Decker Colony near Austin, the heavily retouched, startled-looking matriarch had been so determined to have her photo taken with her brood that her wishes were honored, even though she passed on to her Maker before the photographer arrived.

Those ethnic groups who did not start their own towns often congregated in cities where there were already others like themselves, which often meant they shared the same skills. At one time, it was estimated that half the grocers in Beaumont were Italians. The ruddy tavern keepers in the photo *(opposite)* were Belgians, most of whom located to the lower Rio Grande valley.

After the Civil War, a wave of destitute Southerners came to live in the one area of the Confederacy not devastated by conflict. As the century closed, however, a curious pattern took shape; the tide of immigration that had turned Galveston into the second-busiest port of entry in the United States (behind only New York) began to ebb, both from abroad and from the rest of the United States. From the close of the frontier to the discovery of oil, there was little reason for anyone to go to Texas, and those who did went to the cities. Most of the southern emigrés remained poor dirt farmers, and the economy of the towns was heavily dependent upon rural agriculture. Thus while the rest of the United States entered the Gilded Age, Texas became a backwater that even reverted, in the cases of tenant farmers and laborers in the company towns, to a virtually feudal economy.

The Political Pendulum:
From Progressive
to Conservative
and Back Again

FOREIGN or homegrown, the status of the Texan in the great American melting pot had altered by the opening of the 1900s. Galled by the Civil War and humiliated by occupation, Texans rejoined the Union only to find themselves twenty years later about the last people in the country left holding the bag of populism when it was found to be full of hot air. Where Texans once postured their independent self-assertion, now they were, if anything, a bit testy over being regarded as buffoons. And the country had left them behind; the war with Spain in 1898 had made the United States—at least the North—an industrial and imperial power; Texans economically were still eating the dust of Reconstruction. Congress and the Supreme Court were regarded distantly and with suspicion, as those bodies generally protected the interests of powerful corporations, which did not play well with reform-minded followers of Jim Hogg. In the eyes of Texans, the Court partly atoned for that, however, with the case of *Plessy* v. *Ferguson*, which at least endorsed the segregation of blacks.

While the Progressive party itself had never actually controlled the state, its accomplishment lay in having forced the regular Democratic party far enough to the left to make its positions palatable to most of the reformers. After two terms of Hogg and two terms of his equally populist successor, Charles Culberson, the mood was changing. Partly, this was a result of the national populist collapse finally reaching the Red River, but more particularly in Texas it was a shift soon confirmed and cemented by the huge influx of cash that followed the discovery of oil. When the tenant farmers and hog callers who had always looked for a champion of the common man suddenly found themselves with six- and seven-figure bank accounts, they lost no time in familiarizing themselves with the design on the other side of the coin.

One man in Texas saw this coming and strove to engineer the state government to lead the change, not react to it. Edward M. House of Houston, a smooth and canny mover within the smoke-filled rooms, had masterminded the careers of Hogg and

By the time of the Galveston Storm, GOVERNOR JOSEPH DRAPER SAYERS was already an experienced relief administrator, having overseen aid disbursement after the Huntsville penitentiary burned down in 1899, and then after a Brazos River rampage killed nearly three hundred people and flooded some twelve thousand square miles. When the scope of the Galveston disaster became clear, Sayers arranged with the army to transfer fifty thousand rations and ten thousand tents, organized a work force of four thousand laborers (paid $1.50 a day from $1 million in relief donations), and arranged Red Cross aid with Clara Barton. Nor did he neglect to point out the region's considerable reinvestment potential to a deputation of eastern moneybags.

Sayers was a tough customer on any front. He had arrived in Texas in 1851 at the age of ten, was a classmate of Sam Houston, Jr., at the Bastrop Military Institute, and in the Civil War was wounded twice—and returned to the battle on crutches. After one term as lieutenant governor, he spent fourteen years in Congress before kingmaker E. M. House aided his gubernatorial bid. He was sixty-two when he stepped down in 1903, and before his death at eighty-seven had garnered a formidable legal practice, chairmanship of the Industrial Accident Board, and a regency of the University of Texas.

Culberson, and had diverted—and disarmed—the populist flood by channeling it into the mainstream. Then he turned his energy toward changing the Texas political climate into one more hospitable to the needs of business. The man who occupied the governor's mansion at the opening of the new century had already been there two years. Joseph Draper Sayers was a former congressman and a southern gentleman, a Confederate veteran in fact, and also a protégé of Colonel House. His successor, S. W. T. Lanham, who served from 1903 to 1907, was hardly distinguishable from Sayers in either background or philosophy, and together their legislative program struck a balance of good sense and good manners.

In the early years of the century, the state's tax burden weighed most heavily on real estate, especially farms, which caused discontent among those farmers whose

When the cash generated by the petroleum industry was added to the wealth already present from cotton and cattle, the result was a new phenomenon to most Texas cities—whole neighborhoods of impressive upper-class homes. This street was in Amarillo.

sentiments were still heavily progressive. The sudden exploitation of natural resources brought about by Spindletop—it could not properly be called "industry" yet—provided an alternative. And while the Sayers and Lanham regimes rejoiced at its health, they also levied new franchise and gross-receipt taxes on pipelines, railroads, and sleeping-car companies, which almost doubled the value of the state's tax rolls.

On the other hand, financial laws were passed that made the management of money and the conduct of business easier. Creation of state banks had been banned by the Texas constitution of 1876, a result of lingering suspicions that dated back to Sam Houston and Andrew Jackson. The existing patchwork of national banks and private banks and factors was abysmally inadequate to the monetary explosion that followed the oil boom, until an amendment in 1904 finally made provision for a state banking system. The financial vacuum was quickly filled by the chartering of some five hundred banks over the next five years.

Attempts had been made in repeated sessions of the legislature to reform the election code, which as it existed lent itself to all kinds of fraud. Under the leadership of Judge Alexander Terrell, beginning in 1903, amended in 1905, and not finished until 1907, a vastly superior code known as the Terrell Election Law supplanted it. State and local nominating conventions with their chicanery and shenanigans were abandoned in favor of primary elections, followed, if necessary, by a runoff of the top two candidates if no majority emerged from the first. It also required candidates to file financial statements so the public would know where their campaign money came from.

Also on the progressive side, both administrations passed laws to the advantage of organized labor—exempting unions from antitrust regulations, banning blacklists and payment of wages in company scrip redeemable only at the company store, and, for the first time in Texas, regulating wages and hours in some industries and limiting some child labor. What the legislature gave with statutes, however, they tended to take away with appropriations—or the lack of them—that would have enforced them. It was a balancing act.

One commonly held tenet of the newly wealthy business class was that the once-exalted common man was now white trash and could no longer be trusted to vote intelligently. A poll tax was passed in 1902. Although it arguably reformed the system by ensuring that only properly qualified and registered men could vote, its greater intent was quite simply to dilute the voting power of the poor—again, a balancing act. The strange thing about the poll tax, though, was that the farmers and laborers whom it was intended to discourage actually supported it. These one-time progressives had found a new outlet for their reformist zeal: prohibition. And they were counting on the poll tax to tamp down the vote of the Mexicans and Germans, who mostly saw the antidrinking movement as a silly excess, which it was.

Prohibition, which may be defined realistically, if not politically, as the gnawing dread that somewhere, sometime, someone in Texas was taking a drink, had been on the political scene for years. But, it was only the activity, or outrage, of colorful crusaders—sharp-tongued, civilly disobedient, and usually affiliated with the Women's Christian Temperance Union—that made it a cause célèbre. Texas had governed the consumption of alcohol for many years by local option, the same way it governed every other issue on which the state was too broad and diverse to arrive at any consensus. Under this system, those counties that wished to ban the presence of whiskey, or wine or even beer, had already done so. They were "dry." The goal of the prohibitionists was to foist the same ethic on those counties that were still "wet." They did not give up, of course, until Prohibition was not only a state but a national accomplishment, but it was in the early 1900s that their voices first became shrill.

The Sayers and Lanham years were the last real era of good feeling in state politics; Lanham was reelected in 1904, having spent, according to the statement required by the Terrell Election Law, twenty dollars. By 1906, however, the sentiment had shifted again. The dying but still-eloquent former governor Hogg had grown increasingly

The hatchet-wielding temperance crusader CARRY NATION was born in Kentucky but had long lived in Texas, in Brazoria County. Her first husband died a drunkard. Her second, a preacher, was beaten during the Jaybird-Woodpecker War, and they left the state. Texans followed her escapades, however, and in the fall of 1902 students at the University of Texas contacted her, complaining (in jest) of drunken law professors and asking her intervention. To their amazed delight, she got off the train in Austin with her hatchet, smashed some glass, and gave the stupefied faculty members a formidable dressing-down. Unaware that she'd been had, she fell for the same prank again two years later.

critical of their probusiness stance, and, for the first time in a long time, Colonel House was not at the center of things, brokering deals. Hogg encouraged his boyhood chum, Palestine lawyer Thomas M. Campbell, to make the run, but he did not live to see Campbell victorious.

Taking office in 1907, Campbell wanted to see to it that Texas's wealthy paid something closer to their fair share of taxes, and he tried to win passage of a state income tax. The best he could get out of the legislature, however, was a small inheritance tax. He did fare better on other fronts. Typical of the reforms of the Campbell era was the so-called Robertson Law of 1907, which required life-insurance companies to invest within Texas three-quarters of their Texas-generated profits. The statute was a sure crowd pleaser, intended as it was to spur an influx of capital. Texas was only following the lead of other states. The amount at stake was in the neighborhood of $40 million, of which less than $1 million had stayed in the state before the law was passed. The law's actual benefit to Texas came from an aspect that was the last thing its framers expected. Foreign—which in this context meant out-of-state—insurance companies simply packed up and left rather than comply with such a law. Texas suffered, but only briefly, for the law served as a kind of tariff that allowed Texas-based insurance companies not only to flourish but to become national powers.

THOMAS CAMPBELL was just the man to reestablish the populism of the great Jim Hogg, as the two had been boyhood buddies and were raised on adjoining farms in Cherokee County. Although he at one time had been general manager of the Great Northern Railroad, he received Hogg's dying benediction for the gubernatorial race, and campaigned loudly against corporate interests and the previous two administrations, which had sheltered them. Disappointed in the more conservative legislature that hampered his second term, Campbell later ran for the Senate; he was defeated and retired from public life. He died in 1923.

There was a national financial panic in 1907, which led to another Campbell reform measure, a state-supported insurance fund on bank deposits, which operated with much success for twenty years. It was also on Campbell's watch that the legislature created state health and medical boards, as well as passed a prototype pure food and drug law. Local government was improved by statutes that allowed cities to regulate utilities, and by giving school districts greater power to levy and spend taxes.

Campbell's best marks came with his vigorous enforcement of antitrust legislation, strengthened with a new act that he signed in 1907. It brought its biggest dividend in a huge legal battle known as the Waters-Pierce Case. National petroleum titan Standard Oil of New Jersey had long since repented its folly of ignoring the Spindletop oil possibilities, and it began doing business in Texas through its subsidiary, the Waters-Pierce Company. To avoid antitrust difficulties, papers were filed showing the latter to be an independent corporation. The lie was exposed in a legal wrangle in Missouri, and Texas attorney general Robert Davidson brought suit to revoke its Texas license and collect about $5 million in penalties. The case was simple enough, but the president of the company was a friend of Texas senator Joe Bailey, and the court battle was paralleled by a feud fought largely in the press by Davidson and Bailey, the latter's character becoming by far the hottest political issue of the day.

The Waters-Pierce Company lost its case but appealed to the state supreme court and ultimately to the Supreme Court of the United States. It still lost. Payment of its fine, $1,808,483.30—delivered in small bills in a wheelbarrow pushed up Congress Avenue—was intended as a show of contempt but had the effect of publicizing the company's downfall; its remnants were then broken up in receivership and sold at auction.

Although Texas's first two governors of the 1900s were Confederate veterans, neither held more vivid memories of Reconstruction than SENATOR JOSEPH WELDON BAILEY *(left)*, who was born near Vicksburg, Mississippi, about the time it fell to the Union siege. He was twenty-two when he settled in Gainesville, whose public fell in love with him over his Fourth of July oratory and sent him to Congress in 1890. Tall and strong, he affected an air of western showmanship with his long Buffalo Bill hairstyle. As a Dallas journalist observed of Bailey, "of heroic build, smooth face, long hair and longer coat, all at variance with prevailing styles, he struck me as a political masher, a sort of statesmanlike dude stuck on his intellectual shape."

He was hard to figure, though. He supported war with Spain but eloquently opposed the acquisition of colonies as being inconsistent with a free republic. He was progressive, but in the minds of many voters tainted himself at the time of his succession to the Senate by becoming involved with the Waters-Pierce Oil Company. In the days before popular election of senators, the legislature did not appoint him to the post until a hearing *(right)* absolved him of wrongdoing. His term was clouded, however, and, although he was selected to serve a second stint, the fact that he told a second investigation that he had received no fee for representing the company, without mentioning large personal loans made to him by Henry Pierce, resulted in his being pressured to resign. While amassing further fortune from his law practice, Joe Bailey continued to try to influence public affairs, usually guessing wrong. He supported an income tax, opposed prohibition, and when he ran against Pat Neff for governor in 1920, was shown the door by the voters. To his credit, he did come out of retirement to support Ma Ferguson in her opposition to the Ku Klux Klan. He died in 1929, crestfallen that Texas Democrats had actually delivered their state to Herbert Hoover.

Sanding the Social Edges

Schools for white children in Texas cities kept up pretty well with the rest of the United States, but there was an appalling discrepancy between those and the schools of the rural districts. In the countryside, one-fifth of them were not yet divided into grades, remaining one-room holdovers of the frontier era, when one teacher taught all the grades. Improvement was impossible until a state constitutional amendment passed during the Campbell years raised the ceiling on taxes that rural districts could levy.

EDUCATION, and the idea of its importance, was somewhat slow to catch on in much of Texas. Partly, this was because the Reconstruction Republicans and carpetbaggers had always been advocates of education, and any part of their program was still squinted at. (This was particularly true of black education, but, by the turn of the century, illiteracy in that population had declined from more than three-quarters to less than half.)

It was not until 1915—the year that Southern Methodist University opened in Dallas—that mandatory attendance in all schools was standardized at two months per year from ages eight to fourteen. Once that pill was swallowed, the national standard of nine months from ages six to sixteen was quickly put in place. That sufficed until the age of women's suffrage brought a host of educational reforms. There were private academies for those who could afford them. The most fashionable of the finishing schools for girls was opened by Miss Ela Hockaday in Dallas in 1913. She grounded her program on four principles: scholarship, character, courtesy, and athletics. The latter category might seem strange, but it gave Miss Hockaday's graduates the self-possession to sail through almost any situation without embarrassment. Report cards evaluated the students at such skills as "behaves in a ladylike manner at all times," and "speaks in conversational tones." Discipline could be politely savage. Once, two girls tiptoed into the kitchen in the middle of the night to snack on some Grape-Nut ice cream, only to be nabbed by their flashlight-wielding headmistress. Miss Hockaday was unflappable: "Oh, girls, you must be hungry. Well, this is certainly no way to eat. Put those spoons down." She awakened a maid, then had her dress and set the finest ware on the table. Miss Hockaday supervised the unfortunate creatures in gorging on ice cream to the point of illness. Her method worked, however, and the Hockaday School became a staple supplier of students to such colleges as Vassar and Radcliffe.

Social improvement was doomed without books, and Texas ended its frontier era with fewer than a half dozen public libraries in the entire state. Even at its premier repository of learning, the University of Texas, the library was housed in one corner

Urban life or rural did not make much difference if you were the right age.

of the chapel. In Tyler, at the first statewide meeting of the Texas Federation of Women's Clubs in 1898, delegates agreed that remedying this deficiency should be their first crusade. Fortunately for them, this was just the time that Pennsylvania steel magnate Andrew Carnegie turned his philanthropic largesse to the same issue, and Texas benefited enormously. A Carnegie library was not that hard to get. A community, whether through its government or its civic groups, would provide a building site and pledge an annual budget of 10 percent of the building cost. Dallas, San Antonio, and Houston opened two such libraries each, and by the time the last one in Texas was built in Vernon in 1917, thirty-four Carnegie libraries costing a total of $645,000 dotted the map from Clarksville to Pecos. Most of the communities, however, were already in arrears on their budget agreements.

One quirk of obtaining a Carnegie library was that Mr. Carnegie himself had to approve its architecture, and he favored Greek Revival. From the time the first one in Texas opened in the little town of Pittsburg in 1898, they tended to be two-story brick structures with Ionic or Corinthian columns outside and wood floors and sixteen-foot pressed tin ceilings inside; this one in Sherman was typical. Twenty of Texas's thirty-four were later demolished. Only a handful of the survivors still serve as libraries; some house local history museums.

At the behest of the Texas chapter of the Colonial Dames of America, Texas's famous bluebonnets became the state flower in 1901, long before Onderdonk started the craze of landscapes composed around them. Known as "buffalo clover," among other names, until pioneer women were struck by the flowers' resemblance to tiny sunbonnets, they turn vast acres of central Texas and the Hill Country into a lush blue-violet carpet every April.

Throughout the frontier era, when the Anglo population was occupied in riding and roping and planting cotton, interest in the arts was centered in the German and other Central European communities of the Hill Country—a tradition crowned in 1898, when Frank van der Stucken of Fredericksburg was invited to conduct the New York Philharmonic. Eight years later, pianist Olga Samaroff of San Antonio made her debut in the same city. Of greater permanence to the local identity, San Antonio artist Julian Onderdonk produced a canvas in 1910 called *Bluebonnet Scene*, a landscape of rugged hills that featured the Hill Country's lush carpet of violet-blue lupines. Unwittingly, he created a genre with which, to his undying chagrin, he was forever linked as "the bluebonnet painter."

Non-German Texas was even slower in establishing any kind of theater tradition, and at the turn of the century the state was, for all intents and purposes, a cultural backwater. An occasional big billing did come through, as when the great Sarah Bernhardt performed her American farewell at Galveston's Opera House in *Camille* in April of 1911. For the most part, however, visits such as that by Lillie Langtry to the late Judge Roy Bean's saloon late in 1903 served only to highlight Texas's general cultural dereliction.

Beginning in 1900, when electric train service linked the north Texas cities of Denison and Sherman *(above)*, the long-haul steam locomotives of the frontier era began losing competitive ground in passenger traffic to the so-called interurbans. The busy schedule and frequent stops of the electric trains were ideally suited to commuters; Fort Worth and Dallas were connected in 1902, and most other major cities were eventually served by more than five hundred miles of track. It was only the advent of cheap automobiles and improved highways that put them out of business.

For a number of years, neither interurbans nor horseless carriages threatened the business of thriving saddleries such as this one *(below)* in Austin.

Eventually, the major cities began to find the time and the means to support artistic endeavors. A fine arts museum was opened in Houston in 1900; Dallas inaugurated theirs in 1903 and a symphony orchestra in 1907—only seven years after music as an academic study was introduced to the public schools there. Houston did not get around to starting a symphony orchestra until 1913, the same year Lillian Eubank of Abilene sang her debut at the New York Metropolitan Opera. (In the more Germanic San Antonio schools, free violin lessons had been offered since 1893.)

In popular music, the era of the cowboy ballad had waned, and other endemically Texan musical genres began to find their voices. In 1899, a thirty-one-year-old African American from Texarkana named Scott Joplin published his "Maple Leaf Rag," a song with a distinctive syncopated style which he called "ragtime." It became a craze, but most of the money and popularity was gained by Anglo performers of his music, a fact that Joplin bitterly resented.

Scott Joplin (left) and Blind Lemon Jefferson (right) were two distinguished black composer-musicians produced by Texas around the turn of the century. Closely akin to Jefferson musically was Huddie Ledbetter, born in Louisiana but raised in Texas, who during his hard life became well acquainted with the prison systems of both states. It was in prison that "Leadbelly" was discovered by folklorist John Lomax, who arranged his release so he could perform such blues classics as "The Midnight Special."

This culture also produced traditional singers of great quality, such as baritone Jules Bledsoe, born in Waco in 1898. It was he who played the lead in Eugene O'Neill's *Emperor Jones* and sang "Ol' Man River" in *Show Boat* on Broadway.

The first song to carry the appellation blues—the "Dallas Blues"—was published in 1912, the work of Hart A. Wand. But the blues became more associated with and almost synonymous with Blind Lemon Jefferson. Sightless since his birth near Wortham in 1897, his music led him to sing in that curiously indiscriminate blend of venues unique to the African-American culture. His music spoke to the heart of the black cultural experience, and, whether he sang in churches or in brothels, the people listened.

While ragtime and other African-rooted genres became accepted as part of the national musical milieu, it was still true that when the rest of the country thought of Texas and music at the same time, they thought of the cowboy and his lonesome ballad. This penchant was reinforced by two events in 1910: first, the publication by folklorist John Avery Lomax of *Cowboy Songs and Other Frontier Ballads,* and the debut in the moving picture theaters of an El Paso native, Tom Mix. Tellingly, Lomax had to obtain financial backing for his *Cowboy Songs* from Harvard University; it was beyond the wigs at the University of Texas to recognize such endemic music as a legitimate art form. Mix appeared in the first of no fewer than three hundred films that became known under the collective heading of Westerns. The cowboy had been a national cultural icon before, thanks to decades of romantic dime novels, but the veritable torrent of horse operas on the silent screen cemented the image as never before.

Even more phantasmic—so some would argue—than the cowboys' transition from bunkhouse to movie theater, was that they began to find religion. As a general proposition, religion in Texas evolved somewhat as a function of urbanization. In the larger cities, the most influential congregations were those of moderate, mainstream denominations—Lutheran, Catholic, Presbyterian, and Episcopal. In the smaller towns and even more so into the rural areas, dominance had been rapidly achieved by more vigorous and fundamental churches—Methodist, Baptist, and Church of Christ, in a roughly ascending order of doctrinal shrillness—which competed fiercely for the souls of the sparsely populated ranches. But, in the midst of their cacophony, one extraordinary tradition began. At Fort Davis, from where the last Texas Apaches had been routed, the Bloys Camp Meeting Association was incorporated in 1900. The post's chaplain, William B. Bloys, 120 pounds and frail, had doggedly visited all the far-flung ranching communities of the trans-Pecos, preaching to whoever assembled. In an important practical concession to the area's isolation, he baptized those seeking it into whatever church they wanted. He began meeting with a few local ranch families for a week every August at Skillman's Grove, sixteen miles west of the fort. Eventually, he bought the property—for two dollars an acre—and organized an interdenominational (Presbyterian, Baptist, Methodist, and Christian) association to host an annual week-long gathering. In time, Bloys built an electric-light plant, but he still planned the meetings around the full moon in order for people to be able to see at night. They ate, they prayed, but no collection plate was ever passed. Services were not always as polished as they were back east—as, for instance, when Blind Meriman the piano tuner fell into the well-ditch during the Baptists' immersions, or when several of the ranchers' dogs upset dinnerware while treeing a wildcat, but at least it was religion, willingly attended, and for west Texas that was progress. Attendance first topped one thousand in 1913.

Along with its interdenominationalism and dependence upon truly voluntary contributions, Bloys infused his association with one other idiosyncrasy: It had to act by consensus. Decisions had to be unanimous. This came back to haunt him when, in old age and increasingly shaky health, he sought to retire. The decision was, by custom, unanimous: "Sit down, Bloys! There'll be time enough to elect your successor when you're gone." He went in 1917, aged a biblically correct three score and ten.

The Cowboy Camp Meeting Association, founded by REVEREND WILLIAM BLOYS, shown here with his wife, was an institution of unprecedented adherence and even gained some imitators. This photo of the faithful gathering was taken either at a Bloys meeting or one of the soon-to-follow Paisano Camp Meetings, which took their name from the Spanish diminutive term for *roadrunner*, used in this sense as *companion*.

The Booming Southeast

RELIGION had an even tougher time gaining a toehold in the rough-and-tumble oil towns of southeast Texas. Further discoveries after the fabulous Lucas gusher—a second strike in the same area, then at Sour Lake in 1903, and then elsewhere in the state, such as at Electra in 1911 and Burkburnett in 1912—established Texas as a formidable economic power among the states. But religion was not the first thing on the mind of most of the drillers, roughnecks, and speculators who flooded into each new boomtown.

A much brisker business was done by the bordellos, such as the one pictured on page 25, in the southeast Texas town of Batson during its boom year of 1905. The ladies smiling and waving from the balcony seem convivial enough, but, according to one patron, "they were just has-beens, drunkards, dope fiends, and what have you. There was some young girls mixed up in there, but most of them were old cats that'd been kicked out of the higher class. . . . They was just as tough as a boot." Often beaten and stabbed on the job, the boomtown hookers gained a reputation for looking out for one another, and for being model patients when professional care was required.

Venereal disease, needless to say, was rampant—often well over 50 percent in any given bunkhouse. In the camaraderie of roughneck life, a dose of clap was a badge of manhood, but it was a daily occurrence to see men enter the outhouse, grab the doorframe, and shriek as they tried to urinate. And in the ignorance of the time—that the disease was over when the first symptoms went away—most cases remained untreated.

And then there were the saloons, one of which might come into existence with no more capital than laying a plank over a couple of barrels. The nicer and more permanent-looking establishments did not appear until later; for the first few years, no proprietor would risk putting a mirror behind the bar, because he knew it would soon be shot out. A thriving boomtown would have several drinking establishments—the big players typically patronized one, the journeymen another, and the down-and-out still another. Brawls erupted over disagreements and sometimes just out of a need to blow off some steam, but, whether in earnest or in fun, they could be brutal. One man whose wife encouraged him to get up after he had been knocked down was observed playing possum to spare himself further battering. Alcoholism was so common as to be not worth remarking; a fellow on a binge was said to be "taking Christmas." The proprietors could be every bit as rugged as the patrons, but one establishment in Humble, north of Houston, gained such a reputation for cheating and roughing up its customers that the latter decided to take revenge. "One night we got a bailin' line and put it around the saloon and put a clamp on it with a hook. When the log train come by, we hooked it on and scattered that saloon about four hundred yards down the track."

But fortunes could be made by braving such dark places. Very early in the oil boom, one Granville Humason devised an improved drill bit of rotary cones that could dig ten times faster than the existing ones and even grind its way through solid rock. Presumably in need of money, he sold rights to the new bit for $150 in a bar to a Spindletop contractor named Howard Hughes, who by the time he died in 1924 had parlayed his Hughes Tool Company into a $2 million concern, which he left to his pilot/playboy son. Like most barroom history, the story has many variations, but it was Hughes who applied for the Rock Bit patent in November of 1908, and the quest for oil was advanced immeasurably. From deals made around turn-of-the-century Beaumont grew such U.S. corporate titans as Gulf, Mobil, and Texaco.

Drinking and violence both were at least partly occasioned by the living conditions, which were appalling. One doctor in the Beaumont of the Spindletop era complained that all the water came from cisterns and could not be drunk until the tadpoles had been strained out of it. Residents suffered constantly from malaria,

The moral depravity of the boomtowns was not the only thing that made them seem like living in hell. Gas blowouts and other accidents sometimes resulted in apocalyptic fires. When the smell of natural gas hung too thickly in the town, cooks might wait for a breeze to freshen the air before lighting stoves.

Gas blowouts, when they occurred, left a distinctive inverted cone of craters; one left a hole 2,200 feet deep.

typhoid fever, and dysentery. "Water was worth more than oil," the doctor remembered. "You could buy water, but the containers would get contaminated. It was hard to keep them sterile."

In the cafés and boardinghouses, according to one roughneck, "The only safe thing to eat was ham and eggs. You could watch them cut the ham and see them break the eggs." Still, the flies were so thick that it was common to eat with one hand and fan flies with the other. One patron, dining with three friends, cut his bread into four pieces, spread them with an appalling salve that was supposed to be butter or oleo, and ran a pool on whose bread would attract the most flies by the end of the meal.

In the hotels and boardinghouses, men were stacked almost like cordwood. One man who had paid a dollar to sleep in a chair remembered having to pay another dollar for a second chair on which to put his feet. When the boardinghouses were so full that not even a chair or desk could be let, men would sleep outdoors, congregating for warmth in winter around wellheads where gas was being flared off.

The gas gave a particular touch to the impression that life in a boomtown was life in hell, for the gas was heavily impregnated with sulfur, and the smell of brimstone could choke a man more than a mile from the field. The irony was, the foulest gas was the least dangerous; fresh gas right from a well could strike a man unconscious before he could flee, and could kill him as he lay there.

Some workers managed to find sufficient housing to bring their families to town, but it was a rough life for the women and children. The mortality rate from cholera and typhoid was high, exacerbated by the fact that in a boomtown there might be no doctor worthy of the name. Large doses of castor oil were credited with saving many young lives. Boys who were tough and adventurous, though, grew up to relish their early lives. "Kids didn't fare so rough," recalled one. "People didn't pay no attention to kids. . . . [The men] didn't care what they said in my presence, or what they done. I seen lots of things that it wouldn't be safe to tell. But I wasn't in any danger."

As on the frontier, it took the arrival of the wives and children for religion to become established, and, even then, Bible meetings were often as not disrupted by pranks. In one case, a dog with tin cans tied to his tail was given a good whack and set off down the church aisle. "That," recalled one of the culprits, "was more fun than doing a criminal act." Men who began taking part in services frequently did so uncomfortably. One man whose tongue tangled over Old Testament names acquired the habit, when called upon to read a passage, of pausing briefly to assay whether to tackle a particularly Hebrew moniker. If he couldn't, he would call him Jim and proceed with aplomb.

With their new technology in hand, wildcatters fanned out across the countryside like ants. They struck oil at Brownwood, two counties southeast of Abilene, and at Petrolia (felicitous name) near Wichita Falls. The price, of course, plummeted. (When black gold spewed from wells being drilled on the arid Waggoner Ranch, the millionaire cattleman growled, "Damn the oil; I wanted water!")

However, oil was not the only staple on which east Texas depended. Sawmills had been among the very first business concerns started by the Anglo settlers while still under Mexican rule, and with the opening of the twentieth century the timber in-

As much as the sale of oil benefited the Texas economy, it was only with the beginnings of their own refinery system that the state began to make the transition from internal colony to national power.

In an age in which one was expected to do for oneself to get ahead, JOHN HENRY KIRBY *(above left)* possessed the dual abilities to work hard and make the right connections. Born in 1860 near Peachtree Village, in heavily forested Tyler County, he dropped out of Southwestern University for want of money before attaching himself to Woodville's state senator S. B. Cooper, who got Kirby a senate job and sponsored him in reading for the law. Eastern money rewarded his legal ability with further employment managing large timber interests. During the financial downturn that began in 1893, Kirby had the good sense to buy land while it was cheap, and built his first sawmill in Silsbee in 1896.

Kirby's housing of laborers, many of them African Americans *(above right)*, in company towns was a practice that seems inherently abusive to today's sensibilities, but his own reputation was one of dealing honestly and evenly with them, which resulted in generally good labor relations. Blacks in all areas of labor, however, were chronically intimidated by the knowledge that those who did step out of line would come in for rough treatment. Those suspected of really egregious crimes against whites—most typically the rape of a white woman—could be meted truly revolting deaths. A whole series of photographs taken, from various angles, of "The Burning of the Negro Smith, Greenville, 7–28–1908" *(facing page)* attests the public approbation of such incidents.

Burning of the Negro Smith,

dustry grew quickly. This was due in large part to the acumen of Tyler County lawyer John Henry Kirby, who in July of 1901 chartered Kirby Lumber Company and endowed it with fabulous assets by a stunning stratagem. Kirby knew that eastern money was now desperate to get in on the Texas oil action, and by currying favor in the right places he came up with investment capital to acquire vast acreages of pine forest. By seeing to it that the Yankees were kept happy in their quest for oil, Kirby gained control of some eight *billion* board feet of saw timber. Eventually, Kirby Lumber came to employ some 16,000 workers, cutting and sawing trees from the 368,000 forest acres the company owned. Life could be rough for those laborers, though. The redlands of east Texas had also been known since the early days as a remote place where justice, legal or social, could be hard to come by for the poor and noninfluential. Much of the timber labor was done by blacks, who often lived in company towns. These were a shameful reminder of the worst abuses of the Gilded Age, in which workers rented company houses and shopped in company stores, and might even be paid in company scrip, barely a level above serfdom.

Eighty miles to the west of Beaumont, an economic surge of a different sort was taking place. Ever since the days of the Texas Republic, the city of Houston's attempts at prosperity—not to say regional hegemony—had been stymied in Galveston's important shipping connections. Galveston, however, was now fighting for its life in the wake of the 1900 storm; its citizens passed almost unanimously a $1.5 million bond issue for the construction of a seventeen-foot-high concrete seawall to prevent

While most of Texas was reveling in the various oil booms, the city of Galveston concentrated on rebuilding from the hideous destruction of the great storm of September 1900. The exigencies of the situation demanded a city government that could act without lengthy debate and delay, and surviving leaders empowered the governor to appoint a mayor and four commissioners, each of whom had both legislative and executive authority within his own department: police and fire, water and sewage, finance, etc. That left little say for the people in their city affairs, and the Texas supreme court later ruled that the officials had to be elected. The commission form of city government, however, became a favorite of progressive reformers and spread across the country. It lasted in Galveston itself until 1960.

The vast sums spent on rebuilding the city included the erection of the granite seawall and a causeway to the mainland, repairing or replacing virtually every structure in town, and (pictured here) raising the city's elevation by pumping sand from the floor of the Gulf. The first phase of the latter task was completed in seven years; eventually some 30 million cubic yards of sand were dredged in. The effort so exhausted the community that economic leadership of the region was seized by Houston, which had been Galveston's rival and second fiddle for two generations.

a recurrence of the disaster. But when the bonds went begging on the markets, the people had to buy them up themselves. Further bonds to raise the elevation of the entire city—which cost four times as much as the seawall—also came out of local pockets, although Governor Lanham offset some of it with state money. The improvements were a success, as was proven by a second hurricane in 1915 that cost only a handful of lives in Galveston. But the city's economy had been bled dry.

Business leaders in Houston sensed the opportunity and laid plans to administer Galveston a coup de grâce by dredging a deep-water ship channel out of Buffalo Bayou. With a seaport, Houston's superior road and rail connections would draw enough shipping out of Galveston to strand the latter as a commercial backwater.

The Army Corps of Engineers, however, refused the project until Houston solved its unhealthy water situation. Buffalo Bayou had always served the city as both a drinking supply and sewer, and Houston was notorious for its "bowel complaint." After wells were dug for fresh water, an engineer named Alexander Potter designed and built a remarkably advanced sewer system, collecting and filtering waste through rock, gravel, sand, and coke before allowing it to drain into the bayou. The system began operation in 1902, and Potter answered challenges to its efficacy by drinking a glass of effluent.

An eighteen-and-a-half-foot channel was finally opened in 1908, with a turning basin located where the old town of Harrisburg had been. Improvements to the channel began almost immediately. Federal money matched funds raised by the Houston Navigation District, and a deeper channel of twenty-five feet was opened in 1914,

Houston's rise to economic leadership began with a primitive-looking dredge scooping mud from the bed of Buffalo Bayou.

Even as Houston concentrated more on heavy industry, the ship channel also increased the city's dominance in the marketing of cotton. This warehouse stretched for a quarter of a mile—the longest in the world.

In 1906, attention was diverted from the oil boom when a small towboat labored into Sabine Pass with this stunning catch, a ninety-foot bull sperm whale. A quick-thinking Port Arthur chamber of commerce paid a thousand dollars for the carcass, and charged the curious two bits a head for a close-up view. It was a gold mine—special trains rolled out to Sabine Pass creaking under hordes of sightseers—until the smell finally grew stronger than their curiosity. A local taxidermist then bought and mounted the body, at enormous expense to himself, only to be spurned and called a fraud by the same public. With no odor to assault them, they refused to believe that anything could grow that large.

As Houston became an industrial power, its new rival, Dallas, became a business and retailing center. Neiman Marcus department store opened in 1907; among its later retailing innovations were the first regularly scheduled fashion shows in the United States, starting in 1926.

as the mayor's daughter scattered white rose petals on the water and said, "I christen thee Port Houston. Hither the boats of all nations may come and receive hearty welcome." A cannon boomed, fired with a remote switch by President Wilson in Washington, D.C. Further improvements were made, and by 1920 Houston surpassed Galveston in shipping tonnage serviced. No sooner was Galveston vanquished than Houston began to feel the sting of a new rival for the state's economic hegemony: Dallas, where the word was that if the Houston boosters could suck as hard as they could blow, they wouldn't need dredges to deepen the channel.

The Tamed Domain

TEXAS'S frontier heritage of paying state debts or luring new settlement with public domain—land to veterans, land to homesteaders, land to the railroads; three million acres to one consortium alone to pay for the capitol—had become so ingrained that by the turn of the century Texas was seriously underbidding her hand insofar as the value of land was concerned. A homestead law of 1897 actually reduced the minimum price of farmland to $1.50 per acre, but the law that supplanted it in 1906, which required prospective owners to seal bids, brought offers ten to fifteen times that amount. This realization came late, however. Lands whose sale was to finance state asylums were gone by 1912; most of the public school lands were in private hands by 1920. Even some of the former kingpin cattle operators, when they saw the spike in land values, sold advantageous tracts to speculators and so parceled themselves, eventually, into insignificance.

Overall, the ranching industry began a decline right about 1900, which did not level off until 1930, when the active herd numbered about 5 million head—about half that of its heyday. Farming, however, began to increase, moving north and west through the Panhandle on land once reserved for grazing cattle. It was, however, a particularly hard scrabble to get crops out of the hardpan of the Staked Plains, and the more so for want of water. It was bad enough to live in a soddie and dig roots for firewood, but the necessity of hauling water from sometimes remote sources was intolerable. As muttered one woman who upended her bucket in trying to get off a water wagon, "Oh, God, how I hate country where you have to climb for water and dig for wood."

That complexion began to change significantly when a drought in 1909 to 1910 depressed land values. A Hereford real estate agent named McDonald dug a pit in a low spot called Frio Draw and found water. That, and a drilled well near Slanton the following year, signaled irrigation of the high plains. This changed its face forever, because the soil of the Panhandle proved to be superb for the cultivation of cotton. It needed only water. Throughout the early 1900s, some observers warned of what they perceived to be a fundamental weakness in Texas's agricultural portfolio: its ever-growing dependence on cotton. By 1910, about half the acres that were planted in anything were in cotton. Cotton was an east and central Texas crop, however. Early efforts to introduce it into the Panhandle were unsuccessful. Although ranchers had by and large accepted agriculture since the close of the open range—and indeed many of them had begun farming operations of their own—they drew the line at cotton.

One aspect of farming the Panhandle that is often forgotten today is that no operations could commence until something was done about the prairie dogs that already lived there. No one was interested in hunting them; although they are just as acceptable for food as rabbits or squirrels, the word *dog* attached to them discouraged the appetite. There were too many to shoot—at least 500 million of them on ninety thousand square miles—anyway. Drowning them was tried in areas where that seemed possible, but one rancher drained an entire stock tank over a prairie dog "town." The last of the water disappeared a half hour later, after which the little rodents popped up as frisky as before. So the Staked Plains were dotted for a time with teams of prairie dog poisoners *(above)*. Working from isolated camps, they scattered buckets of lethal grain, often followed by a second application of poison gas.

When attempts at irrigation revealed that the Panhandle was underlaid by a vast aquifer of fresh water, it seldom occurred to those pumping water for their crops how it got there. Years of wasteful depletion, with no more prairie dog burrows to replenish the supply, resulted in a freely falling water table and a great deal of worry about how much longer irrigation could continue.

Experimental plots planted in the ranching country were trampled or plowed under. West Texas was for white people, and the claim was "Cotton brings niggers." It turned out they were wrong, for growing cotton in the Panhandle required irrigation, which required lots of money and machines, which left blacks right out of the picture. Thus by 1928, there were 17 million acres of cotton, worth $450 million, much of it in the northwest corner of the state.

With more people and more intensive use of the land came greater notice of its once-obscure natural phenomena, one of which was a mile-long outcropping of flint thirty-five miles north of Amarillo. Study by geologist Charles Gould and others eventually revealed that the rock had been chipped for spear and arrow points for at least twelve thousand years. Alibates flint has also turned up in archaeological digs hundreds of miles away—suggesting that not only was this the source of some of the first stone in the Stone Age but also comprised some medium of trade or commerce.

A small creek near the quarry had been previously named for local rancher Allie Bates, a fact unknown to Dr. Gould when he deduced the present spelling in 1907.

Pastoral pursuits took on a different complexion in the Hill Country west of Austin and San Antonio. The sheep ranching that endured such hostility from the cattlemen during the frontier era now flourished, supplemented, thanks to some timely tariff protection, by the production of mohair from a vast herd of goats. Charles Schreiner, a French immigrant and Civil War veteran, gained the upper hand in this industry; his people were tending sheep and goats on some 600,000 acres by 1900. He ran his operation from the town of Kerrville, which benefited from his philanthropic nature, and where his general store—one of the largest in the Southwest—became a staple of the local economy. Old-guard cattle ranchers who merely scratched their heads

By the time the first telephone rang in Lubbock *(below)* in 1902, it had a population of about three hundred, having struggled to attract settlers ever since rival town-boosters had called a truce and settled on the site in 1891. The need for a marketing center to service the region's ranches eventually overcame the aversion to dust storms, grass fires, and northers, and the town prospered.

One of Lubbock's earliest leaders was cattlewoman MOLLY ABERNATHY *(inset)*, who had ranching heritage on both sides of her family tree. Her first husband had the sharp eye and good fortune, in the age of diminishing public domain, to find and file on a vacant string of land between two railroad surveys, one mile wide and a hundred miles long. He settled twenty-four families on "The Strip" before provoked neighbors had him murdered in 1900. Molly, however, quadrupled the size of her own operation, made money on her herd of registered cattle, and invested in downtown properties in Lubbock. Her marriage in 1905 to real estate developer Monroe Abernathy (for whom two more towns were named) brought further resources to the family. Molly helped found the Business and Professional Women's Club in Lubbock, and was a legend by the time she died in 1960.

Most prominent of the Hill Country sheep and goat ranchers was Charles Schreiner *(inset)*, whose holdings stretched eighty miles, from Kerrville to Medina. One of his philanthropic projects was the establishment of a prep school and junior college for boys, whose land and endowment (more than half a million dollars) he entrusted to the Presbyterian Church.

over central Texas's enthusiasm for sheep and goats were utterly dumbfounded by an explanation by one early mohair producer, William H. Haupt. "In fine, the goat never butts you like sheep. With kind treatment, he is sensible, intelligent, docile, 'a thing of beauty,' and even a companion with whom one can spend a social hour." One hopes, at least, that most of his ardor was for the commerical potential of mohair production, of which Kerrville became the leading center in the United States.

Changes in the Valley

WEST of the rapidly industrializing eastern part of the state and south of the sprawling cattle concerns of the middle Gulf Coast lay the Rio Grande valley. Separated from Corpus Christi by a hundred miles of ranches and scrub brush, and two hundred miles south of San Antonio, the region had passed through the frontier era in sleepy isolation, except for outlaws from the north fleeing the law, and banditry and cattle rustling from across the river. It was border country both geographically and socially.

What little economy the region had dodged a bullet in 1903, when the army proposed to shut down Fort Brown. It was left to a freshman congressman, John Nance Garner of Uvalde, to try to convince Secretary of War William Howard Taft that losing the army would wreck the local economy. "Mr. Secretary," said Garner, "it's this way. We raise a lot of hay in my district. We've got a lot of stores and we have the prettiest girls in the United States. The cavalry buys the hay for its horses, spends its pay in the stores, marries our girls, gets out of the army and helps us develop the country and then more replacements come and do this same thing. It *is* economics, sir. It *is* economics."

While his fast talking was the beginning of a brilliant political career, development in the valley was given a more meaningful push by the arrival of the St. Louis, Brownsville & Mexico Railroad the following year, 1904, and by an increase in irrigation that turned the semiarid pastures into a lush green paradise of vegetable farms and citrus groves. This latter enterprise, which was still of modest proportions in 1910, fairly exploded in 1914 with the introduction of grafting—the technique of patching branches of improved fruit varieties onto the trunks of hardy native stock.

With the train came Anglos and their money, which upset a social-class balance that had spanned generations. After the Texas revolution in 1836 and the war with Mexico in 1846, Mexican landowners, many of them possessing substantial holdings, left for the border area, sometimes after being summarily divested of their holdings and given compensation. As wealthy Anglos—or, more accurately, enterprising Anglos who became wealthy—took control of the ranch country, they also assumed the traditional obligations that Spanish *patróns* had owed to the *peóns* who worked the ranches: sympathy, security, caretaking. The difference was that the new Anglo *patróns* parlayed that relationship into political control over their *peóns* in a way that seems less savory now than it did then. According to one observer, "The Mexican naturally

The year the railroad arrived—1904—was also the year that the head-busting border village of Six-Shooter Junction *(left)* incorporated, under the more prosaic name of Harlingen. It was named after the Dutch city that was the ancestral home of Uriah Lott, president of the railroad *(right)* that brought the twentieth century to the valley. It was one of the few perks that Lott got; he died in poverty in Kingsville in 1915. The town itself was the project of Lon C. Hill, who had moved to the area in 1901, then strung twenty miles of wire so he could have a telephone in his house, graded the road hubs, and promoted the place. An inveterate town builder, Lon Hill bought another site in 1904 and named it Lonville—it became Mercedes— and also was in on the incorporation of McAllen. "The Chief," so called for his long black hair and imposing bearing, volunteered his services to the government during World War I, and died in 1935.

inherited from his ancestors from Spanish rule, the idea of looking to the head of the ranch—the place where he lived and got his living—for guidance and direction." On the great King ranch, "The King people always protected their servants and helped them when they were sick and never let them go hungry, and they always feel grateful, and naturally [their votes] don't need any buying. . . . I suppose they control 500 votes."

After arriving in Congress in 1903, it took JOHN NANCE GARNER only six years to become Democratic whip, and then Democratic majority leader, before being elected Speaker of the House in 1931.

Deeper in the valley, Hispanic ownership of the land was still common, but the relationship between *patrón* and *peón* was the same. One Anglo, James B. Wells, did carve out a veritable empire in the border country. Like the Kings, he looked out for his workers, "whose notes he has endorsed and paid, whose babies he has played with, whose tangles he has untangled, and whose troubles he has made his own for

Railroads and town boosting contributed to the modernization of the valley, but it was irrigation that turned the brush country and Rio Grande jungle into a farm owner's paradise.

more than thirty years." And by the election of sympathetic sheriffs, often Hispanics themselves, the bosses were able to dispense a kind of informal, off-the-record justice, which, on the one hand, gave Hispanics more lenient treatment than they could expect from the state of Texas, but, on the other hand, made the bosses' word absolute law. The system that became known as "boss rule" was accepted, however, because free participatory democracy had never been part of the Spanish and then Mexican systems; the *peóns* did not miss what they had never had.

Such security came at a price even beyond political loyalty, however. Wages were low—Jim Wells himself encouraged a potential investor in the valley, saying that "an abundant supply of good labor . . . could be obtained at 50¢, or less, per man, per day." Here, too, there was good effect and bad. The ranch laborers received benefits from their *patróns,* whether Anglo or Hispanic, that extended far beyond wages, but the continual payment of only subsistence wages perpetuated the cycle of dependence. The new Anglos—the ones who came on the train with money to invest but no understanding of how the system worked—engendered increasing discontent among the *peóns,* who became surly, worked halfheartedly, and thus perpetuated their negative stereotype.

All was not paradise in the valley towns, either. Citizens complained of black troops stationed at Fort Brown, and a race riot wracked Brownsville in 1906. The Texas Rangers sent Bill McDonald, who brazenly disarmed two of the soldiers and gained his famous reputation—as described by an observer—that he would charge hell with a bucket of water.

The other side of paradise, of course, was "stoop labor," inevitably done by impoverished Hispanics who looked to the *patróns* of the great estates for their livelihood, and then, with the arrival of the Anglo bosses, for their political cues.

The Pursuit of Gregorio Cortez

GREGORIO CORTEZ

OUTSIDE the protection of the great estates, life for Mexican-Americans in Texas, and for rural Hispanics especially, could be dicey. Probably no case history embodies their plight—the prejudice they had to endure, the cultural gulf that prolonged divisions, and the complexities of their relations with Anglos—better than does the flight, capture, and trial of Gregorio Cortez Lira.

His life up until June of 1901 might have been that of any Hispanic laborer. Born on a ranch south of the border in 1875, he was the seventh of eight children; in 1887, the family moved to Texas, to the little town of Manor, just east of Austin. Married and a father by the age of sixteen, Cortez took ranching and farming jobs all over central and south Texas, nearly always traveling and working with his older brother, Romaldo. Well-built and handsome, and with the family living in Manor, Gregorio cut something of a romantic swath. After ten years, the brothers settled down—insofar as it could be called settled—as tenant farmers on adjoining tracts on a ranch near Kenedy, in Karnes County, about fifty miles southeast of San Antonio. Romaldo and his wife were childless; Gregorio and his wife, Leonor, now had four children, aged ten, eight, five, and three.

On June 12, 1901, ten days short of his twenty-sixth birthday, Gregorio Cortez's odyssey began. The sheriff of neighboring Atascosa County, alerted to a horse theft, followed a trail to the Karnes County line. He informed Karnes County's popular three-term sheriff, Brack Morris, who took up the case, having been informed that the suspect was "a medium-sized Mexican." Morris quizzed several Mexican families in the vicinity, including one Andrés Villareal, who informed Morris that he had recently traded a horse to Gregorio Cortez in exchange for a mare. Cortez's apologist and only biographer, the folklorist Amerigo Paredes, assumes that Morris went to the Cortez place to question him about the mare, which Cortez had legally acquired. Since he did not swear out a warrant for Cortez, and had left a deputy to look around Cortez's stock pens a half mile from the house, it is equally possible, however, that he was more interested in the horse Villareal had disposed of.

It was one o'clock in the afternoon, and Cortez was lounging with his wife, mother, and brother on the porch of his home; the children were still eating the noon meal inside. Sheriff Morris pulled up to the gate in his surrey, accompanied by a deputy, and Romaldo went out to see what they wanted. When he returned, he told Gregorio, *"Te quieren."* Both men knew English very well, but whether they were suspicious of the lawmen and wanted to communicate without being overheard, or whether they simply spoke Spanish in their home, the result was tragic. One of Morris's deputies, Boone Choate, spoke just enough Spanish to translate badly. "Te quieren" means literally "you are wanted," but means idiomatically "they want to talk to you." As Choate relayed it to Morris, however, Romaldo had informed Gregorio that he was a wanted man.

Then there was a second misunderstanding. Gregorio approached, and Morris asked whether he had traded a horse to Andrés Villareal. Cortez said no. In English, a mare is a female horse; in Spanish, the distinction is sharper. A horse is a horse—*caballo*—not a mare—*yegua*. Cortez had traded a mare, not a horse, but Morris thought he had caught Cortez in a lie, and so informed him he was under arrest. Then there was a third misunderstanding. Cortez protested in Spanish that he could not be arrested for doing nothing wrong. As Choate garbled it to Morris, he had said, "No one can arrest me." Morris pulled his gun, and Romaldo, who was unarmed but much larger than Morris, ran toward him to tackle him. Morris shot him in the face, at which point Gregorio pulled a revolver from the back of his belt and shot Morris. When the sheriff continued firing, Cortez plugged him twice more. Choate raced on foot to the stock pens, where the second deputy had been left, and they lighted out on foot for Kenedy to get reinforcements.

In Texas, there was only one end for a Mexican who had killed a sheriff. In such danger, Gregorio Cortez displayed from the first a wiliness to be reckoned with. Loading his family into Morris's surrey, he sent them to stay with a friend in Kenedy. He knew a posse would stop them and so he told his ten-year-old daughter, Mariana, to tell them they were from another ranch, closer to town. The ruse worked, and meanwhile Cortez and the wounded Romaldo mounted horses and hid in the brush, planning to make their way to a doctor in town that night. This trip took until one o'clock in the morning, because for the last five miles Romaldo was too delirious to stay on his horse, and Gregorio had to carry him.

Cortez knew that posses would be expecting him to run for the border, so, leaving his two horses in the brush, he set out northward to get help from his relatives around Austin and then to flee to north Texas. By eight that morning, he had reached the town of Runge and stopped for breakfast, horrified to discover that this was Morris's hometown and people were gathering for his funeral. Skulking under cover, it took him a day and a half to walk some eighty miles to the house of a friend, Martín Robledo, near the town of Belmont, near Gonzales. He told Robledo what had hap-

GREGORIO CORTEZ is posed with a whole squadron of guards. His vilification in the newspapers was sometimes tinged with an odd mixture of admiration and sympathy, but his legal troubles were exacerbated when his wife, who apparently caught on to his raffish philandering, deserted him and refused to provide an alibi at his retrial.

pened, and Robledo agreed to hide him for a few days. That afternoon, however, the footsore Cortez was resting barefooted on the porch when the house was rushed in a pistol-blazing ambush led by Gonzales County sheriff Robert Glover at the head of several deputies. It seemed that back in Karnes City, Cortez's family had been discovered, and his wife, while being questioned "under pressure," had told authorities his plan.

Cortez killed Sheriff Glover, and one of the deputies died in the gunfight, probably in a cross fire created by another member of the posse. The lawmen did wound Robledo's wife and one thirteen-year-old boy; all the Robledos were taken into custody, and the wounded boy was strung up by his neck "until his tongue protruded" to see whether he would talk, but they let him down when he had no answers. Cortez had fled barefooted into the brush full of thorns and burrs, and, after tearing his vest in half to make shoes, he lay concealed for the duration of the gunfight and while posses combed the area on all sides of him.

The press sensationalized the incident with all the gusto they could: One lone, scared Mexican became a gang of merciless desperadoes. Hundreds of men were deputized into posses and a thousand-dollar reward was posted. With his northward escape cut off, Cortez fled south and for the next week, much of it on the back of one heroic little brown mare, led authorities on a crookedly brilliant, erratic chase that was covered day by day in the papers. He was captured on his birthday, June 22, near the town of Cotulla, only thirty miles from the border. Much exculpatory evidence emerged at his two trials; he was acquitted of the murder of Morris but convicted of killing Glover, and was sent to prison. He became a folk hero to the outraged Hispanic community, and diplomatic efforts on the part of their leaders secured a pardon for him in 1913. He died at forty-one, three years later, and was buried in Anson.

Who Will Save the Alamo?

Recognition of Texas history and the importance of its example to the rest of the country came from PRESIDENT MCKINLEY himself, who during a swing through Texas in May of 1901 stopped in Houston to address the Daughters of the Republic, and met Mary Jones, the widow of Texas's last president. He also made a pilgrimage to the Alamo, where he delivered the speech shown here.

MANY writers have noted that Texans have an awareness of their history and heritage that is unsurpassed by the people of any other state in the Union. While the Texas State Historical Association was founded as early as 1897, much of that awareness on the part of the general public dates from the first decade of the twentieth century, sparked and fueled by a virulent controversy that became known as the Second Battle of the Alamo.

This controversy began only four days after Spindletop, when a nineteen-year-old San Antonio society girl named Clara Driscoll wrote a letter to the editor of the *San Antonio Light*, deploring the deteriorating condition of that shrine of Texas liberty, the Alamo. Over the years, the compound had been alternately ignored and commercialized. The state of Texas had purchased the chapel from the Catholic Church as early as 1883, but the remainder of the complex, the fortress where most of the fighting had taken place, had become integrated into the building of the wholesale grocery firm of Hugo & Schmeltzer. That company was negotiating with a New York syndicate to demolish the structure and build a hotel—which in the business climate of the day was a very popular idea. Only women and sentimental fogies would give a thought to the historic stones that supported the grocery warehouses.

Clara Driscoll was a Texan to the core—both her grandfathers had fought at San Jacinto; her father, Robert Driscoll, was a millionaire rancher whose spread, the Palo Alto Ranch, was headquartered near Corpus Christi but spilled into three neighboring counties. It bordered on the King Ranch, and the King family were friends of the Driscolls. Clara, however, had grown up in boarding schools in New York, and then attended the Château Dieudonne convent near Paris. She was bright and she knew how to get what she wanted, whether by charm—her looks were stunning—or influence.

The Daughters of the Republic of Texas, a historical organization founded in 1891, had been negotiating for the warehouse property for years but could not raise the funds because it was prime business property in the heart of downtown San Antonio. No one was going to let them have it cheaply just because some silly battle had taken place there almost seventy years before. In 1903, with the New York negotiations nearing fruition, Clara took charge. Becoming chairman of the Daughters' Committee on Alamo and Mission Improvements, she wrote a letter to Charles Hugo, of Hugo & Schmeltzer, on her father's stationery, which Hugo would be sure to recognize. The result was that she presented her personal check for $500 for a thirty-day option on the property adjoining the chapel in order to buy time to raise another $5,500 for an extended option. This would allow time to raise the $75,000 purchase price for the whole three acres. With demolition delayed, the Daughters launched a fund-raising subscription, and Clara left for Austin to lobby the legislature for an appropriation to fund the option. She turned on the charm, with the result that a handsome young representative from Uvalde named Hal Sevier not only introduced the bill to give her the money but began courting her as well. Both houses passed five thousand dollars for the purpose, but Governor Lanham sent it back with his veto. The legislature was about to adjourn, and there was no time to refute his excuse that there was no "Alamo fund in the state revenue account to which the five thousand dollars

By the time CLARA DRISCOLL finally bought the Alamo out from under the wrecker, the endless wrangling had sapped her interest, and she turned to writing musicals and romantic novels. She married Hal Sevier in 1906, and they honeymooned in Europe for three months before becoming social fixtures in New York and then Austin, where Sevier founded the *American* newspaper. With the deaths of her father and brother, Clara became a powerful businesswoman and eventually overshadowed Sevier. She contributed heavily to Democratic party candidates, which was not the only reason Franklin Roosevelt made Sevier ambassador to Chile in 1932. She divorced him in 1937 and resumed using her maiden name, dividing her time among the ranch, her Corpus Christi penthouse, and palatial home in Austin—Laguna Gloria—which she later gave to the city as an art center. When she died in 1945, Clara Driscoll was accorded the singular honor of lying in state beneath the dome of the Alamo chapel.

could be charged." When the time came to ante up, the Daughters found they had fallen far short in their fund-raising. Once again, Clara Driscoll made up the difference personally, this time almost $3,500.

If the purchase was to continue, a twenty-thousand-dollar payment had to be made the following winter, and the Daughters redoubled their fund-raising efforts, this time seeking one dollar from every schoolchild in the state, for which each would receive a short history of the siege and a photograph. They raised about seven thousand dollars, which still left Clara in the lurch for the rest. Watching from a distance was her father, who quizzed her about her intentions. Without hesitating, she declared she would pay for the whole thing herself if she had to, at which point Robert Driscoll indulgently assured her that funds would be available. To put the matter to rest, she presented Hugo & Schmeltzer with another check and signed five promissory notes. The legislature finally made an appropriation for the purchase as well, and when the state accepted title to the Alamo complex on August 30, 1905, it vested custody of the property with the Daughters of the Republic.

All of which was well and good, but the seeds of further controversy lay in Driscoll's view that the heart of the complex—the squat baroque chapel—was all that need be saved. "All the unsightly obstructions around it," she wrote, "should be torn away." In other words, what she had bought was a vista across which to see the Alamo chapel properly enshrined. The convent wall hidden by the Hugo & Schmeltzer grocery was not, in her view, contemporaneous with the revolution, or historically significant. This brought her nose-to-nose with the tiny but formidable Adina De Zavala, a middle-aged spinster schoolteacher, granddaughter of the provisional vice president of the Republic of Texas, a founder of the Daughters of the Republic, and Clara's erstwhile ally in the campaign to purchase the Hugo & Schmeltzer property.

Miss De Zavala's vision for the property included a history museum and Texas Hall of Fame, making use of the entire complex, including a reconstruction of the convent wall, which, she believed and insisted, had been a scene of fighting during the siege. It began as a modest disagreement, but as each woman's cause gained adherents an open war erupted between the "Driscollites" and the "De Zavalans." Astonished bystanders saw the local Daughters split into two chapters, each claiming to be the successor to the original, with control over the Alamo complex.

Clara Driscoll had originally agreed with De Zavala's plans for the property, but she had become distracted by love and society, and left for New York to get married to Hal Sevier. With the Daughters having failed repeatedly to come up with hard cash even to get their hands on the property, how they intended to finance De Zavala's scheme struck the Driscollites as thoroughly impractical. Besides, a firm that intended building a hotel on the north side of the property began interfering; calling De Zavala's patriotic fervor "misguided," they offered to tear down the Hugo & Schmeltzer building for free. That would have ended the argument in favor of the Driscollites, who then sent a smith to the Alamo to change the locks, but he decamped when the five-foot Miss Adina arrived, shotgun in hand. She maintained her involvement at increasing sacrifice to herself, for she had nothing like Driscoll's money, and when she was criticized for neglecting her teaching duties she resigned her job with the school district. The feud climaxed when the De Zavalans heard that the Driscollites intended leasing the Hugo & Schmeltzer building as a vaudeville and variety theater. Miss Adina locked herself in the place and refused to budge, at which point the Driscollites resolved to let her starve. San Antonio was speechless.

The sheriff arrived with an injunction to evict her, but she refused either to read it or to listen to it. The sheriff left two deputies, with orders that De Zavala could

ADINA DE ZAVALA lost the court battle over control of the DRT but won the war over preservation of the contested portions of the Alamo complex. Through fierce protest and adroit manuever, she prevented the Driscoll faction from demolishing much of the convent wall that was later established as having been standing at the time of the siege, as she insisted it had been. After the "Second Battle of the Alamo," De Zavala turned her attention to saving the Spanish Governors' Palace, which was reduced to housing a junk dealer; over the succeeding years, she saved from demolition the houses of Francisco Ruiz, a signer of the Texas Declaration of Independence, and early Texas figures Jose Antonio Navarro and John Twohig. In addition to writing prolifically on historical subjects, she led a search for, and believed she had found, the site of the Mission San Francisco de los Tejas, the first Spanish installation in the country. She never married, but she served in numerous historical capacities before her death at ninety-three, in 1955.

leave but that no one else could enter. Sympathizers brought her coffee and dough-nuts, but the authorities refused to let her have them. Eventually, they allowed her a drink of water, but the peephole in the door was too small to pass a glass through, and so the liquid was poured through it and into her mouth. A compromise was reached the next day, by which time title to the property reverted to the state. In 1912, the Hugo & Schmeltzer grocery was torn down and the convent walls were rebuilt on the original foundations; subsequent research proved that the convent walls were an integral part of the 1836 battle. Thus it was that both women, whatever their eventual state of enmity, had played crucial roles in preserving the most important relic of Texas's independence.

The Alamo chapel as it appeared in 1902, with part of its controversial appendage seen to the left.

GOVERNOR LANHAM worked up little enthusiasm for preserving the Alamo, but he did turn out for the dedication of the Confederate Heroes' Monument on the capitol grounds in Austin in 1905. Also present for the occasion were Frank Lubbock, who served a term as Texas governor during the Civil War, and John Reagan, one of Texas's preeminent frontier-era statesmen, who served Jefferson Davis as post-master general of the Confederacy.

The monument itself was by far the most elaborate on the capitol grounds, for, to turn-of-the-century Texans, the Civil War was far from a dead issue. It had been only forty years since the event; as elsewhere in the South, many people still had bitter memories of it. Most Texans of voting age had endured the oppression and insult of Reconstruction, and the irony was utterly lost on them that while nursing such venom for that period they had lost care so completely of a very proud history of revolution and independence.

SAMUEL W. T. LANHAM was the last rebel veteran to serve as governor of Texas, having joined Kershaw's Regiment at the age of fifteen. He had been wounded at Spotsylvania but had served throughout the war. Having come to Texas by wagon train, Lanham and his wife, Sarah, settled in a log cabin in Weatherford in 1868, and supported themselves by teaching school in their home. Lanham had little education himself, but his wife prompted him nightly on the following day's lessons. He learned quickly, read for the law, and was admitted to the bar the following year. As district attorney in 1871, it was Lanham who prosecuted the Kiowa raiders Satanta and Big Tree for the Warren Wagon Train Massacre. From 1882, Lanham spent most of the next twenty years in Congress, before becoming governor in January 1903.

Lanham won a second term easily—his financial report, required by the Terrell Election Law, listed a total campaign expense of twenty dollars. His commitment to education continued; during his administration, two important colleges were founded in San Marcos and Denton. He died in July of 1908, some three weeks after Sarah.

C. W. Post: Social Reformer and Millionaire Rainmaker

WHILE Galveston and then Amarillo tinkered with their new forms of city government, a completely different experiment was taking place in remote Garza County. Distressed by the prevalence of tenant farming in the Great Plains, Michigan cereal millionaire Charles William Post set out to prove that the American farmer could, given half a chance and an even break, thrive independently. In 1903, Post bought a huge tract—by one tally $3.50 per acre for 213,324 acres—astraddle the Cap Rock east of Lubbock.

Post divided his farmland into quarter sections and built a complete farm on each—house, barn, well, windmill, and fences—which he then offered for a low cash down payment and low interest. Taking a cue from the land speculators who were filling up the Rio Grande valley, Post ran excursion trains out to his experimental settlement; those who bought farms didn't pay a fare. It was no Utopia, however. When he first began building in each section, Post constructed the house on each of the four farms at the point where the quarter sections cornered together, so the families would have neighbors within hailing distance. Quarrels among them, however, prompted him to begin locating the houses in the middle of each farm—half a mile apart.

When the time came to lay out a town to support the growing population, Post envisioned it atop the Cap Rock, but had to move it a few miles east because of a state law that required county seats be located not more than five miles from the center of the county. Post City was begun in 1907; the entrepreneur offered houses there on similarly generous terms as the farms: he sold a $1,500 house for $250 down and $25 per month. In a year, he had fifty takers; by the time he died, the latter-day impresario had settled some twelve hundred families.

Post hired an impoverished young Scot named George Sampson as chief stonemason, and the crews provided Post City with amenities rare for its time and place: electricity, a waterworks, and a sewage system. Post took an intense interest in all the work. "He was a wonderful person," recalled Sampson. "You wouldn't know he was rich by the way he acted." Before it was done, the town boasted a cotton mill, a steam laundry, the Algerita Hotel, and even—Post and Sampson being good Scotsmen—a three-hole golf course. They even concocted a putting surface of oil and sand when no grass could be found suitable for a green. When they played each other, Sampson usually beat Post, and went on to design golf courses professionally. (The locals, however, were less familiar with Scottish culture; at one social event where music was provided, the sheriff arrested band members for indecency, but then apologized and let them go when it was explained to him that, in Scotland, kilts were not considered provocative.)

CHARLES WILLIAM POST, born in Springfield, Illinois, in 1854, was a thoroughgoing exponent of the Gilded Age; emblematic of the times, he dropped out of college to enter business, and by age thirty had founded the Illinois Agricultural Works and given himself a good case of "nervous disorder"—not unlike stress. To recuperate, he bought a ranch near Fort Worth, Texas, but then also opened a wool mill, developed real estate, and remained ill. In 1890, he checked into a sanitarium in Battle Creek, Michigan, but improved only after turning to Christian Science. In Michigan, his developments in the manufacture of breakfast cereals brought fame, further riches, more stress, and a sizable dose of noblesse oblige, with its attendant contradictions.

Although a vigorous proponent of the open shop and a virulent antagonist of organized labor (he served as president of both the American Manufacturers Association and the Citizens' Industrial Council), Post was generous with his own people. To encourage home ownership among the working class, he built snug homes and sold them to his employees at low cost and interest.

C. W. Post's interest in his town extended to the minutest details. When the Algerita Hotel *(above)* opened, he instructed the cooking staff, "If you have fricasee *[sic]* of chicken with peas, call it that—don't call it fricasee aux pois *[sic]* . . . don't try to make the cowpunchers think we are a bunch of frog-eating French." Nor did his entrepreneurial spirit flag. Waiters were required to inform guests that Post's celebrated coffee substitute, Postum, was available if they desired it. He was even more direct with his cereal products: Grape-Nuts were always to be made available in a covered dish on each table.

One of the engineering feats of the new city was its celebrated "Forest of Windmills" *(below)*, which channeled the water supply into a concrete reservoir.

Post intended to spend a good portion of his retirement in his namesake city on the plains. His first house *(above)* was quite modest, but he later ordered construction of this startlingly modern twenty-room dwelling *(below)*. Post, however, never lived to inhabit it. After eight years of colonizing and rainmaking at Post City, he grew disgusted with his own failing health. In California, he underwent an appendectomy in 1914 that was apparently successful, but he took his own life shortly thereafter.

The most remarkable aspect of Post's retirement was his three-year fascination with the art and possibilities of rainmaking. Even the most industrious and resourceful farmer could not prosper if his crops burned to the roots, and prolonged drought threatened to ruin the whole colony. Post thought it curious that during the Civil War thundering artillery duels were often followed by thundering rainstorms. Accordingly, he arranged the first of his "rain battles" in June of 1911, suspending two-pound charges of dynamite—168 sticks in all—from kites, and the high wall of the Cap Rock echoed the explosions. Nothing happened. He repeated the experiment on June 30, and to his delight the skies opened; it rained, off and on, for ten days. *Harper's Weekly* published his article about it the following year.

"Battle Butte," an outcropping of the Cap Rock above Post City, was the site of many of the eccentric millionaire's attempts to stun rain from the clouds with dynamite.

Over the next three years, Post staged a total of twenty-three rain battles, which cost him about fifty thousand dollars. When his method of lighting the fuses to the dynamite and then trying to launch the kites proved to be a little risky, he settled for placing the charges along the rim of the Cap Rock. Sometimes the experiments worked and sometimes they didn't, but Post died convinced that he had found a way to wring bounty from the heavens.

Farmers all over Texas were quick to realize the applications for machinery that didn't need horses to pull it. Sometimes old-style plows were merely hooked up to the back of an automobile *(above)*. When real tractors did arrive *(below)*, they looked more like clodhopping locomotives.

Texas Embraces the
Flying Machines

The first military flight, and one of the very first flights of any kind in Texas, was accomplished by Lt. Benjamin Foulois on March 2, 1910, at Fort Sam Houston, near San Antonio. Note tents and uniforms.

TEXANS, perhaps because of the vast distances that were a part of their everyday life, were undoubtedly among the first people anywhere to appreciate the possibilities of flight. In fact, there are very insistent stories of a German inventor named Jacob Brodbeck of Gillespie County, who in the years immediately following the Civil War designed a flying machine powered by a coiled spring. In his version, the wings were movable, and although he lived long enough to learn of the Wright brothers' accomplishment, he died convinced that his machine would have worked just as well.

Also fascinated by the concept of movable-winged aircraft was William Downing Custead, a cousin of Buffalo Bill Cody who lived in the tiny settlement of Elm Mott,

Lieutenant Foulois's swashbuckling pose with his SC-1 Wright pusher belies the fact that he was chosen to head the air division because he was built like a jockey and had little weight to carry aloft.

near Waco, working as a Katy Railroad dispatcher. After years of tinkering with larger and larger models (some of which may have been the source of persistent rumors about flying contraptions in the Waco area before the turn of the century), he chartered the Custead Airship Company in April of 1900 with $100,000 in capital. His early prototype was constructed of bamboo, chicken wire, and oilcloth, but since it kept shaking apart, the bamboo was replaced with tubular steel. The great hurdle in the design of airships with flapping wings was the air resistance on the upstroke, which negated the power generated on the downstroke. Custead solved this by building an airship with two thirty-foot wings consisting of cloth slats that opened on the upstroke to allow the air to pass through, then snapped shut from the force of the downstroke. The engine he installed was designed to pump the wings in a six-foot stroke at a rate of three per second. J. L. Bergstrom of Waco swore he saw the craft lift off the ground in a tethered test, but apparently it never attained free flight. Custead moved to Connecticut and then New York to find further backing for his project, but, frustrated by his lack of success, he eventually moved to Hawaii and became a nudist.

Perhaps the first airplane indisputably worthy of the name to appear in Texas—at this time flying machines did not fly from one event to another but were hauled by rail—did not fly, as it happened. Ned Green, the railroad czar who also treated Texas to its first horseless carriage, brought a Wright model to Dallas for the tourists to gape at during the 1909 fair. It was the following February, though, that aviator Otto Brodie gave Dallasites a demonstration in his Curtiss. At almost exactly the same time, French "birdman" Louis Paulhan gave people in Houston a demonstration of flying as a publicity stunt for the Western Land Company. In the audience watching Paulhan pilot his French-built Farman biplane was Houston machinist L. L. "Shorty" Walker, who was already hard at work building a Bleriot Model XI in his garage. There is no irrefutable documentation, but it is almost certain that Walker flew it, on the same field as Paulhan, in the autumn of 1910.

By this time, the military was already interested in developing its own applications for the flying machines, and had acquired—after some bidding chicanery to get the plane it wanted—a Wright Model A, which promptly crashed during trials, grievously injuring pilot Orville Wright and killing his on-board observer. This plane was cannibalized for spare parts, and a second plane soon emerged, passed its trials, and was delivered to the army as SC No. 1—SC standing for Signal Corps, the branch of the service that was given charge of the new air division.

In February of 1910, Lt. Benjamin D. Foulois, U.S. Army, arrived at San Antonio's Fort Sam Houston with his craft and spare parts all packed into seventeen large crates, with orders as simple as they were strange-sounding: Teach himself to fly. He'd had a total of fifty-four minutes of instruction from the Wright brothers; beyond that, however, it was learn by doing. Foulois's rough-and-tumble landings kept the plane constantly in the shop (he finally suggested that the Wrights replace the skis with wheels, which helped considerably). Although the army allotted $150 for maintenance in the last quarter of 1910, Foulois spent a further $300 out of his own pocket to keep SC No. 1 airborne. By the end of the year, he had made over sixty flights, and in 1911 the budget zoomed to $125,000, which allowed the purchase of two Curtiss Model Ds and three Wright Type Bs. Its place in history secured, the often-crunched SC No. 1 was returned to the Wrights, who presented it to the Smithsonian Institution.

Texans in the Ring
and on the Field

By the opening of the 1900s, most of Texas's 620,000 African Americans had not ventured far from their antebellum roots. Out west, however, blacks nonetheless comprised a fair percentage of the working cowboys. BILL PICKETT, said to be of mixed black-Indian-Anglo heritage, was born sometime around the end of the Civil War, and worked the ranching communities north of Austin. Once while loading cattle onto a railcar in Taylor, Pickett bulldogged a runaway steer, not just grappling its horns but biting its tender upper lip as well.

Developing a no-hands version of this accomplishment, Pickett joined the Miller Brothers 101 Wild West Show, and for decades the "Dusky Demon" was a show-stopper. At his Madison Square Garden debut, his hazer was an Oklahoma boy named Will Rogers. Pickett retired in 1930 but was killed by a stallion two years later. Although he invented neither bulldogging nor the now-defunct variation of lip biting, Pickett's technique and showmanship landed him in the Cowboy Hall of Fame.

APART from aviation—and Texas was becoming a haven for stunt-flying "bird-men"—sports in Texas was usually associated with those skills that developed on the frontier—riding, roping and other rodeo skills, and marksmanship. Leading performers in the latter category included a husband-and-wife team from San Antonio, Ad and Elizabeth Toepperwein, who enthralled audiences at the Saint Louis World's Fair in 1904. Ad was a veteran of Buffalo Bill Cody's Wild West Show. Using a .22, Elizabeth (her nickname was "Plinky") once shot at small wood blocks tossed into the air twenty feet away. Of two thousand blocks, she missed five. (Also at the Saint Louis World's Fair, by the way, was one Fletch Davis of Athens, Texas, a cook who wowed fairgoers with his concoction of ground beef grilled and served in a bun with condiments. He called it a "hamburger.")

AD and ELIZABETH TOEPPERWEIN made a sensation with their trick shooting at the 1904 World's Fair.

Gradually, however, Texans began to make their mark in the mainstream of American sport. John Arthur Johnson, a looming black janitor in Galveston, began supplementing his income with under-the-table money for boxing matches. In 1901, he took on a Jewish Pole named Joe Choynski, lost, and both men went to jail for violating legislation that outlawed professional boxing. While locked up, however, Choynski taught Johnson the finer points of the sport, and after regaining his freedom Johnson became a legitimate contender for the heavyweight title.

The reigning champion since 1899 had been Jim Jeffries, who retired undefeated in 1905. Tommy Burns of Canada took the title in November of 1906. As Jack Johnson fought his way past other contenders one after another, Burns, who stood only five feet seven, ducked a bout with him as long as he could. The great John L. Sullivan loudly touted that his protégé Kid Cutler could put Johnson in his place, so the whole boxing world was watching when Johnson knocked him out on the first punch. A meeting with Burns was now inevitable, and Johnson beat him in Sydney, Australia, in December 1908, to become heavyweight champion of the world.

The title was clouded, however. Johnson's detractors—and he had many—claimed that the succession had never left Jim Jeffries, who had no right to give his title away. But the real issue was racism. Johnson was raucous and obnoxious. From the time he bought his first automobile in 1904, he drove like a madman and sneered at his hundreds of citations and collisions. Worst of all in the eyes of his detractors, he split from his black wife and took up with a succession of white women. White sportsmen hated him, a bile only made more bitter by the fact that he kept winning, and a search was instituted for a Great White Hope who could topple him.

Once it was obvious that no new blood could get the job done, it was probably inevitable that Jim Jeffries would be talked out of retirement. He and Johnson met in Reno, Nevada—the only state in which prizefighting was legal—on July 4, 1910, and Johnson beat the living daylights out of him, after which his title could not be disputed. Johnson's winnings from the Jeffries fight amounted to more than $100,000, the largest purse ever taken by anybody in any sport. Still on the lam for other prizefighting violations, however, he absconded with the money and headed for Chicago. There, he opened his Café de Champion the following year and accrued still more enemies for his fast living, wild nightclub, maniacal driving, and his preference for white women. He finally stood trial, was convicted and sentenced to a year in prison, but Johnson fled to Europe in the summer of 1913 rather than do time. The coming of the Great War hampered his ability both to arrange matches and pursue his second career as a stage actor.

Further seekers of the Great White Hope finally mounted a challenger in the person of Jess Willard, and a bout was arranged in Havana for April of 1915. Jack

WORLD'S CHAMPIONSHIP BATTLE, JULY 4, 1910
ROUND 2

THE KNOCK-OUT

Jim Jeffries probably had no business climbing into the ring to take on Jack Johnson in 1910, certainly not in the July heat of the Reno desert. Jeffries was five years into his retirement, and before he resumed training had ballooned to over three hundred pounds. He trained vigorously, but Johnson administered a hideous beating. As seen in these photos, Jeffries's wariness in the second round had become fatigued desperation in the fifteenth, before going down for the count.

When his own time came, however, Johnson proved equally reluctant to give up the ring. Johnson was thirty-seven and nearly spent from fast living when, in April of 1915, he went to Havana to defend his title. Jess Willard KO'd him in the twenty-sixth round.

One of Jack Johnson's first promoters was ALBERT LASKER of Galveston. Son of German Jewish immigrants, Lasker was an accomplished newspaper writer by the time he was out of high school, and was only seventeen when he arranged the bout with Choynski. After writing speeches for a Republican congressional candidate named R. B. Hawley (he won, stunning achievement that it was in Texas at the time), Lasker went to Chicago and established his career in the advertising business.

Or, rather, he founded the business of advertising. Up until this time, for respectable companies, advertising meant taking space in newspapers. It was Lasker who invented the concept of the ad campaign to convince people to buy things they didn't know they needed. Products he handled for his clients—Kleenex tissues, Frigidaire appliances, Wrigley chewing gum, Sunkist oranges, Quaker cereals ("shot from guns" was his phrase), Palmolive soaps, and Van Camp's pork and beans—became household names. His firm—Lord and Thomas—also devised commercial radio sponsorship, put "Amos n' Andy" on the air, as well as the first so-called soap opera, "The Story of Mary Marlin," and gave a break to an unknown named Bob Hope, on a show sponsored by Pepsodent toothpaste.

Although it would be decades before the connection between smoking and health was established, Lasker handled accounts for both Lucky Strike cigarettes and the American Cancer Society. This genius of hustle never lost his taste for sports, and he was a part owner of the Chicago Cubs.

Johnson was now thirty-seven and had grown—for him—soft with the good life. Still, it took Willard twenty-six rounds to knock him out.

Johnson never mounted a comeback. He acted and fought bulls in Europe and Mexico before returning to the United States in 1920 to serve his time. Afterward, he fought in exhibition rounds and made personal appearances—including, sadly, the sideshow at Coney Island—until he was killed (appropriately enough) in a car wreck in 1946.

Jack Johnson, however, was not the only African American Texan to make a name for himself in sports. Throughout the early 1900s, Bill Pickett amazed rodeo and Wild West show crowds with his no-hands bulldogging of steers. In 1911, Andrew ("Rube") Foster, a native of Calvert, founded the Chicago American Giants, a forerunner of the Negro National Baseball League.

Baseball was probably the most popular sport; the Texas League of Professional Baseball Players had been established as early as 1887, but it sputtered through almost

Even Texas towns that could not afford to field Texas League teams managed to put together semiprofessional or amateur teams that competed fiercely for the hometown honor.

The term *Texas leaguer*, a base hit that drops between the infield and outfield, stemmed from Ollie Pickering, when he played for Houston, once going seven for seven, all of them single bloopers just above the infield.

The commercial rivalry between Houston and Galveston was perhaps matched only by the growing football intensity between the University of Texas and Texas A & M. Up until 1911, UT had never bothered to designate a mascot, but in that year the team's manager, Steve Pinkney, was chasing rustlers during the border troubles. There he happened to spy a longhorn steer, dark orange and white, with a vaguely Texas-shaped blaze on its forehead. He convinced alumni to purchase the animal, and the Texas Longhorns were born.

A & M and UT established a spirited home and home-series tradition, and in the 1916 season the Longhorns upset the Aggies 21–7, which so delighted the alumni that they decided to brand the score on the hapless steer the following Texas Independence Day. The Aggies got wind of the scheme, however, and, in February 1917, six cadets combed south Austin until they discovered the mascot's lair and branded the beast with a huge 13–0, the score by which the Aggies had quashed UT in the game previous to the last.

In an effort to mitigate the damage, the steer's galled UT handlers altered the brand to form the letters BEVO—the name of a popular nonalcoholic beer of the time—which became the name of that and all subsequent UT mascots. This particular animal ended its days in 1920 as the main course of a barbecue to which football players of both teams were invited.

annual reorganizations until the North Texas and South Texas circuits united in 1907. Over the next forty years, no fewer than two dozen Texas cities—not just the major ones but the likes of Denison, Corsicana, Greenville, Paris, and Cleburne—fielded teams for at least a few years. Eventually, they were all bought out by national teams, who continued to use them as farm organizations.

Football also gained popularity, especially on college campuses. By the time the Southwest Conference was formed in 1914, some football rivalries in Texas had already become traditional—foremost among them an annual grudge match between the University of Texas and Texas A & M. The latter's pride and mainstay during those early years, Harry Warren Collins, who stood six one and weighed 190 pounds, led the Aggies to an undefeated season in 1917; they weren't even scored against in eight of their games. Even "Rip" Collins, however, later opted for professional baseball, and spent eleven years with the New York Yankees.

As sport diverged from merely organized frontier skills, women began to find outlets for wholesome exercise. Whether whacking golf balls on the links *(left)* or deep-sea fishing *(above)*, proper attire was mandatory. At Ela Hockaday's private school for girls in Dallas, an emphasis on sports gave young women a sense of accomplishment and self-possession that was all too often denied them in the professional arenas.

Prewar Politics

THE Sayers-Lanham era was now entirely over insofar as it represented any age of good feeling. Their probusiness philosophy, though, was about to return for another go. Tom Campbell's more populist administration, as represented by the collection of the Waters-Pierce fine and more than $200,000 in other antitrust penalties, so stung the business community that they made sure the electorate knew that out-of-state capital was being frightened away, to the detriment of Texas's development. Campbell was reelected in 1908, but he had to contend with a more conservative legislature that stymied most of his initiatives.

This close split of power between progressives and conservatives increased the friction over the other principal issue between them: prohibition. Campbell and his progressives favored it, and a referendum held the year of his reelection mandated the legislature to submit a prohibition amendment to the state constitution for the people to vote on. The legislature, which was conservative, probusiness, and wet, took no action except to strengthen the local-option laws that were already on the books. Thus, by the 1910 election, the wet-dry hysteria overshadowed everything else. The man who triumphed in the Democratic primary for governor was a wet, Oscar Branch Colquitt, who had run unsuccessfully four years before, but he now found the times more in his favor. He ran on a platform of what he called "legislative rest," giving business a breather from the relentless hounding of the Campbell years. "Baileyism" was also an issue, of course, as the debate over Texas's tainted senator continued. Colquitt was smart enough to say little, knowing that two other entries in the primary would split the anti-Bailey vote, which could, in this tight four-way race with no clear favorite, swing the result to him. He was right.

Statutes affecting people that were passed in Colquitt's administration were mostly of a humanitarian nature—a hospital for tuberculars and a home for Confederate widows were established; the school districts were put on a better financial footing; restrictions on child labor were tightened. The most important area of agreement between the two camps concerned prison reform. Texas prisons were still among the most brutish in the nation, and Colquitt had run for office very vigorously on the promise to end the worst abuses. During the campaign, he demonstrated the use of the "bat," a five-foot whip that ended in a knot of three-inch rawhide straps. The burly candidate hefted the instrument only with difficulty but gave a violent display of how it was used. The impression made on the electorate was so profound that

Tom Campbell, after Colquitt's election, enacted this reform before even leaving office. But the big issue was prohibition, and it would not go away.

Under local option, 167 Texas counties were already completely dry. Sixty-one had at least some dry precincts, and only twenty-one were completely wet. The enemies of alcohol, however, were grimly determined to bring the sinning territory to heel. Even the legislature was split almost right down the middle—seventy-four

Everything a working governor needs: an oak rolltop desk, four telephones, and a spittoon with a straw mat—heavily spotted—to protect the carpet from near misses. OSCAR BRANCH COLQUITT was born in Georgia but raised in northeast Texas, and worked a succession of menial jobs before entering the newspaper business. His formal education was rudimentary, but he later read for the law and was admitted to the bar, in addition to owning and publishing the paper in Terrell. After two terms as governor, he ran for the Senate, but because of his history— anti-Wilson, antiprohibition, pro-German—he failed to unseat longtime senator Charles Culberson, whose health was rapidly failing. He was eighty when he died in 1940, but he was still working—for the Reconstruction Finance Corporation.

drys and sixty-nine wets—and in 1911 it looked as if a statewide alcohol ban would finally become a reality. But the movement was derailed by a rump defection in what became known as the Whiskey Rebellion. Eleven state senators retired to a hideout in Bandera County, denying the senate a quorum until the end of the session. They were led, oddly enough, by that body's only Republican, Julius Real from the German counties, who, even more oddly, did not himself imbibe. He merely thought that other people had the right to if they wished.

A prohibition amendment eventually was submitted to the voters in July of 1911. The stumping for and against it was the most hysterical the state had seen since the

Although Texas was rightly famous for its cattle industry, the little town of Cuero in the south-central part of the state became the focus of a thriving turkey industry. With demand being largely seasonal, birds were rounded up from area ranches shortly before Thanksgiving and driven toward the city abbatoirs. The leading rancher of the area, Isaac Egg—happy name—could be counted on to drive in some ten thousand birds alone. Beginning in 1912, the city turned this into a festive event, the Cuero Turkey Trot, with bunting along the main street, a parade presided over by royalty (the Turkey Sultan and Sultana), automobiles and women decked out in turkey feathers, and turkey races. Seen here in one early Turkey Trot, is Governor Colquitt, in top hat, pictured nearest to the camera, presiding over the annual running of the birds.

frontier campaigns involving Sam Houston. The drys assembled a statewide onslaught of speakers from former Governor Campbell to the best-known religious leaders and moralists in the state. Governor Colquitt led the wet forces and was heard with equal or greater interest; shortly before the election, 7,500 people gathered in Dallas to listen to him, followed by 10,000 in Fort Worth the next day. In the end, forced statewide prohibition was turned down by the people, but by only six thousand votes out of nearly a half million cast. The dry forces claimed election fraud, but local option continued to be the governing law. Oddly, after all this, Colquitt's downfall almost came in a tempest against the adoption of a particular history book for use in the public schools. The book contained a photograph of Abraham Lincoln. Ignoring the barely latent animosity that remained from Reconstruction, Colquitt declared, "I want the truth of history taught. . . . I had rather resign . . . than have my children studying a textbook in the public schools of Texas with Abe Lincoln's picture left out of it, and I am the son of a Confederate soldier."

The fury Colquitt stirred up over Abraham Lincoln did not make his reelection in 1912 any easier. Running against him in the primary was state supreme court justice William Ramsay, who stumped to strains of "Dixie," rhapsodized about Confederate veterans, and won the support of most of the newspapers. Ramsay was also an ardent prohibitionist, and he took to referring to the governor as Oscar "Budweiser" Colquitt. It was not a pretty race in a state where gubernatorial reelection had been a traditional courtesy, but Colquitt won out—216,000 to 180,000. In the general election, the governor was reelected ten to one over his Republican opponent. Also running, incidentally, as a Prohibitionist-Republican was Andrew Jackson Houston, second son of the legendary Big Sam, but he finished a lame fourth, behind both a Republican and a Socialist. It was his third and last try for a term in his late father's house; in no contest for the seat did he poll more than six thousand votes.

Colquitt took the voters' sentiments to heart, and his second term saw the passage of a broader slate of reform legislation, especially in the field of labor. An eight-hour day was granted to state employees, an employer liability act was passed, and the employment of women in certain industries was limited to no more than fifty-four hours a week or ten hours in any one day. And Standard Oil of New Jersey, still not completely extricated from the Waters-Pierce mess, had to fork over a half-million-dollar antitrust fine.

For some time since, state politics had been getting on without onetime kingmaker Edward M. House, who had engineered the campaigns of Hogg and his successors. House had gone on to richer pastures, delivering the Texas delegation to Woodrow Wilson, the governor of New Jersey, in a tensely fought, smoke-filled Democratic National Convention in Baltimore; he then stayed on to manage Wilson's campaign. Wilson took House deeper into his confidence than any other adviser, and almost

The camera-shy Col. Edward M. House *(left)* of Houston was captured in a re-flective pose during the height of his influence. Born in Houston three years before the Civil War began, his father sent him to a private school in Connecticut to receive a better education than Reconstruction Texas could offer. He formed a bond there with the son of Indiana senator O. H. P. T. Morton, through whose favor young House met a number of leading political figures. It was by House's own ability, however, that he won their respect. Upon returning to Texas in 1880 to manage his share of the family estate, he indulged a passion for back-room politics that wed shrewd maneuver with a sense of public responsibility.

It was Governor Hogg who awarded him the honorary title of colonel—a cross that that he patiently bore—but he would not accept an official position either from Hogg or the governor's three successors. He first met Woodrow Wilson in November of 1911, and they took to each other at once; after delivering the 1912 nomination to Wilson at a badly fractured convention, then managing during the campaign to keep the Democratic party united while Taft and Theodore Roosevelt fed on each other, House could have had any office in Wilson's gift. He chose, however, to continue to advise privately. When in Austin, House ran his operations from his striking house on West Avenue *(right)*—now demolished.

until the end of Wilson's term the quiet, canny, deal-making pragmatist was at the President's side and probably was the second-most-powerful man in the country.

Although he was not cut from the brawling western mold Texans would have preferred, they found much to like about Woodrow Wilson. He was a populist, but a schoolteacher, which made his brand of populism more respectable than it had been for a while. And, more importantly, he advocated an aggressive foreign policy; with the newest Mexican revolution two years under way, the thought of the federal eagle glaring at the Rio Grande was a comforting one. Wilson was not universally popular among Democrats in Texas, especially among the bosses in the valley, but their distaste was more a personal matter than one of policy. Jim Wells was heard to utter the words *boob* and *schoolmarm* when referring to Wilson, but, for unity's sake, Governor Colquitt convinced Wells that a nice financial contribution could preserve his influence in federal circles.

During the campaign, House even assumed responsibility for Wilson's personal safety. He sent a telegram to Quanah, Texas, for ex–Texas Ranger Bill (one riot, one ranger) McDonald to "bring your artillery"—his .45 and his automatic. McDonald disapproved of the Secret Servicemen's practice of carrying .38-caliber revolvers, and one of them had the nerve to protest that they could kill a man just as well. "Yes," snapped McDonald, "if you give him a week to die in." Wilson was enchanted.

He needn't have worried about carrying Texas, which voted for him four to one, and Texans, under the sponsorship of Colonel House, began an ascendancy to power in the executive branch that almost matched their control in Congress. Albert Burleson was made postmaster general, a powerful position for its patronage possibilities, and

Colonel House may have been genteel enough to move in Washington society, but when it came to Woodrow Wilson's personal safety he sent for a crusty Texas Ranger, CAPT. BILL McDONALD.

Thomas Watt Gregory became attorney general. House, for his part, learned to use his power judiciously, and distanced himself, and the President, from home-state politicos (such as Jim Wells), whom he considered petty and venal. One of Wilson's important allies on the Hill proved to be a thirty-one-year-old freshman representative from the Fourth Congressional District named Sam Rayburn. Back in Texas, Rayburn had risen to speaker of the state house in only three terms, and in Washington he began turning heads immediately with his abilities as an orator and—more to the purpose—parliamentarian.

Georgia O'Keeffe

GEORGIA O'KEEFFE's penchant for plain dress in an era of bows and frills expressed her quest to discover the beauty hidden in the ordinary and the unnoticed. A flower, for instance, "is relatively small," she explained in a 1939 catalogue statement: ". . . nobody sees a flower—really—it is so small—we haven't time—and to see takes time like to have a friend takes time. If I could paint the flower exactly as I see it no one would see what I see because I would paint it small like the flower is small. So I said to myself—I'll paint what I see—what the flower is to me but I'll paint it big and they will be surprised into taking time to look at it. . . ."

AMARILLO in 1912 was a bustling cow town of fifteen thousand; and as with other small ex-frontier cities in which some citizens aspired to cultural advancement, the process was tedious, ongoing, and not universally appreciated. In August of that year, a plain-dressed, gothically dark young woman disembarked at the train station to become the supervisor of drawing and penmanship of the six public schools.

Georgia O'Keeffe was twenty-four. Born in Wisconsin and reared in Virginia, a background of "open fires and a lot of brothers and sisters—and horses and trees," she was slim but full-figured, with an angular face, long nose, and a strong chin framed by ample coarse black hair. Beneath a high, prominent forehead, full eyebrows hedged thickly above hollow, deep-set dark eyes that conveyed any emotion—rage, disdain, quest, mischief—with stunning penetration. In an era of frills and corsets, O'Keeffe's attire was severe: black dresses, white collars, straight lines. Her visage seemed already a metaphor for one aspect of her later art: drawing the eye to the essential beauty in a forbidding landscape.

Independent—sometimes rudely so—and intimidated by the credentials and society of the other art teachers, O'Keeffe took up residence not at a boardinghouse respectable for young single women but at the rowdy Magnolia Hotel on Polk Street, where she got a truer feel for the time and place in which she found herself, observing cowboys just in from the ranches as they ate and drank, played cards, and consorted with painted women. Nearby, the Grand Opera House was featuring a burlesque, *Miss Behave*.

Also of concern to colleagues and neighbors, O'Keeffe often took long walks, alone, out on the prairie, sometimes guiding herself back late at night by the city lights radiating into the sky. The Texas plains spoke right to her artistic core; it was "the only place," she later recalled, "where I have ever felt that I really belonged— that I felt really at home." After a summer of teaching in New York, she turned down a better job for more money in order to return to Amarillo.

The welcome, however, did not last. Beginning in 1913, the state of Texas required that courses be taught from textbooks that had been approved by a selection committee. It was a positive reform in some respects, but art at this time was taught, especially in the public schools, by imitation: copying. It was a method against which O'Keeffe had rebelled as a student herself, and which had even caused her to abandon art entirely for a time. Only when she studied with an associate of the influential Arthur Dow, who theorized that art is better related in its abstract elements—masses of light and dark, presented in the context of two-dimensional Oriental decoration, rather than in mere "nature-imitation"—did she resume her career with renewed energy. Such art, however, was more than the public schools of Amarillo were ready for.

Rather than subject her students to a methodology that she found useless, she defied the superintendent, refused to order the approved books, and encouraged the pupils to draw the things they saw every day—doors, weeds—teaching them to see, really see, as well as draw. And she found her pupils receptive; she was particularly arrested by the work of her Mexican students, whose simple drawings divided space into flat planes of bright colors and seemed almost to prove the validity of Dow's

Two weeks after ensconcing herself at the Magnolia Hotel, O'Keeffe was interrupted at an evening domino game by shooting in the street outside. The guests crowded into the doorway in time to see a man stalk by holding a smoking sawed-off shotgun. One woman standing by O'Keeffe asked him what the trouble was. He replied. "Nothing. I got him."

These two views of Amarillo express well the difference between what other people saw and what O'Keeffe saw. This somewhat later view of POLK STREET *(above)* depicts the hive of daily activity in which the busy and the self-involved were caught up every day. O'Keeffe perceived it more in its elemental geometry— as in the aerial view *(below)*—of titanic planes of sky and earth.

theories. Adult eyebrows, however, rose when she guided her elementary students in hefting a pony onto her desk for them to draw.

Regarded as eccentric and unsociable by her colleagues, O'Keeffe undoubtedly spent some of her quiet hours in recalling a meeting, or near-meeting, in New York five years previously. She and some other students had visited the celebrated 291 gallery, the center for American progressive art, which was lorded over by the indomitable photographer Alfred Stieglitz, who treated them abruptly. The grumpy old man fascinated her. "Do you know," she later confided to a friend, "I believe I would rather have Stieglitz like some thing—anything I had done—than anyone else I know of."

Tired of feuding with the superintendent and anxious to explore where her Texas inspirations would lead her, O'Keeffe left Texas after the 1913 to 1914 term for further study in Virginia, South Carolina, and with Dow himself in New York. Her two-year exile to Amarillo had radicalized her own artistic thinking, and she sent a roll of abstract drawings to her friend Anita Pollitzer for comment, with the instructions that no one else see them. Pollitzer was so struck by them that she disobeyed and showed them to Stieglitz. "Finally," the great impresario reputedly said, "a woman on paper," and he exhibited them. Aghast, O'Keeffe stormed the 291 gallery and demanded they be taken down, but Stieglitz talked her out of it.

With this approval, O'Keeffe returned to Texas in the fall of 1916 to teach at the West State Normal College in Canyon, just south of Amarillo. When not teaching fashion design and interior decoration, she hiked the vast palette of the Palo Duro Canyon. The thousand-foot drops that once sheltered Indians from the cavalry and then sheltered Goodnight's cattle from the northers now sheltered this bony young woman who reveled in the beetling simplicity of sheer cliffs of brown, red, white, and ocher, occasionally emitting unfeminine echoing whoops at the sheer splendor of it. "That was my country," she said once. "Terrible winds and a wonderful emptiness." She heard that Stieglitz kept one of her revolutionary drawings, *Blue Lines*, inspired by the upward-yearning crevices of Palo Duro Canyon, over his own table.

Instead of remaining in her boardinghouse, where she nearly gagged at the pink wallpaper in her room, O'Keeffe soon approached Douglas Shirley, a physics professor at West Texas State, and his wife, Willena, to rent the upstairs room in their home, which had a three-windowed dormer that faced east and commanded an uncluttered view of the sunrise. In the Texas dawn, she related, "The light would begin to appear and then it would disappear and there would be a kind of halo effect, and then it would appear again." She assayed it endlessly, and her Canyon years produced many *Light Coming on the Plains* studies.

Her colleagues at West Texas State tried to overlook her strangeness and respect her, sobered by the testimony of students who found her an inspired and inspiring teacher. Some succeeded, but artistically they were not on her plane. She asked the Shirleys for permission to paint the trim of her east-facing dormer black, to frame the dawns; they said no. Once she showed Douglas Shirley an interpretaton of Palo Duro, and all he could say was, "It doesn't look like the canyon to me." O'Keeffe protested that it showed the way she *felt* about the canyon. "Well," said Shirley, "you must have had a stomachache when you painted it!" She tolerated their moronics, and occasionally even showed them a piece of artwork and let them guess what it was, sharing the joke with them when she told. She was not humorless; she could mimic other faculty wickedly, and when something struck her fancy she erupted in great peals of laughter. Deep down, however, she grew alienated. At least in distant New York, the great Stieglitz championed her work with his unique vigor. He now wrote her incessantly.

In the pre–World War I Texas Panhandle, the Old West was not gone beyond recall. Down on the floor of the Palo Duro, an eighty-one-year-old CHARLES GOODNIGHT (*left*) still ran the JA Ranch, and he hosted Canyon city's social event of the season at his house (*right*) a few weeks after O'Keeffe's arrival. As several hundred towns-folk cheered, bow-wielding Comanche and Kiowa Indians whom Goodnight had brought over from their reservation rode down and killed one of his buffalos. Both nostalgia and steaks were appreciated by all.

Gossip also swirled about her personal affairs. She allowed an attorney friend to visit her, unchaperoned, in her room. Willena Shirley put a stop to that, but then O'Keeffe allowed one of the West Texas State students, Ted Reid, to drive her out onto the plains to sketch or study the light—sometimes moonlight. To her colleagues, such behavior was partly offset by the force with which she could defend her artistic principles. O'Keeffe gave a Faculty Circle lecture on Cubism, and to her mischievous delight provoked such an intense discussion that time was deducted from the music teacher's discourse on Wagner.

The end of Georgia O'Keeffe in Canyon came not over her private life, which appears to have been quite blameless, but over her politics, or lack thereof, at the advent of World War I. She was not subversive, by any means, but unthinking parroted jingoism irked her, and rural Texas was not a hospitable place to think philosophically—at least out loud—on the nature and causes of war. Not only did the idea of war sicken her; she was an artist. That wasn't just what she did; that's who she was. "What does patriotism have to do," she challenged a colleague, "with seeing a thing as green when it is green and red when it is red?"

During the patriotic fervor of the Great War, none were too young to express their devotion. State law mandated that schoolchildren receive ten minutes of instruction every day in "intelligent patriotism."

In Canyon, as elsewhere, flags were displayed and bunting hung from front porches. West Texas State did its part, offering degrees to male students who enlisted before their final exams, and O'Keeffe offended patriotic faculty by counseling her students to finish school before enlisting. During a chapel lecture, a history professor tortured Nietzsche, to O'Keeffe's thinking, to fuel an anti-German harangue; she jumped to her feet and demanded to know whether he had ever even read Nietzsche. The hall buzzed, and from that time her Texas days were numbered.

The horrible epidemic of influenza that ravaged the whole country that year swept into Texas with the winter northers. O'Keeffe had never enjoyed robust health, and, despite the papers that she layered under her dresses to block the winds, she took sick. Granted a leave of absence for the spring semester, she agreed to teach summer sessions and left to recuperate with a friend in south Texas. Back in Canyon, however, the rumors whirled that she had been fired for subversion, and the newspaper intimated that her illness was not really that serious.

Stieglitz, however, was alarmed about her health, and, with his own career in a perceived decline, he sent a young protégé to Texas to persuade her to come to New York. She loved what the Texas landscape imparted to her, but her professional impasse seemed insuperable. With the word now that Stieglitz not only desired her presence but needed her, she quietly entrained for the East in June 1918. They married six years later.

Georgia O'Keeffe's art was far from finished in its evolution. The levitating skulls and titanic flowers for which she became so famous lay in her future, but it was the Texas panhandle, with its huge vistas and high clarity, that gave her a new way of seeing, and, in her vision, the seed was planted to magnify the beauty found in the commonplace.

Texas's Own Battleship

This panoramic view of the launching ceremonies for the superdreadnought USS *Texas* captured the advent of a new era in battleship construction.

PERHAPS because of their history of having once been an independent republic, with their own navy, Texans had always maintained a lively interest in American naval vessels with strong Texas connections. The last ship named for the state, the Atlantic flag of Teddy Roosevelt's Great White Fleet (which had ridden out the 1901 hurricane in Galveston harbor), had been retired and sunk as a gunnery target. Since that time, battleship architecture had undergone a radical metamorphosis. Gone was the bristling grab bag of different gun sizes and calibers, outdated by Great Britain's revolutionary HMS *Dreadnought*, mounting a main battery of huge twelve-inch rifles and a bare minimum of secondary armament. Every naval power on earth joined the race to improve on the *Dreadnought* concept, and when in 1911 the United States Navy laid the keel of a new USS *Texas*, designed as the largest and most powerful battleship the world had ever seen, the interest from Texas was keen.

Texas and her sister, *New York*, trumped the world's other fleets by mounting ten fourteen-inch guns in five twin-mounted turrets, with a secondary battery of five-inch guns in main deck casemates and a smattering of three-inch mounts for lighter duty. Her construction took almost three years and cost a then-astronomical $6 million. After joining the fleet in 1914, she made a port call to Galveston, where she was swarmed with incredulous visitors and presented with a magnificent silver service for the officers' wardroom.

With the entry of the United States into the war, *Texas*, *New York*, and three other battleships steamed to Great Britain, where they operated as the Sixth Battle Squadron of the British Grand Fleet. *Texas*, however, was tardy. Under her full-load displacement of 35,000 tons, she ran aground off Block Island. Standard efforts to free the stricken goliath failed and when she was finally powered off the mud—as the crews of tending vessels shouted, "Come on, *Texas!*"—she had to return to New York for repairs.

Cleaving a ten-foot bow wave and with coal smoke billowing from her funnels, *Texas* on her sea trials in 1914 pushes up to speed. Although she was designed to be the first capital warship to attain twenty knots, the contractors failed to outfit her with the planned turbines, and *Texas* was hampered throughout her life with reciprocating engines that, although among the very largest ever built, were obsolete even at the time they were installed.

In her patrols with the British, the monster guns were never fired in anger; the Germans had already had a taste of fleet action at Jutland, and the *Hochseeflotte* did not challenge again. Her only action came on January 30, 1918, firing five-inch rounds at a periscope, only to heel hard over to avoid a German torpedo. She was, however, one of the vessels that escorted the German fleet to their surrender at Scapa Flow, and she returned to New York the day after Christmas.

Shortly after the war, *Texas* took part in a bit of history that presaged the passing of her own era. In March 1919, the first airplane ever to be launched from an American battleship, a Sopwith Camel, was catapulted aloft from her number-two turret.

Undisputed mistress of the seas, *Texas* was the most powerful warship in the world when she joined the fleet in 1914. Even her crew was implanted intact from an older battleship being stricken from the list, rather than being assembled from scratch. She is shown here during or just after her tour with the Royal Navy, as seen by the bearing compass painted around the number-two turret and the clock-like range finder on the forward cage mast. Although only three years had elapsed since the photo taken on her sea trials, numerous other additions to her super-structure had been piled amidships, signaling the end of clean-line battleship design.

Border Mayhem

Throughout the second decade of the twentieth century, the last thing Texas citizens wanted to see was the sudden appearance of bandolero-hefting *insurgentes* in their town. A call for Rangers was sure to follow.

THE problem of crime along the long border with Mexico had existed literally since independence. What began as a show of disdainful machismo to the breakaway Texans—the cattle rustling, thievery, and murder—soon evolved into a livelihood for Mexican *jefes* on the outs with their government, such as Cheno Cortina in the 1850s. By no means was it a one-way operation, and it was certainly fed by the racism and discrimination of Anglos on the north side of the river. Nevertheless, tensions that had never entirely abated rose dramatically when the Mexican Revolution, which began in 1910 against the repressive regime of Porfirio Díaz, had repercussions that spilled over into Texas almost from the beginning.

Indeed, some Texans got to witness the first outbreak of fighting. Díaz had held power for thirty years, a period of increasing industrialization, brought about by increasing foreign investment, but also a period of increasing class division and foreign domination. Supremely confident, however, Díaz offered to stand for election in 1910 and dared the liberals and intellectuals to take their best shot. They fielded Francisco

Madero, a thirty-seven-year-old idealist, a native of Coahuila State but educated at the University of California. During the campaign, Díaz had Madero jailed, and he won the election. Upon his release, Madero fled into Texas, raised his standard, and became the brains of the revolution, directing the insurgency in part from hideouts in San Antonio and even Dallas.

El Paso was uniquely important to him. He was well regarded there and could organize and recruit, plus it was just a stone's throw across the river from the important city of Juárez, which was only lightly held by federal forces. On February 6, 1911, about fifteen hundred rebel troops planted themselves outside Juarez, opposite El Paso's ASARCO smelter. There they were soon joined by about five hundred more, following the lead of an ex-bandit once named Doroteo Arango but who had rechristened himself Francisco ("Pancho") Villa. Madero, who by now had proclaimed himself president, arrived with still more men on April 2. The doings were watched with fascination from El Paso, binoculars raised, Kodak cameras clicking. Women in white bustles, carrying parasols, gazed just across the narrow river at the fiercely stereotypical mob of insurrectos—all mustaches and stubble beneath impossibly huge sombreros, weighted down with crossed bandeleros of cartridges, hunting knives thrust through their belts. Sympathizers threw them money and even cookies.

To oppose Madero's three thousand men, the federal commander had a garrison of only seven hundred, but they held the advantage of position, fortification, and artillery. In an attempt to avoid bloodshed, the two sides negotiated on neutral ground—El Paso's Sheldon Hotel—but the talks broke off on May 7. Late the next morning, rebel commanders opened battle, without Madero's permission, and for three days Ciudad Juárez was a bloodbath. The firing was clearly audible in El Paso, and from rooftops, balconies, and railcars El Pasoans strained to follow the action. Soldiers from Fort Bliss tried to prevent citizens from approaching too close, but by the end of the fight five Americans had been killed and fifteen wounded by stray bullets.

The Díaz government had already begun to crumble, from multiple factors; when the dictator gave up and subscribed the Los Tratados de Ciudad Juárez, Madero became president of Mexico and was later affirmed in an election. Texans were relieved that the struggle—a short one as Mexican revolutions go—seemed over and that the good man had triumphed. But Díaz, at least, had known how to survive. The idealistic Madero lacked his brutality. Pancho Villa and another rebel *jefe*, Emiliano Zapata, spurned Madero's leadership and conspired with the head of Madero's army, Victoriano Huerta, who overthrew Madero and had him murdered. Huerta controlled the country for a while, but Villa and Zapata turned on him, too, and when joined by still another insurgent leader, Venustiano Carranza, all fighting Huerta and one another, chaos reigned utterly. (Enlisting briefly as a Huertista, incidentally, was Gregorio Cortez, pardoned from Texas prison.)

Huerta gave up the struggle in 1914, and of the remaining contenders, Carranza emerged on top, his position acknowledged by the United States and eight Latin countries. This was enough for the others, except Pancho Villa, who was galled to the core. He decided to call attention to his outrage by staging raids into American territory in 1916. He devastated the town of Columbus, New Mexico, and his forces also crossed the Rio Grande at different points into Texas.

This was the last straw for Texans and most especially the Texas Rangers, fifty-six of whom were on duty in the valley trying to keep a lid on the cross-border rustling. They were already boiling over an incident the previous year that is usually politely forgotten in modern history books but that struck the populace like a bomb at the time. Early in 1915, there was taken into custody in McAllen one Basilio Ramos,

The Texas Rangers were not without their own problems during the border troubles. The practice of hiring men into the organization on the basis of patronage rather than ability began with Colquitt, but it was a practice increasingly abused by both Ferguson and Hobby. The exigencies of bandits on the border, prohibition at home, and war abroad swelled the Ranger organization to several hundred, many of whom were unqualified and unsuitable, to the disgust of hard-riding veterans like those pictured here: CAPT. FRANK HAMER, at right in the tie and dark hat, learns tricks of the trade from CAPT. CHARLES STEVENS, at center with binoculars. This photo was taken near Tomate Bend in 1918, on the trail of Mexican bootleggers who had been smuggling liquor across the border.

The particular brand of *rinche* on their tail was of little moment to the border Hispanics, who often wound up just as dead. Often they were bandits, and often not; especially after publication of the Plan of San Diego, they seldom lived long enough in custody for this to be discovered. Typical of Ranger reports of this era: "We have another Mexican, but he's dead." German agents, one of whom was probably the instigator and possibly the author of the Plan of San Diego, operated freely in Mexico, further complicating the Rangers' job of keeping the border quiet.

a Huertista and onetime beer distributor in Duval County. On his person, he carried a blowhard irredentist political manifesto called the Plan of San Diego, which called for the redemption to Mexico of the American Southwest. All Anglos over the age of sixteen were to be slaughtered, along with Mexicans who had sided with them, and the country turned over to loyal Mexicans, blacks, Indians, and even Japanese. The invasion was to begin at two in the morning of February 20.

Ramos soon jumped bail to Matamoros and left Mexican-Americans in the valley to deal with the hideous consequences of the outrage he had ignited. Up to this time, Rangers were merely rough in their treatment of Hispanics suspected of involvement in the border trouble; after the Plan of San Diego, it was simply a race war and an open season on any Mexican caught in the open armed or without a verifiable excuse for his activities. Hundreds of them died—lynched or, more usually, shot "while trying to escape," as the saying went. In one case, a civilian constable conveying three prisoners to jail had them appropriated by Rangers, who gave him a receipt. The prisoners were found dead a day later.

From the other side of the river, border Mexicans reacted with understandable rage that had nothing to do with the ongoing revolution. Raids into American territory increased, until by June of 1916 three American soldiers were killed at San Ignacio.

The army finally sent Gen. John J. Pershing into Mexico with a force of the Tenth Cavalry to find and throttle Villa, and also sent Captain Foulois to the border from San Antonio with eight airplanes to help patrol the lonely stretches of brush country. That duty was so arduous, however, that within a month six of the planes were out of service and the other two were so dilapidated that Foulois burned them. "I didn't want to take a chance," he wrote, "that somebody would order us to keep flying them." The Tenth Cavalry did most of the chasing, catching few, but when the Villistas did manage to turn the tables and nab one of Pershing's men, treatment was no less brutal than what they suffered from Texas Rangers. Sam Robertson, one of Pershing's scouts, was captured, then beaten and dragged behind a horse. (Left to die, he was rescued and lived to receive the Congressional Medal of Honor for services in France.)

By July of 1916, most spleens were vented, although isolated clashes with American troops continued until they were withdrawn. The border returned to an uneasy calm, but more than a thousand people had died, most of them innocent victims.

By the time of the Mexican border trouble, the army's old Wright pusher planes were too flimsy to be used. Captain Foulois burned his last two to keep someone from being killed in them.

When it came to chasing bandits, the difference in effectiveness between the army regulars depicted here and the Rangers shown previously is revealed at a glance. The army was accustomed to well-ordered troop movements against a large and organized enemy. *Insurrectos* and bandits alike were guerillas; one outlaw said he could hear the soldiers creaking and clattering a mile away, and so he simply melted into the brush. Texas Rangers operating by stealth were far more efficient.

The army did not return from Mexico empty-handed. They had in tow hundreds of Chinese refugees, descendants of imported laborers from the days of the transcontinental railroad in the United States. They had emigrated to Mexico to become merchants, but once the revolution started every tinhorn *jefe* who gained control of a town demanded the loyalty of the Orientals, and many were punished severely for their willingness to trade with all factions equally. To escape the continual browbeating, the Chinese took up with the U.S. cavalry, and most of them eventually settled around San Antonio.

Farmer Jim Ferguson

A new face appeared on the political scene for the primary season of 1914, James E. Ferguson of Temple. He was forty-two years old, the son of a Methodist preacher. He had made his money in banking, but he was so slick, it was hard to pin him down on just what he was. Farmers thought he was a farmer, an image he cultivated, for the rural vote was still powerful. He was a lawyer, and had served a stint as city attorney in Belton. But most of all, during the 1914 primary, he was an extraordinary stump speaker who could enthrall audiences while saying absolutely nothing.

Baileyism was still an issue, although less so since he had resigned, to the relief even of his supporters, in January of 1913. Prohibition was still a highly volatile topic. The drys had lost the last round in their quest for an amendment to the state constitution, but they found sufficient comfort in the razor's margin of the defeat to redouble their effort and their rhetoric. And, they had a powerful new friend in Morris Sheppard, whom the legislature had sent to the Senate over "Budweiser" Colquitt's objection when Bailey quit. "I shall oppose [liquor]," he swore, "because I hear the cries of children who are hungering for bread. I shall oppose it because I see a mother's wasted face, her pale lips pleading with the besotted figure at her side. . . . I shall oppose it because its abolition will mean a new stability for the Republic, a new radiance for the flag." The prohibitionsts wore him like new armor.

Ferguson was as frankly wet as a candidate could be, but surprisingly this was not fatal to him among the rock-ribbed, for two reasons. First was the perceived hypocrisy of his opponent. Tom Ball of Houston was an ex-congressman, and touted his favor of prohibition. Ferguson took pleasure in pointing out that Ball belonged to the Houston Club, a private cabal of wealthy wets. Ball protested that he was a member only for its literary pursuits, and Ferguson took even greater pleasure in pointing out the Houston's Club's expenditures the previous year had totaled $112 for reading materials, and $10,483 for liquor—to say nothing of $361 for poker chips and cards.

More potently, Ferguson had found an even more emotional issue: land reform. When C. W. Post had founded his namesake town in Garza County, it was to provide relief to the growing number of tenant farmers. Although that experiment in setting the yeomen on their feet was successful, it was an isolated benevolence; elsewhere in Texas, more and more farmers were stuck on land they did not own. It was a long history. Before the Civil War, tenant farming was known but quite rare. Fifteen years of the rigors of Reconstruction had thrown more than a third of Texas farmers into tenancy, and by 1910 the figure had crept up to over half—and that was after ten years of mostly good crops. Prices fell in 1911, then came national recession, a drought, and, worst of all, war in Europe shattered the export market for Texas cotton, which was two-thirds of the entire annual sale. Cattle did not fare much better. Farmers and ranchers who were going broke but did not wish to leave the land indentured themselves into tenancy, a situation the remaining wealthy landlords took advantage

Like his predecessor, whose campaigns he had assisted, JAMES E. FERGUSON was ill-educated, and spent his early years as a vagrant laborer and field hand all over the western half of the country. He returned to Bell County to better himself, farmed, entered law practice, and founded the Farmers State Bank in Belton, which he later sold in favor of the Temple State Bank. His entry into the gubernatorial field was serendipitous—he suggested in an editorial that it was time to elect a businessman, preferably Tom Henderson of Cameron, but discovered he had named his own poison when Henderson and other influential Democrats said he should run himself. After his impeachment, he remained something of a factor in state politics; he stumped during his wife's last bid for office in 1940, and died four years later.

of by squeezing cash bonuses from tenants beyond their traditional share of one-quarter of the cotton and one-third of other crops. Ferguson promised a law to ease the burden on the sharecroppers, and waged a brilliantly folksy campaign. As a conservative lawyer and banker, he made ten speeches in the urban areas to reassure business interests, then stood on nearly 150 stumps in the country and small towns, emphasizing relief for the tenant farmers. In the end, voters overlooked his wetness and gave him a victory over Tom Ball that was comfortable enough also to defeat the (seemingly) biennial referendum on submitting the prohibition amendment.

Ferguson as governor continued to find ways to enact genuine reform without alienating—for a while—the intellectuals and business people. His tenant reform measure was enacted but was largely unenforceable because the state faced legal difficulties in interfering in private contracts. The prison reforms of previous administrations had made the Texas penal system only slightly less barbarous than before, and Ferguson instituted a vigorously liberal program of pardons and paroles that not only cut state prison costs but solidified his support among the disadvantaged. Another innovation of Ferguson's administration was the creation of the Texas Highway Commission in 1917. Perhaps even the governor himself believed it would be a mechanism to reform the process by which contracts were let for the construction of state highways, but almost from the start it turned into a nest of cronyism and corruption that helped topple the Ferguson dynasty years later.

He also alienated thinking women with his disdain for women's suffrage, which he displayed to the extent of standing his wife, Miriam, up at the Democratic National Convention in 1916 to read a minority report hostile to the concept. The more direct source of his downfall, though, was his constant meddling in the affairs of the University of Texas. Although often painted as antieducation, Ferguson did sign a bill enabling the distribution of free textbooks in rural schools, and during his administration the state even opened small colleges in Stephenville, Arlington, Commerce, Nacogdoches, and Alpine. But Ferguson was a dictatorial bumpkin when it came to the educational "big boys." In addition to trying to get fraternities abolished, he had ordered the UT president, R. E. Vinson, to dismiss certain faculty members whom he regarded as, among other things, useless "butterfly chasers." Vinson refused, and Ferguson attempted to wrest Vinson's dismissal from the board of regents. They refused, of course, and Ferguson tried to ditch uncooperative members of the board. Finally, in June of 1917, he vetoed the entire appropriation that the legislature had voted for the university—$1.5 million.

Ferguson's feud with the university probably broke no laws, but powerful alumni in and out of the legislature felt they had endured quite enough buffoonery, and marked the governor for removal. The following month, he was called to testify to a grand jury, and by fishing different waters it was learned that he had received a

Students and faculty at the University of Texas had a predictable reaction to Governor Ferguson's antiacademic polemics. This protest at the University of Texas followed his veto of that school's budget appropriation.

$150,000 loan, and Ferguson was cited for contempt for declining to name the source. When he later revealed that it came from the state brewery association, shock waves rippled across the entire state.

He was indicted on nine counts, including misappropriation of public money, and while nothing came of that, the legislature quickly transformed them into twenty-one articles of impeachment. After a three-week trial in the state senate, Ferguson was convicted of ten specifications, such misfeasance as depositing state money, at no interest, in banks that he partly owned, and paying a personal note with money diverted from the college in Alpine. The whole process was remarkably swift. He was removed from office in late September 1917, and the lieutenant governor, William P. Hobby of Houston, a newspaper publisher, was sworn in as his successor.

Hobby had also opposed statewide prohibition, but once the United States entered the war he did sign a bill forbidding liquor sales within ten miles of a military post. That whole issue was obviated by the passage of national Prohibition. (It was Morris Sheppard, thin-lipped and righteous but in every other respect a fine senator, who introduced the amendment to the federal Constitution.) While Hobby took steps to improve Ferguson's Highway Department, he showed himself no less bashful in his ability to find posts for his supporters in organizations such as the Texas Rangers. Unlike Ferguson, Hobby endorsed women's suffrage, which provided him a larger volunteer force when he decided to seek a term of his own. Opposing him in the primary was, of all people, Farmer Jim Ferguson. His impeachment had specifically disqualified him from ever holding state office again, but Ferguson did have one technicality in his favor, that he had resigned the day before his conviction, which arguably nullified the whole process.

Lacking much in the way of a real issue, Ferguson ridiculed Hobby personally, at one point making fun of his looks. Hobby frankly admitted that he was short and sail-eared, but at least he knew, he said, what money was his and what belonged to the people. Hobby was having tennis courts built at the governor's mansion, about which Ferguson sniped that a cow pen might be more productive. Droll and unflappable, Hobby was surprised at Ferguson's interest, since as far as he knew the only thing Ferguson had ever milked was the treasury. In contrast to the shady finances and "loans" of Ferguson's, Hobby distributed to the press a tally of all his campaign contributions and their sources, from 50¢ to $2,000 each, for a total of $80,500. The largest donors were himself and his brother, accounting for $11,685. Declaring, "I have no secrets connected with my campaign or my administration," Hobby also gave the press itemized expense sheets.

The campaign was a bitter one. Many of the party functionaries were Ferguson appointees and knew where their bread was buttered, and former governors Colquitt and Campbell—whom Ferguson called "the two most arrogant and ignorant fools

WILLIAM PETTUS HOBBY's early life was as sedate as Ferguson's was peripatetic. He found employment at the *Houston Post* when he was sixteen, and while he worked in the circulation department he gained a love of journalism from the paper's reporters, among them William Sydney Porter (better known for his short stories under his pseudonym, O. Henry). Hobby went on to own and run the *Beaumont Enterprise*. Like Ferguson, he was a wet, believing that prohibition detracted from more meaningful matters, and rode Farmer Jim's coattails to election at twenty-five to the lieutenant governor's chair. While Hobby retired from public life after his term in the governor's mansion, he remained an influential journalist. He branched out into radio, and bought the *Houston Post* in 1939. He wound up among the Texas conservative Democrats who split with Roosevelt over the philosophy of the New Deal and the decision to run for a third term. He died at eighty-six, in 1964.

on the top side of God's green earth"—campaigned for Hobby. With war under way, both sides tried to tie the other to German connections. Hobby had appointed Jacob Wolters, a descendant of a prominent Texas German family that included veterans of San Jacinto, as commander of the Texas National Guard; Ferguson referred to him as a "full-blooded German." Wolters defended himself with able indignation and insinuated that the mysterious $156,000 loan whose source Ferguson refused to discuss might have come from German agents. Ferguson was livid, declaring in a speech in Athens that "any man who makes that charge against anyone, even a free nigger, is the worst slacker and traitor there is." After it all, Ferguson was walloped two to one in the primary, and it was Hobby who oversaw the remainder of Texas's contribution to the war effort.

T-Patchers and
Tough 'Ombres

Lᴀꜰᴀʏᴇᴛᴛᴇ, Wᴇ Aʀᴇ Cᴏᴍɪɴɢ: the Thirty-sixth (Texas) Division parades through Fort Worth before shipping out for France.

Oꜰ war interest to Texans, similar to following the exploits of their battleship, was the recruitment of two infantry divisions composed predominantly of Texans. Soldiers of the Texas National Guard were organized as the Thirty-sixth (Texas) Division on July 18, 1917, adopting for their insignia a distinctive T (for Texas) patch, which gave rise to their nickname. Their first units arrived in France at the end of May 1918 but did not see combat until October 6, when in the Champagne sector of the Meuse-Argonne offensive they managed to wrest Rheims from the grip of the Germans. In twenty-three days of battle, they suffered 2,600 casualties.

Other recruits from Texas and Oklahoma were organized as the Ninetieth Division on August 25, 1917. Units began embarking for France in mid-June 1918, and on station there, adopted as their insignia a T-O (Texas-Oklahoma) patch, later accepted as the acronym for Tough 'Ombres. They fought in the Villers-en-Haye and Puvenelle sectors of the Lorraine, as well as in the Saint-Mihiel and Meuse-Argonne contests.

Defending a machine-gun nest.

A wounded T-Patcher pauses for a breather.

After suffering some 9,700 casualties, the Tough 'Ombres were selected for occupation duty inside Germany, and they were not shipped home until May of 1919.

The photograph on page 103 shows the Thirty-sixth Division parading in review in Fort Worth prior to being shipped out. The photos on the following pages comprise a short album of views snapped by soldiers of the Thirty-sixth and Ninetieth divisions during various stages of licking the Kaiser—in action, in pain, in victory, and in fun.

Accepting hot chocolate at a Red Cross station.

Receiving decorations from General Pershing. Note T patch on the shoulder.

Soldiers of the Ninetieth (Texas-Oklahoma) Division become some of the brawniest women in the history of French theater.

Victory at last. Tough 'Ombres gather behind their banner in an occupied German village.

The Great War
Comes to Texas

GEORGIA O'Keeffe was not alone in feeling the lash of overzealous patriotism during the Great War. Up until the moment the United States entered the fray, it was not at all unusual to find Americans who were sympathetic to the German side of the European squabble. In fact, it was pretty respectable; former governor Colquitt was an open sympathizer. Once Wilson asked for a declaration of war, however, a wave of anti-German fervor swept the country. In Texas, the 1918 gubernatorial contest was peppered with charges of German sympathy, and the movement reached the nadir of silliness when Governor Hobby vetoed the fiscal appropriation for the German department at the University of Texas. While this was a relatively harmless manifestation, the suddenly correct hatred of Germans and all things Germanic sometimes had hideous effect on the large population of German Texans who lived mostly in central Texas and the Hill Country.

While it was patriotic nationally to be anti-German, what happened in Texas was that it legitimized anti-German loathing on the part of Anglo-American Texans, which had surfaced from time to time ever since the establishment of the German colonies in the 1840s. During antebellum times, the slave-beating cotton planters of east Texas despised the German newcomers, not only because they wouldn't own slaves but because they were industrious, thrifty, and shrewd and soon outstripped the Anglo-American Texans in economic status. During the Civil War, the sympathies of German Texans lay largely with the Union, which gave Confederate Anglo Texans license to brutalize and occasionally hang German settlers anywhere they could be caught. More recently, the German counties had been indefatigably Republican in their voting habits, cause enough for suspicious loathing; now with war, the gauntlet had to be run again. Bank accounts were squinted at for their ability to buy war bonds, and, reputedly, even enlistments were strong-armed if not outright shanghaied. It was a disgrace, but such were the times, and it still remains a shunned topic of examination.

Woodrow Wilson's reelection slogan—"He kept us out of war!"—eventually played him false. Germany's resumption of unrestricted submarine warfare and, more importantly for Texas, their blatant stirring in Mexico's ever-simmering pot, made the decision to fight a hugely popular one. Some 200,000 young Texans rushed to volunteer, including the entire 1917 class at Texas A & M—an institution that contributed no fewer than 2,200 military officers to the effort.

At home, few questioned the need for the food regimen called "Hooverizing"—no pork on Thursdays and Saturdays, no meat on Tuesdays, and no wheat on Mondays and Wednesdays. Those who could not buy Victory Bonds and Liberty Bonds at least scraped up enough for some War Savings Stamps. "Give Till It Hurts" was not criticized.

With its vast stretches of vacant real estate, Texas hosted a concentration of army training bases, but it was aviation that made the most lasting impact on the state's prestige and economy. Observing three years of war in Europe had done little to modify the U.S. military's thinking about airplanes, or their combat potential. At a time when France and Germany had five hundred flying machines apiece, the U.S. Army had twenty-one, still attached to the Signal Corps, for their entire utility was seen in reconnaissance. Not until 1916 did the army move to establish a training base for pilots. Lieutenant—now Captain—Foulois had been forced from San Antonio

Lt. George E. M. Kelly, for whom Kelly Field was named, was British by birth but joined the U.S. Army after being refused by the British and Canadian armies. He saw duty in China and the Philippines before transfering to the new Air Service; he was taught to fly by Glenn Curtiss himself. Kelly was killed on May 10, 1911, while attempting to land his Curtiss Type IV Pusher on the Fort Sam Houston parade ground. He hit too hard and fast, wrecking the landing gear. The plane bounced about thirty feet high as Kelly managed to steer it clear of a line of tents before it crashed again; he was thrown from the wreck onto his head.

Preparation of Kelly Field, which involved plowing under cotton fields and cutting away and smoothing over mesquite thickets, created an enormous dust problem. Oiling the dirt was considered but decided against, as it was thought the land might be returned to farm production in the future. As seen in this photo taken on the airfield, some early student pilots had more to learn than others.

when an air crash killed one of his pilots and caused the commanding officer of Fort Sam Houston to forbid him further use of the parade ground for aerial training. From his new base in Maryland, Foulois recommended a return to San Antonio because of its generally better flying weather. (This was done, in spite of the fact that a political maneuver in Congress required the base be located in the North or East.) In March 1917, land was leased, 627 acres of cotton fields and mesquite brush southwest of San Antonio, and construction begun on Kelly Field, named for the aviator killed in the Fort Sam Houston crash. The first planes landed on April 9, and the following month a further fifteen-hundred-acre tract was added. A fleet of Curtiss JN-40 "Jennies" was brought in and operations commenced.

The army was slow to enter aviation, but when they did, the war effort spurred them into shocking efficiency. Kelly Field became the reception center for the whole Air Service, accommodating more than 32,000 officers and enlisted men, with some 1,562 pilots produced by the end of the war. (Twenty-seven others died in training crashes.) Indeed, Texas became the hub of U.S. military aviation, with nine different air bases in Dallas, Forth Worth, Wichita Falls, Waco, San Antonio, and Houston. In them, it seemed as though every possible ramification of air war was explored, from advanced combat training to the release of passenger pigeons to carry messages from cockpit to base.

More Boomtowns

Texas oil strikes were not purely a turn-of-the-century phenomenon. In fact, major discoveries followed one after another, and fortunately for both the national war effort and Texas economy, rich fields were brought in just in time for the fight— at Ranger and Desdemona in 1917, Breckenridge in 1918, and at Panhandle beginning in 1918. Desdemona *(above)* was pumped dry in only a few years, and, however much activity is seen here, became a ghost town thereafter.

The effort of the United States in the Great War had required immense expenditures of lives and money and—of particular importance to Texas—energy. While the great gushers of the early twentieth century had launched the Texas economy on a sea of oil, that overproduction had wrecked the market, which began to decline after 1905, even as other fields were being discovered one after another.

Perfectly timed to meet the war effort were titanic oil strikes near the village of Ranger, about halfway between Fort Worth and Abilene, and at Goose Creek, in Harris County, south of Houston. The water of the latter stream had long been noted for its natural sheen, and in August of 1916 a gusher blew in at 8,000 barrels; another one almost exactly a year later belched out 35,000 barrels a day.

Ranger, with a population of only about six hundred, was situated in a series of barren, rocky whalebacked hills. Until that time, there was no proof that oil lay under any of the interior plains, but on October 21, 1917, one W. K. Gordon struck petroleum that blew out of the ground as greenish black as liquid malachite. Overnight, Ranger became "Roaring Ranger," as ten trains a day unloaded speculators, merchants, prostitutes, gamblers—the whole milieu of the boomtown had been shipped west; in two years it had a population of thirty thousand. There were more women in the boomtowns now than there had been during the earlier strikes, trying to care for husbands and families in conditions that the passage of time had not improved. Floors could not be mopped until the mud and oil were chipped off with a hoe. That was about the best use for the hoe, since salt water spewing from the wells killed the gardens. In the beauty parlor, a seat with a newspaper in it meant that its previous occupant was a prostitute. One woman on trial for killing her husband pled justifiable homicide, for making her live in such a place. She was acquitted.

As exploration continued, some wildcatters had luck that was positively amazing. Hugh Roy Cullen found oil southwest of Houston in 1921 on land that had yielded fifty-two dry holes, and he parlayed it into a fortune of hundreds of millions. His method was to acquire abandoned fields and drill deeper than anyone else had. In fact, there was a joke that when he died, he would lean out of his coffin and say, "No, boys, better go a little deeper." That, and his imprecise but uncanny summary eyeballing of surface geography and its probable geology, made him the wonder and envy of all his peers.

Nineteen seventeen also brought an oil strike of a different sort—workers in the field walked off their jobs. A still larger discontent was brewing, however, for the encroachment of wildcatters and drilling rigs into the erstwhile ranching empire highlighted an interesting cultural neurosis of the day. The fact was that two of the great lynchpins of Texas's economy, oil and ranching, coexisted uneasily. To those raised on the ranches, cattle were more than an occupation; ranching was a way of deeply felt living, and the infusion of city people and machinery disoriented them. Of course, the cattle industry had been in decline since the opening of the century; the ranchers needed the money oil brought but resented the intrusion into their pastoral existence. One of the most telling vignettes of the era was of the plains rancher who had leased drilling rights to the land surrounding his house. Sitting on his front porch at night, drinking whiskey, he took potshots with a .22 at the lights on the rigs, growling with each shot, "Sons of bitches."

Oil money was crucial to the survival of the ranches, however. The larger spreads especially were in trouble, and, in the case of the King Ranch, were later reduced to going out looking for oil companies to drill on their land.

The Suffrage Movement

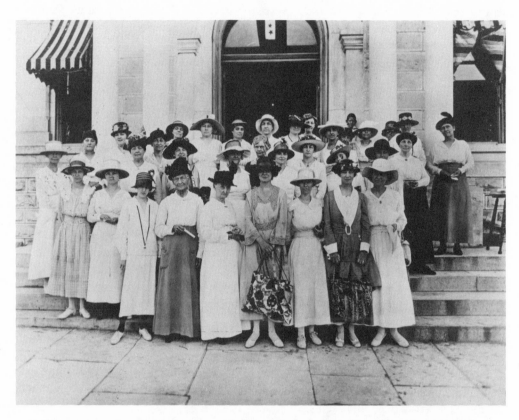

The masses of women who assembled to register to vote, like those *(above)*, belied opponents' arguments that most females did not care about suffrage one way or the other. Something closer to the real reason behind men's opposition to—and fear of—women voting is probably revealed in the propaganda photo *(facing page)*. Ex-senator Joe Bailey admitted as much when he said, "It would be useless to talk to a woman about the great and fundamental principles of the government. . . . To her way of thinking no man should be permitted to do anything which she thinks a good man ought not to do, and she would promptly proceed to pass a statute . . . punishing him if he did not obey."

BECAUSE Texas's history as a Spanish colony and then Mexican province left her a legal system in which the status of women was more enlightened than in the Anglo-derived common law of the United States, the movement for women's civil rights in Texas had less ground to make up than elsewhere in the United States. In fact, Texas women nearly got the vote in the state's 1868 Constitutional Convention, but from that time the advantage of heritage was overbalanced by the sheer intransigence of many state legislators. A similar proposal in the 1875 convention never even made it out of committee; and except for some desultory drumbeating by the Women's Christian Temperance Union in the eighties and nineties, the issue lay mostly dormant until 1903.

In February of that year, three sisters, Annette, Elizabeth, and Katherine Finnigan, organized the Equal Suffrage League in Houston. In the following month, Carrie Catt, president of the National Woman Suffrage Association, created a stir with a lecture in Houston, and soon after a state chapter was organized with Annette Finnigan as president. Their legislative efforts were not effective, however, and the organization petered out when Miss Finnigan moved from Texas. Not until 1913 was it reorganized and a women's suffrage bill introduced into the legislature. It was never voted on, but momentum was now building, and over the next two years the number of local women's suffrage clubs grew from eight to twenty-one. In the 1915 session, a resolution was entered supporting a constitutional amendment, and while it gained a majority in support, it fell three short of the two-thirds needed for passage.

Lobbying for the vote for women was an arduous task. One earnest suffragette was greeted by one cold blast after another by a particularly obstinate senator: "You ought to get married and tend to a woman's business."

"But I am married," she replied.

"Then you ought to be having children."

"I have five. How many would you suggest that I have?"

"Then you should be home taking care of them."

"They're in school and their grandmother is there in case they get home early."

"Then you should be home darning stockings!"

The lady who exhibited such equanimity in the face of such boneheadedness was Jane Yelvington McCallum of Austin, who went on to serve two governors as secretary of state.

As later secretary of state to governors Moody and Sterling, JANE YELVINGTON McCALLUM was, in effect, Texas's chief clerk, in charge of official paperwork—from publishing the laws, to attesting to the governor's signature, to registering corporations. In this capacity as chief keeper of documents, McCallum performed one service to the state of which she was particularly proud: finding and preserving the Texas Declaration of Independence of 1836.

ANNIE WEBB BLANTON knew her opponent for the state school superintendency, having succeeded him as president of the Texas State Teachers' Association. Following her term in office, she returned to private life to stake out a brilliant career, including a doctoral degree from Cornell, and eventually the chairmanship of the Education Department at the University of Texas. She was a three-time vice president of the National Education Association and was a founder of the Delta Kappa Gamma professional society. She died in 1945, aged seventy-five.

By 1917, repassage of a suffrage resolution was certain, but the real question was whether the supporters could husband enough votes to override an equally certain veto from Governor Ferguson, who was wholly unsympathetic to the cause. Ferguson's sudden impeachment—in which the ladies played an enthuasiastic role—removed that obstacle. Governor Hobby proved to be a vastly more enlightened customer than Farmer Jim. When in March of 1918 a women's suffrage amendment was attached to a bill regulating state primaries, Hobby signed it, giving women the right to vote in nominating conventions and state primary elections. Woodrow Wilson wired his congratulations, and in return, Texas women voiced support for the federal constitutional amendment with such volume that Carrie Catt referred to them as her heavy artillery.

That was all progress, and in the fall elections of 1918 the suffrage organization felt strong enough to flex some muscle in its first statewide contest. The first job, of course, was to work for Hobby's reelection, but they also made their own run for the office of state superintendent of schools. The candidate was a reluctant Annie Webb Blanton, an educator from Denton who had made a good name for herself as president of the Texas State Teacher's Association. Those who knew her, professional colleagues, the people in Denton, and even the *Denton Chronicle* supported Blanton staunchly, but the campaign turned ugly. The leading candidate, W. P. Doughty, was a Ferguson man, a liability that the women exploited with great skill. When Doughty labeled her an atheist, Blanton retorted that if Doughty had "carried his candidacy to the Creator in prayer as earnestly as I have, he would not have been endorsed by the breweries." It was a nastily effective double-barreled load, first in tying him to the Ferguson brewery-loan scandal, and second in tacitly impugning his patriotism, as prohibitionists had since the beginning of the war condemned beer drinking as a Germanic vice. Many county organizations deleted Blanton's name from the primary ballot, and only the specter of a lawsuit got her on the general ballot in November. Still, she won, and not to put too fine a point on it, soon after the inauguration the editor of the *Denton Chronicle* received a package from Blanton, with a note attached: "I think you are the only editor of a paper to receive a box of fudge made by a state superintendent of public instruction."

Crowning decades of lobbying and agitating, suffrage leaders witness Governor Hobby putting his signature to the law giving them the right to vote.

In January of 1919, both the state house and senate passed suffrage resolutions; and when the federal amendment was submitted to a special session the following June, Texas became the first state in the South to grant full voting rights to women. With their cause won, the Equal Suffrage Association, far from resting, transformed itself into the Texas League of Women Voters. Three hundred and six thousand Texas women were registered to vote and given a quick political indoctrination through special schools headed by a lady with the felicitous name of Nell H. "The Ramrod" Doom. Moreover, they organized a coalition of six statewide women's groups, including the Texas Federation of Women's Clubs and the ubiquitous Women's Christian Temperance Union, into a Women's Joint Legislative Council. From their office in Senate Committee Room 5, they marshaled through the legislature a formidable slate of bills on education, birth registration, prohibition (naturally), and prison reform. Their opponents in the capitol branded them—not without admiration—the Petticoat Lobby, a grudging recognition that, on balance, in the years since that key regrouping in 1913 the suffrage movement in Texas had posted a record of accomplishment heartily envied in the other camp.

It took only until 1922 for the first woman to be elected to the Texas House of Representatives, Edith E. T. Wilmans, representing the Fiftieth District in Dallas County. She served only one term before trying to advance to the governor's mansion, but she was knocked out in the primaries of both 1924 and 1926. She tried to win offices at various times over the next quarter century but was never accepted back into public life. The first woman in the state senate proved more durable. Margie Elizabeth Neal was from Carthage, in the otherwise-conservative bastion of deep east Texas. The fact that the people there were willing to vote a woman into office said much for her formidable accomplishments, which included being the first woman to hold a seat on the executive committee of the state Democratic party, and she had been a delegate to the Democratic National Convention in 1920. She won her senate seat in 1926 at age fifty-one, and returned for three additional terms; subsequently as a New Dealer she worked in the National Recovery Administration and the Social Security Administration. She lived to ninety-six.

Unrest and Reform

WHEN World War I finally ended, when all the shooting—if not all the suffering or the dying—was done, it was a Texan, General Pershing's bugler, Hartley Edwards of Denison, who sounded the plaintive notes of "Taps" into the quiet of the Compiègne forest at 11:00 P.M. on November 11, 1918.

Five thousand one hundred and seventy Texans had died in the service of their country; a third of them had never ventured abroad, having been felled at home by the influenza epidemic of 1918. After giving so many casualties to the "war to end all wars," Texas soon suffered a casualty of the peace: Wilson had sent his trusted Colonel House to lean on the British and French for support of his Fourteen Points, and the two were in Paris for the peace conference. But there, they had a falling-out as bitter as it was mysterious; House returned to Texas, and even after Wilson was crippled by a stroke suffered on his speaking tour in support of the League of Nations, the President's wife, Edith, refused to let House see him. They never met again. It is not unlikely that House, a pragmatist and deal maker, had tried to persuade Wilson to give some ground to Congress to make his League of Nations more palatable to them. That, however, was a point of principle to which Wilson could not accede—a stubbornness that cost him his health as well as his League.

House was only one casualty of the peace. While victory was being gained abroad, the sense grew at home that things were not quite right, that inequities too long neglected had to be tended. There were ample warning signs.

By 1920, Texas's industrial sector was poised to overtake agriculture in economic importance, a transformation that, though unthinkable before the war, was accomplished during that decade. This led naturally to rapid growth of the cities and, inevitably, spawned a labor movement. Unions did not have much of a history in Texas. The Screwmen's Benevolent Association in Galveston was one of the oldest, going back to 1866, and at one time had been quite powerful because of the unique skills required to compress cotton bales into ships' holds. Technology, however, had outmoded their trade, and the Screwmen's Association had disbanded by 1924. In 1886, the Knights of Labor had thirty thousand members in Texas, but the failure of their rail strike presaged their decline. A Texas State Labor Union was not organized until 1905, but it only lasted four years; Texas labor really took root in 1900, when six city trade councils were granted charters by the American Federation of Labor, and a steady growth began.

When ten thousand oil-field workers walked off the job in 1917, they idled much of the industry for three months, striking as much for union recognition as for higher wages and better conditions. They ended the strike in a better financial position, but the union was not accorded any standing. The postwar period also saw some ten strikes in the transportation industry, eight in metal trades, and chemical plants were shut down six times. Texas had more than five hundred locals of the United Mine Workers, and they walked out three times. Shipbuilding was halted seven times. When ten thousand building tradesmen struck in Dallas in 1919, it was only one of twenty-three walkouts statewide in that industry.

One of the most disruptive strikes occurred in 1921, when a nationwide walkout of dockworkers crippled every port in the state. Indeed, labor in Texas was so discontented that when a national rail strike was threatened in October of that year, an actual walkout was averted everywhere else in the country except for that of six hundred International–Great Northern Railroad members of Texas locals.

The agricultural advances made in the valley before the Great War, now aided by restoration of order in the region and the passage of a key state constitutional amendment to provide for the establishment of irrigation districts, led to an explosion of development in the years after the armistice. Especially with other Texas farmers suffering in a postwar depression, immigration from north Texas was heavy, and what had been a landscape of sleepy, dirt-poor transborder haciendas became a hothouse of real estate speculation.

Here, the history makes a curious arabesque. Irrigation cost money, and was most appropriate for large tracts of land. That shut most of the newly arrived small operators out of the market. The speculators, of course, saw the need for an influx of capital, and they did not waste effort showing these emerald tracts to sodbusters who couldn't buy them. Instead, they rolled in special trains—excursions offered often at their own expense—of well-heeled investors who, not surprisingly, knew a good prospect when they saw it. It was not at all unusual for such an excursion to net the realtor a million dollars in sales. The joker in the deck was that this influx of rich landowners into a section known previously for its poverty and lack of ambition gave Texas the greatest disparity it had ever seen of wealth in the closest proximity to the wretchedly poor and ignorant, and mostly, Hispanic. From the *peóns'* perspective, they had traded down to the worst possible economic status. First, they exchanged their Hispanic *patróns* for Anglo political bosses such as Archer Parr and Jim Wells, who at least understood the system and, as the saying went, took care of their people. The northerners who showed up on the trains now in many cases understood neither the local culture nor language. This was a different kind of graft altogether, and one that bore evil fruit for years. Still, in the decade following World War I, the influx of capital and its development doubled the valley's population.

As much as Hispanics, Texans of African descent also chafed under the injustices that were so woven into the fabric of life that their immutability seemed taken for granted. About a quarter of all Texans in the service were black, but they suffered no less discrimination in the military than they did on the outside. Black soldiers stationed at Camp Logan near Houston went on a rampage in August of 1917. A Houston policeman had roughly treated a black soldier and his female companion, then arrested the military policeman, also black, who tried to intervene. Word spread and rumors flew: The black troops were supposed to be marching into town, or, alternatively, the police were marching out to Camp Logan. Eventually there was a confrontation, resulting in sixteen wounded and seventeen dead. Of the 150 soldiers involved, 41 received life terms after courts-martial; 13 were hung in a mass execution.

While labor disputes continued throughout the twenties and political relief for blacks was decades away, a significant reform was achieved on behalf of valley His-

Among the valley's boosters was perennial presidential candidate WILLIAM JENNINGS BRYAN, seen here giving a speech in Mission.

Constant activity by Texas Rangers in the lower Rio Grande valley, while creating friction with the Hispanic population, did tamp down the level of cross-border raiding. Upstream, however, in the arid trans-Pecos region, one notorious gang continued to operate, headed by one Chico Cano and his brothers Manuel and José, who rode at the head of four or five dozen brigands. Splashing across the Rio Grande whenever they pleased, "they were not Carranzistas; they were not Villistas; they were not anything," according to one Presidio County rancher whose son was killed and mutilated by them. They had operated out of the Mexican village of El Pourvenir at least since early 1913. During raids in 1916, they killed one Texas Ranger and tortured a federal customs agent to death. On Christmas Day of 1917, they descended on the Brite Ranch, about twenty-five miles inside the border, terrorized the family living there, looted the ranch store, and killed a stage driver and his two passengers, who had the bad luck to interrupt them. Another raid was mounted on a ranch thirty-five miles south of Van Horn three months later, and this time troops were seen with them, wearing Carranzista uniforms.

Texas Rangers scouting the area found citizens in El Pourvenir and the nearby town of Pilares wearing clothes and using goods taken from the Brite Ranch. In the predawn darkness of March 26, 1918, eight Rangers, under the command of Capt. J. M. Fox, and four local ranchers crossed the river and rounded up a couple of dozen men of the towns. They claimed later that they were ambushed by other residents; all that was known for certain was that fifteen of the Mexican nationals were shot and killed. Representative Canales used the incident as a paradigm of the need to reform the Ranger organization. Captain Fox and his entire company were dismissed from the service, but Canales's call for reform was highlighted even more by the fact that the department was so politicized that they were removed not for the El Pourvenir killings but because Fox and his Rangers were Ferguson men, and Governor Hobby wanted them out.

Pictured here is the Ranger company that replaced Fox's in the Big Bend border country.

J. T. CANALES

panics by Representative J. T. Canales of Brownsville. In responding to the admittedly difficult and complicated series of border troubles since 1910, Texas Rangers often overstepped the bounds of prudent law enforcement and became an instrument of political repression against the law-abiding, if apathetic, Hispanic majority in the valley.

Canales launched an investigation into the Ranger organization at the end of January 1919, which resulted in a major reform of the unit. He was opposed by an array of Ranger supporters who feared a witch-hunt during his public investigation of eighteen charges of murder and malfeasance. But Canales took a wiser tack, providing in his bill to increase Ranger pay, in order to attract more qualified officers to the force. Their number was reduced from one thousand to seventy-six to eliminate political cronies and honorary commissions, and provision was made for statutory redress of grievances against them. That law was a success, but further progress in the political assimilation of Hispanic Texans was slow to occur; it was not until 1929 that LULAC, the League of United Latin American Citizens, was founded in Corpus Christi.

The Twenties and the Search
for a New Identity

THE end of every mighty struggle—in this case, World War I—leaves a people with a great store of righteous energy that must be vented somehow. A nation whipped into a patriotic frenzy cannot, just because an armistice has been signed, suddenly call it all off and return to their homes and fields. A new crusade must be found and pursued until the emotional armory is dissipated, and that crusade is given a greater sense of urgency when, as after World War I, the times are fraught with dissatisfaction and agitation for change. Nationally, in the 1920s, this took the form of the Great Red Scare. In Texas, it took a decidedly more nativist turn—in a political ground swell that was deeply conservative, pro-American, antiforeign (which included blacks and Hispanics), fundamentally religious, and preeminently backward-looking.

Such a tide of sentiment was bound to manifest itself in one organized way or another, and when it did, it was in the form of a resurgence of the Ku Klux Klan. Or rather, it was not a resurgence of the original Klan of Reconstruction days at all, but a completely new body that was much more the spiritual descendant of the Know-Nothing movement of the 1850s. The only thing they borrowed from the old Klan was its hocus-pocus of shrouds, hoods, and burning crosses, and their willingness to draw upon that specter to browbeat minority populations. But where the first Klan had existed to check Negro ascendance, that was only one part of the new Klan's program.

Curiously, the new Ku Klux Klan was sternly, even severely, moralistic in its countenance, and thus drew to itself upstanding pillars of the communities who in other times would not have lent themselves to it. To the utter confusion of northern observers, the Klan even gave shelter to prohibitionists; the alliance, however, was more natural than outsiders supposed: Most prohibitionists were white Protestants, who tended to perceive blacks as drunks, and to regard Germans and Hispanics as Catholics and foreigners, as well as drunks.

Thus it seemed natural, if not inevitable, that the gubernatorial contest of 1920 featured the most spotless goody two-shoes in the history of the office. The kicker was that he had nothing to do with the Klan. People seemed unsure whether Pat Morris Neff of Waco was qualified for office by his solid and successful political

Although enjoying a following throughout Texas, the Ku Klux Klan was particularly strong in the southeastern part of the state. This rally took place in Beaumont.

background or by the moral record that allowed him to say without contradiction that his lips had never been defiled, not just by liquor but by coffee, tea, or tobacco, as well.

In the primary, Neff was opposed by the redoubtable ex-senator Joe Bailey, who had been spooked into running by the specter of a Jim Ferguson run at the presidency itself (which was a bust), and in reaction against times that were changing too fast for him. Bailey ran against women's suffrage and Woodrow Wilson—too late on both counts—but left people wondering what he meant to do at home. Bailey's great personal weakness was his bombast; Neff lost no time in voicing the opinion that the world had produced three mighty egos. "One was Napoleon and Senator Bailey the other two." Bailey, in turn, questioned the virility of any man who had never shot a gun or smoked. His own past unsavory connections were not entirely forgotten, but Bailey won support among the Ku Klux Klan, and won the primary by just two thousand votes. That was not a majority in the four-man race, and Bailey and Neff faced each other in a runoff, where Neff outcampaigned him with such energy that politicos started calling him the Wildman of Waco. In the whole race, he gave 850 speeches—as many as seven a day—in 152 counties, including 37 that no candidate for governor had ever stumped in. He drove in his Ford; he flew in an aeroplane; he even showed up on a mule—and had a ball doing it. His own platform was simple—to make Texas a better place to live—but when asked pointed questions he did not duck them, and in the second primary he thumped Joe Bailey by a smooth eighty thousand votes. The general election, of course, was a mere formality.

The Texas over which Pat Neff presided was now one of rapidly increasing urbanization. Houston, thanks largely to the boon of its ship channel and deep-sea port, attracted heavy industry. By the end of the decade, some fifty companies were located along the channel alone, eight of them refineries. That was a large payroll, and the workers needed to operate those companies rocketed Houston past Dallas as the state's largest city.

Dallas, for its part, took on a different complexion, that of a financial capital. Insurance companies, starting with the Praetorians in 1899 and Southwestern Life in 1903, had long flourished, making Dallas a national leader in that business. During

On July 30, 1923, an important aspect of Texas justice passed into the history books. Apart from the occasional lynching, the last public hanging was of mass murderer ROY MITCHELL, before this crowd of ten thousand in Waco.

When he ran for governor in 1920, PAT MORRIS NEFF had been in politics a long time to have remained so pure. Born on a farm near Waco in 1871, he graduated from Baylor and was admitted to the bar in 1897. He was elected to the legislature in 1900, and in only three years his peers made him speaker of the state house. Later he stood for, was elected, and served six years as Waco's county attorney, where he won an amazing 406 of the 422 criminal cases he tried. To his thinking, the key to deterrence was not severity but certainty; while he did not always seek the maximum penalty, the fines he collected in McLennan County surpassed the total of all the other 253 counties in the state. Typically, he ran for governor at the behest of neither lobbies nor individuals. He was a free American, he said, and could run if he wished. After his tenure, he remained useful to the people; he was serving as chairman of the Railroad Commission during the troubled days of the early thirties, and then chaired the Baylor trustees until becoming that university's president. He was an honored old gentleman when he died at eighty, in 1952. His epitaph read, "I have worked and wrought as best I could."

the Wilson administration, Dallas beat out Houston and a host of other contenders to house a Federal Reserve Bank, which carried important psychological as well as practical advantages in nourishing its business and banking climate. With so much money to lend in a major rail hub, Dallas also became a center for light industry— leather, furniture, cosmetics, publishing, and so on. Of particular importance was Dallas's fashion industry, which burgeoned after August Lorch began producing modestly priced ladies' ready-to-wear in 1924. And, where innovation struck, Dallas's leading retailer, Neiman Marcus, was not far behind. Two years later that store was the first in the United States to institute regularly scheduled "fashion shows," where live models paraded the latest styles before prospective buyers.

Curiously, the men's clothing industry in Texas owed much of its vitality to two Lebanese immigrants. Joseph Haggar centered his business in Dallas but scattered his factories among smaller towns to take advantage of the labor possibilities presented by housewives in need of extra money. Mansour Farah, on the other hand, centered his operation in El Paso in 1920, from where he eventually became the single-largest manufacturing employer in the state.

Many of the causes agitated by the suffragettes became law during Pat Neff's administration, not least of them a major expansion of the educational system. Free textbooks had already come in 1918, and in 1920 the state limit on school taxes was raised, and more and more of the districts began adding a twelfth grade to the program. The underfunded rural schools began to catch up to those in the cities, mostly by a program of consolidating the districts. Texas Tech opened in Lubbock in 1923, the same year that the state assumed control of the so-called Normal Schools and retooled them into teachers' colleges. A need was also identified for a level of education between secondary school and a four-year baccalaureate, and a program of establishing junior colleges began, largely under the auspices of Protestant church denominations.

Pat Morris described his campaign as "one great big bright day," but his tenure saw some of the worst storms that had ever ravaged the state. This tornado descended on Austin in 1922. Three hundred students in this St. Edward's University dormitory saved their lives by fleeing the building and throwing themselves flat on the ground.

The suffragettes had also been vocal on the issue of prison reform. Neff's government benefited from their labor in ending such abuses as the chaining of prisoners by the wrists to hang from walls. (The legal reforms did not extend, however, to Texas's cuckold law, which was tested in a celebrated case in 1922. Under that law, J. O. Sensabaugh of Dallas would have been permitted to kill his wife's lover. When he discovered them in the act, he decided not to kill the man but did render him harmless with a razor. Sensabaugh appealed his assault conviction, which carried a three-hundred-dollar fine and sixty days in jail, claiming defense under the cuckold law. His conviction stood; the law permitted him to kill his wife's paramour, but not to maim him.)

One of the most lasting accomplishments of Neff's administration was the creation of the state parks system. Neff not only signed the law but, not surprisingly for him, endorsed it with a gift from his family, a 265-acre tract in McLennan County that became Texas's first state park.

In the southeast corner of Texas lay a tangled expanse of more than 3 million acres called the Big Thicket. Its massed vegetation resulted from accidents of both geology and climate, and harbored species of plants and animals—pitcher plants and ivory-billed woodpeckers—that were relics of the last Ice Age. Some areas were so impenetrable as to harbor black bears, long after they became extinct elsewhere in the South. So far from attempting to preserve them, hunters vied with one another to kill the last bear in the thicket. It was not until 1929 that an organization was formed to work for the preservation of this unique area.

It is not surprising that in a place like Texas, where within not-too-distant memory a living had to be wrestled out of the land and the elements, and where a man's advancement depended to an extraordinary degree on his own energy and enterprise, the idea that natural resources should be conserved for future generations was slow to take hold. During his presidency, Theodore Roosevelt spurred the national movement with his much-publicized camping trips with the likes of John Muir and his wholesale creation of national forests from the vast tracts of public domain. Texas, however, because she entered the United States as a sovereign nation, retained title to her public lands, thus there was little the federal government could do here.

Such forestry as Texas had began with Temple banker W. Goodrich Jones *(right)* during Farmer Jim Ferguson's administration. A skinny little man in glasses, Jones had witnessed the benefits of forestry science from a tour of the Bavarian Schwarzwald, and he tried to foster the same ethic by planting ranks of hackberry trees for shade along the streets of Temple. Hackberries were widely considered fencerow trash; his size, spectacles, and this peculiar habit made "Hackberry" Jones a town laughingstock.

Undeterred, he started a State Forestry Association, and approached Governor Jim Ferguson—also from Temple—for a ten-thousand-dollar appropriation to commence a state forestry department. Ferguson was aghast. "Why do you need ten thousand dollars?" he wheezed. "Why, for five hundred dollars I can get you a good man to cut all the trees you want."

In a move that recalled the beatification of the bluebonnet in 1901, the legislature in 1927 tipped its hat to another ladies' group, the Texas Federation of Women's Clubs, and on January 31 made a state symbol of the mockingbird.

Pat Neff's sympathy for a state park system was indicated by his keeping a pen of deer on the grounds of the governor's mansion *(left)*.

Neff had his share of failures but took them in stride. Although he had run as a candidate sympathetic to labor, a rail strike in 1922 threatened major disruption. Unwilling to brutalize strikers but under pressure from the Harding administration, which threatened to send in troops, Neff traveled incognito to the center of the trouble at Denison. Upon being told that although work was available, "none of you scabs need apply for it," Neff felt compelled to declare martial law, and the National Guard was on the scene for three months. Also, the legislature was hostile to his attempts to economize the budget, and he was unable to bring about a constitutional convention to modernize Texas's antiquated 1876 document.

Nor did the people completely remold their thinking to Neff's more enlightened social line. The Ku Klux Klan was still a power in state politics, to the extent that a "White Primary" law passed the legislature in 1923, which barred blacks from voting in Democratic primaries—which in Texas meant virtual disenfranchisement. That was also the year that Earl B. Mayfield, a onetime KKK official, won a federal Senate seat over a distinguished four-term incumbent, Charles Culberson. Mayfield's election was also illustrative of the innate shame and hypocrisy that went with Klan affiliation. In the same primary, Mayfield also defeated a former congressman, R. L. Henry, who trumpeted his involvement with the society; Mayfield had the good taste to accept their support tacitly. Klan opponents who weren't fooled attacked Henry as "the bold Klan candidate," and Mayfield as "the cunning Klan candidate."

Flying's the Thing

Investigating all the possible uses of parachutes included attaching them to the tails of airplanes, and opening them during landing to shorten the required runway length.

AFTER the war, the army had no need for the vast complex of air bases in Texas, and all but one—the first, Kelly Field—were shut down before a gradual expansion began again.

Texans' reputation as leaders in aviation, however, continued to gain currency. In 1918, Katherine Stinson, who was only the sixth woman in the world to be licensed as a pilot, flew the first air-mail run from New York to Chicago. But inevitably, some who reached for fame reached too far: In 1920, Ormer Locklear of Fort Worth, who had been the first stuntman to clamber from one airplane to another in flight, was killed while filming a movie called *The Skywayman*. His funeral in Fort Worth drew fifty thousand people. In this age of barnstorming, the tradition became current that one gained legitimacy as a stunt pilot by flying over at least a corner of Texas, and some of its most remote airstrips became stopovers on cross-country flights. In 1924 a plane wobbled aloft from remote Camp Wood in Real County, but then clipped the corner of Warren Pruett's hardware store. A sheepish-looking young aviator named Charles Lindbergh climbed out and apologized.

When the spectacular silent film classic *Wings* was made, San Antonio was the logical place to shoot it. The realism of its action sequences was, especially for its time, breathtaking; two lives were lost in filming it. Released in 1927, the first year that the Academy of Motion Picture Arts and Sciences offered competitive awards, *Wings* won the Oscar for Best Picture.

KATHERINE STINSON of San Antonio was the fourth licensed woman pilot in the country. With her sister Marjorie and two brothers, the Flying Stinsons gained celebrity status, in addition to opening their own flying school to train pilots during the Great War. At a Helena, Montana, air show in 1913, Katherine became the first woman to pilot U.S. mail; she is seen here taking the postal oath in May of 1915 for a special flight from Seguin to San Antonio. Two years later, she flew 610 miles from San Diego to San Francisco, setting a distance record, and then donated her time raising money for the war effort. Her exploits inspired would-be aviatrixes to stage a run on flying schools during the twenties.

Also significant among early Texas aviatrixes was Bessie Coleman, a young black woman from the little town of Atlanta, near Texarkana. Denied admission to U.S. flying schools because of her race, Coleman used money saved from her successful Chicago chili parlor to go to France. She returned in 1921 with a certified pilot's license, ready, as she said, to "put a little color" in aviation. For five years, she was a huge hit at air shows, saving her money to open a flying school for other African Americans. But that was a goal she never reached; she was killed when her plane crashed in Florida in 1926.

During his stay in San Antonio, COL. BILLY MITCHELL had ample opportunity to ponder and test the various military applications of aircraft. His demonstration of an airborne assault generated fewer shock waves than his sinking of the captured German *Ostfriesland*, proving the vulnerability of battleships to aerial bombs.

And it seemed that no sooner had people gotten used to the idea of flying in airplanes than some were jumping *out* of them. The first parachute course was taught army pilots at Kelly Field in 1920, in which the parachutist rode aloft on the wing of the plane, opened his chute, and let it pull him off. The idea of riding up inside the plane and then jumping out did not occur right away. The military possibilties were thoroughly explored; Gen. Billy Mitchell staged a demonstration at the reactivated Brooks Field nearby on April 28, 1929, in which eighteen men jumped from twelve planes at two thousand feet. As they floated down, they were able to unpack machine guns and lay down a withering fire on their landing zone. A Russian field marshal watched in fascination.

Texans raised in this romantic age of flight, when a county fair was not quite complete without a display of aviation, sometimes dreamed of making a mark themselves. Clyde Corrigan (he changed it to Douglas, in honor of Douglas Fairbanks),

The newfangled machines of war gave another unexpected boost to Texas economy. In Europe, zeppelin bombardment had become a feature of the war, when hydrogen-filled dirigibles pummeled rail yards and factories. They were defended against by lofting barrage balloons, also floated with hydrogen. But hydrogen was extremely flammable, and a search was on for another light gas to substitute.

At this time, helium was one of the rarest of elements in usable form. It had long been believed to be an element of the sun but had only been isolated some twenty years before from a couple of rare minerals. When it was discovered that natural gas under the Texas high plains contained from 0.8 percent to 1.5 percent helium, the British government put enormous pressure on the Americans to find a way to extract the rare element and make it available.

The U.S. Navy, acting through the Bureau of Mines, built two helium plants in Fort Worth, where the Lone Star Gas Company metered natural gas from the Petrolia Field, which was .84 percent helium. From the start, the operation was awash in cloak-and-dagger activities. The plants were guarded by troops from Camp Bowie; even the word *helium* was not uttered—it was called X gas. The Petrolia Field played out, but not before a feasible method of extraction was proved, and in December of 1921 the U.S. Navy's C-7 became the first helium-filled dirigible to fly. After the war, the Helium Conservation Act clamped government control on helium production, and the Bureau of Mines built a large complex outside Amarillo to process helium from the fifty-thousand-acre Cliffside field, whose natural gas contains 1.5 percent helium.

Helium did not become available for private consumption until 1937. A majority of the world's proved reserves lie within 250 miles of Amarillo.

born in 1907 into the Irish community in Galveston, wanted to duplicate Lindbergh's crossing of the Atlantic in his own plane, which unfortunately was a rickety Curtiss Robin monoplane. It had neither wireless nor adequate instruments. In New York in July of 1938, he was denied a flight plan to cross the ocean by the Bureau of Air Commerce. Feigning disappointment, Corrigan received a flight plan to return to California, but on taking off, he made a long, banking turn and headed over the ocean. He landed the next day, to a jubilant reception in his ancestral Ireland. "I got mixed up in the clouds," he explained, "and must have flown the wrong way." Corrigan was received by the American ambassador to Great Britain, Joseph P. Kennedy. The director of the Bureau of Air Commerce, whose name was Mulligan, while suspending Corrigan's certificate, had to admit, "It was a great day for the Irish." Corrigan's ticker-tape parade in New York was the wildest since Lindy's.

Such flights, however, remained dangerous. Wiley Post of Grand Saline saw his first aeroplane at a county fair, and in 1931 he flew his plane *Winnie Mae* eastward around the world in just under eight days and sixteen hours. He repeated the trip, one day quicker, two years later, but died when the *Winnie Mae* crashed in northern Alaska in 1935. Also killed was his buddy and fare, the humorist Will Rogers.

The need of helium lift for airships was dramatically demonstrated in 1922 when the navy dirigible C-2 attempted to land at Brooks Field, a new installation in San Antonio for lighter-than-air craft. The C-2, filled with hydrogen, grazed the hangar and evaporated.

Prohibition

At the time federal Prohibition finally became law, Texas was already mostly dry; liquor could be bought, at least legally, in only twelve counties. To the prohibitionists, however, morality could not just be legislated; to them, the old local-option concept was an issue not of free choice but of hypocrisy: They had had quite enough of drunks and beer bibbers being able to cross mere county lines to do legally what they could go to jail for only a few yards away.

Prohibition, of course, had a much greater national complexion, and in all its negative consequences that staked claims to headlines across the country—bootlegging, racketeering, organized crime, murder—the city of Galveston became a hotbed, partly by history and partly by geography.

Galveston's brothel district around Postoffice Street had been a commercial entity ever since Union troops disembarked to occupy the city in 1865. It was still a port city, with a constant number of sailors on shore leave, who had needs both liquid and carnal. Galveston thus developed—indeed, it cultivated—a "live and let live" tradition that was far less moralistic and Victorian, not to say less nosy, than the straightlaced communities of the mainland. They made frequent reference to their "Free State of Galveston." (The red-light district even had the tolerance of the Catholic Church. As Galveston's bishop, Christopher Byrne, put it, "We segregate physical and mental diseases. Let us do the same for moral sickness. . . . As long as man has free will some of us will fall into impurity." City officials thought this approach sensible, and later established a card index to make sure hookers were tested for venereal diseases twice a month.)

The geographical influence was the same as it had been in the antebellum South, during the days when slavery was legal but importation of more slaves was not. Deserted beaches that stretched to the horizon left and right were ideal places for smuggling, and Galveston became the operating center for the whole western Gulf for sneaking hooch into the country. There was even a well-known anchorage forty miles offshore known as "Rum Row," where foreign freighters—many of them British—could pause outside U.S. jurisdiction and let those who dared dart out in speedboats to buy what they wished. Local consumption was not the larger part of the business; most liquor entering Galveston was wholesaled elsewhere in the country. One circuitous importing route began in Canada and stopped in British Honduras,

Throughout the early twenties, the Fergusons' broadsides against the Klan were given weighty moral currency by two Galveston clergymen whom fate had curiously linked together for more than twenty years. Assigned to Galveston in 1896, Ohio native FATHER JAMES MARTIN KIRWIN's *(left)* leadership in disaster relief, his outspokenness against political extremism even when patriotic, his mediation of labor disputes, and his temperance stand culminated in 1922, when Pope Pius XI conferred on him the title of monsignor. British-born RABBI HENRY COHEN *(right)* arrived in Galveston twelve years before the great storm, aged twenty-five. After the hurricane, he led relief efforts, with a shotgun in the crook of his arm, but ministered to the suffering of all faiths and no faith with equal compassion. "To me," he said, "there is no such thing as Episcopalian scarlet fever, Catholic arthritis, or Jewish mumps." In addition to his prohibition and anti-Klan leadership, he was most remembered for organizing a support network—the "Galveston Plan"—that allowed thousands of Jews from around the world to settle in Texas and surrounding states.

The Ku Klux Klan did make a rigorous attempt to organize in Galveston in 1922, when hooded Klansmen materialized at a Baptist revival, donated a hundred dollars, and announced an initiation ceremony. Father Kirwin and Rabbi Cohen appeared together before the city commission demanding—and getting—a denial of the Klan's parade permit. Considering the Klan's estimation of both Catholics and Jews, the two men were natural allies, but such was their moral authority that the city's people backed them up.

before the llegal cargo was unloaded on Rum Row and then shipped by rail (in cars labeled "junk") to Cleveland. That leak was finally plugged by federal agents, but not before half a million dollars' worth of booze had gone through.

Most of the Galveston liquor passed through the hands of one of two organizations, the downtown gang headed by John L. "Johnny Jack" Nounes, who started innocently enough with a keg he had found on the beach, and who later spread his money lavishly around town. He was not the smartest at it; preparing for his second stint in Leavenworth, he was heard to sigh, "It's in again, out again, caught again. Just the same old story. It's too tough a racket to continue." Busted separately was the downtown gang's other leader, George Musey, who skipped bail to Canada and had a falling-out with an associate there, who tipped off the rival beach gang, who hijacked a $210,000 shipment. The result was a shoot-out on Tremont Street that resulted in one dead, one wounded, and one packed off to prison. Gunplay on the streets was a fact of life in Prohibition Galveston, making that city seem to rival Chicago.

The Maceo brothers, Rose and Sam.

The Balinese Room.

The beach gang was led by O. E. "Dutch" Voight, who in 1921 took on two young Sicilian brothers as protégés, Rosario ("Rose") and Sam Maceo. Immigrants from Palermo, they went to barber school in New Orleans before opening a shop in Galveston. For their customers, they would provide a glass of "Dago Red," the demand for which, and for other higher-class drinks, grew to the point that the barbershop became little more than a front for their bootlegging operation. (And no wonder— they got a quarter for a haircut.) In 1926, they opened the Hollywood Dinner Club, providing entertainment from the likes of Sophie Tucker, Joe E. Lewis, Harry James, and Guy Lombardo.

The Maceos were also heavily involved in gambling, and were later implicated— that's as far as legal inquiry often went—in the murder of the ertswhile leader of the downtown gang, George Musey. They remained popular figures in the community, however, opening other establishments such as the Sui Jen, a Chinese restaurant at the end of a pier off the seawall. They later remodeled it as the Balinese Room, one of the most successful private clubs because of a guard who remained stationed at the foot of the pier. Whenever a raid was mounted, the Maceos had sufficient warning to dump illegal gaming devices through a trapdoor into the Gulf. On one legendary and possibly apocryphal occasion, Texas Rangers who crashed into the Balinese Room were greeted by the band playing "The Eyes of Texas" and an announcer intoning, "And now, ladies and gentlemen, we give you, in person, the Texas Rangers!"

The Mexia Raid

THE twin pressures of Prohibition and boomtown rowdiness worked their worst evil on the little town of Mexia, some forty miles east of Waco. In the autumn of 1921, oil first spewed from rigs there, and in short order the population of 2,500 had ballooned to some 30,000, with the inevitable prostitutes, vagrants, and other camp followers. Stills flourished in the surrounding woods, and no fewer than a dozen and a half gaming establishments—including one in the principal hotel—operated in full view of and in contempt of the law.

When the remaining respectable citizens of the town appealed to Governor Neff to send Rangers, he dispatched his new headquarters company captain, Frank Hamer, who had been on duty only a week. Rangers who arrived incognito in Mexia reported that the center of vice was an establishment called the Winter Garden.

Within this place, they reported ominously, "was operated a public gaming establishment, *viz*, a roulette wheel, chuck-a-luck, blackjack, crap tables and various other gambling games. . . . An armed guard was maintained on the road leading from the public highway to the Winter Garden." Patrons entering the establishment were frisked, and undoubtedly took note of additional armed guards behind lattice screens. The county law officers had gone crooked and protected the place.

On Janury 7, 1922, Captain Hamer, at the head of eleven Rangers and federal G-men, shot his way into the Winter Garden while a second force raided another establishment nearby. He managed to corral nearly all the ringleaders while capturing (see below) an enormous store of gaming devices, narcotics, weapons, and some 660 quarts of whiskey. And, knowing a secure bastion when he saw it, he made the Winter Garden his headquarters while he planned how to tackle the rest of the town.

For some three weeks, he operated with little effectiveness at raiding illegal operations, before complaining to Neff that he was hamstrung by the necessity of obtaining search warrants. The local judicial apparatus was so corrupt (it was later learned that some officials were collecting up to $250 a day in bribes) that no sooner did Hamer obtain a warrant than a warning went out to his targets in plenty of time for them to dispose of their contraband. Neff, accordingly, put the area under martial

Military Hdqrs. until the owner comes back.

Perhaps the premier Texas lawman of the twentieth century, FRANK HAMER was born in Fairview in 1884, and grew up in San Saba and Llano counties before, at sixteen, heading farther west with his brother. In Pecos County, he was employed on the ranch of a brother of the notorious outlaw "Black Jack" Ketchum. His role in capturing a horse thief in 1905 resulted in a recommendation to the Texas Rangers, which he joined in the following year. He was a meaty young bear of a man, six feet three and stout, and quickly gained a reputation for character, nerve, and marksmanship. After a two-year stint, he resigned, still only twenty-four, to become marshal of Navasota for three years, before being recruited to a similar job in Houston. He rejoined the Rangers in 1915 and served with distinction during the border troubles. His elevation to senior captain by Governor Neff involved him in every emergency against the public order during that decade. He retired from active duty in 1932 but retained his commission, and a couple of times he was recalled to public service when his private employment as a free-lance corporate strike-breaker allowed. He died in Austin in the summer of 1955.

law in early February and sent units of the Texas National Guard. Within a month of having his hands untied, Hamer had arrested more than six hundred people—many of whom were clamped into a prison camp that had been the erstwhile Winter Garden. He shut down twenty-seven stills and seized more than nine thousand quarts of hooch, broke up a national narcotics ring, recovered more than fifty stolen automobiles, and ran three thousand drifters and shady characters out of town. By the time Neff lifted martial law, according to the National Guard commander, "so scarce [was] liquor in Mexia that during the last week of our stay habitual drunkards were arrested and found in possession of bottles of denatured alcohol labeled in red print 'POISONOUS.' "

Me for Ma

Born in 1875 and reared on a Bell County farm, MIRIAM AMANDA WALLACE attended both Salado College and Baylor Belton College for Women before marrying Jim Ferguson on the last day of the nineteenth century. After one career as the wife of a lawyer and insurance and banking executive, perhaps the greatest accomplishment of her political career was in pulling off her hayseed "Ma" Ferguson act for the electorate. She is seen here in both her guises, as society lady and chicken feeder. The bonnet was a loaner.

JIM Ferguson wanted to make another run for governor in the 1924 primary, but with his people no longer controlling the party apparatus he was not certified for the ballot. However, those who thought Governor Ferguson's impeachment had finally taken him out of the picture had to think again when he held a hotel news conference in which he announced that his wife, Miriam, would run for governor, with himself to be the power behind the throne. Not that Ferguson had ever been a friend of women's political rights—when once asked about women's suffrage, he responded,

"If those women want to suffer, I say, let 'em suffer!" But he also had a motto: Never say die, say *damn!* Thus Ma Ferguson ("Ma"—from her initials for Miriam Amanda) entered the public spotlight, and Farmer Jim became simply "Pa." The real purpose of the campaign—to reelect Jim Ferguson without actually electing him—was no secret. Ma said openly she was running to clear his good name, and they had a slogan: Me for Ma—and I ain't got a dern thing against Pa. The folksiness put on for their campaign played heavily on Texas's still largely rural identity, and photographers asking to shoot some pictures of Mrs. Ferguson were usually provided her—in a sunbonnet, feeding chickens or performing some other farm chore.

The central issue of the campaign was the Ku Klux Klan, whose postwar appeal was approaching its zenith. A Dallas dentist named Hiram Evans had become Imperial Wizard, and, if the Klan candidates did well, he figured to be one of the most powerful men in the state. Ma's principal opponent in the nine-way race was also from Dallas, district judge Felix W. Robertson, who ran with open Klan support. The campaign was an old-fashioned hackeydam, with the Ferguson band playing "Put On Your Old Gray Bonnet," Ma smiling and saying, "Two governors for the price of one," Pa excoriating Hiram Evans as the "Grand Gizzard," and Robertson trying to focus attention on Prohibition, which the Fergusons had opposed.

Robertson won the first primary with a plurality of nearly 50,000 votes, but in the runoff the other candidates went to Ma, who walloped Robertson by nearly 100,000. In the general election, she beat her Republican opponent, a University of Texas law professor (nice touch) named George Butte. The Klan supported him because he was running against the Fergusons, and despite his best efforts to shake them off, they helped him poll far more votes—nearly 295,000—than any candidate of that party had ever won. Ma was sworn in on January 20, 1925, as the first elected female governor in the United States. (A Wyoming woman, Nellie Ross, had taken that state's executive chair only a couple of weeks before, but the Texas election preceded Wyoming's.) As remembered by the Ferguson's daughter Ouida, "All of us piled into the old twin-six Packard, with Mamma at the wheel. It was, incidentally, the very same car in which we had departed from the governor's mansion in 1917. As Mamma pulled up the hand brake under the old porte cochere at the mansion, [she] said, as if addressing the [car], 'Well, we have returned! We departed in disgrace; we now return in glory!' " On the grounds, Ma was incensed to discover that her name had been defaced from the greenhouse she'd had built, and she ordered it restored.

Ma Ferguson, aside from appointing Texas's first woman secretary of state, adopted such a liberal policy of pardons and paroles for prison inmates—nearly 3,600 in her two years—that charges were made that her husband was in charge of selling them. One story ran that one day a gentleman accidently trod upon Ma's foot in an elevator. "Oh, pardon me," he said. Without batting an eye, she replied, "You'll have to see Pa." Her policy was not without sense, however. Since many of the inmates

During the twenties, the legislature sponsored a contest for the composition of a state song. The winners were William J. Marsh, composer, and Gladys Yoakum Wright, collaborating lyricist, both of Fort Worth, whose entry began "Texas, our Texas! All hail the mighty state! Texas, our Texas! So wonderful, so great!" and didn't get any better.

The history of the song is almost as tortured as its performance. By 1924, Pat Neff was so plagued by petitioners wishing their tunes be adopted as a state anthem that he stiff-armed them all with a contest, the winner to be judged by a special commission and rewarded with a one-thousand-dollar prize, if the song was adopted by the legislature. There were 286 entries, including that of Marsh, book-keeper for the Anderson Cotton Company. A middle-aged British subject, he served on Sundays as organist for congregations of various faiths in Fort Worth. (He was himself a Presbyterian, which may account for the tune's similarity to "God of Our Fathers.") Marsh and Wright won, and "Texas, Our Texas" was to have been performed for the first time at Ma Ferguson's inauguration. Marsh was an honored guest, but he listened in horror as the band played Ferguson's campaign song, "Put on Your Old Gray Bonnet," instead. Marsh attributed the slight to the state house speaker, who had supported another entry, and Ferguson had ordered her own song played as a compromise. Official adoption did not come until 1929, after "Texas, Our Texas" survived a second contest of almost a thousand entries.

"Texas, Our Texas" is seldom performed today, having been largely, if infor-mally, supplanted by "The Eyes of Texas." The latter ditty is a piece of student doggerel first sung to UT president William Prather as a prank in 1904, to the tune of "I've Been Working on the Railroad" (or levee, or what have you). Prather had taken to closing his addresses by saying, "Students, the eyes of Texas are upon you!" This was a phrase initiated by either Robert E. Lee ("Students, the eyes of the South are upon you"—which Prather heard often enough while a student at Lee's college) or Sam Houston ("This was passed before the eyes of Texas!"), depending upon one's personal loyalties.

freed were guilty only of liquor violations, she believed the state need not feed them when they could be taking care of their families. Pa's desk did virtually abut her own, and with his constant advice she set about governing the state. To moderate criticism over the flood of pardons, Ma did veto a new prison-reform bill; still, her term was a virtual legislative stalemate, although one notable bill, removing the disqualification of former state officials who had been impeached, thus enabling them to hold office again, was passed but was later held to be unconstitutional.

No Revisionism, Thank You. From the time Texans rediscovered their history in the early 1900s, the topic dwelt in a rosy mist of hero worship, and outsiders— even the lovable Will Rogers—had need to tread carefully when speaking on the topic. Seen *above, left*, in 1926 addressing the Old Trail Drivers Association in San Antonio, Rogers has just recounted how small the herds were when they left Texas but how they increased as they passed through Indian Territory, until "by the time they got out of Oklahoma there wasn't an Indian there that had any cattle left." All had a good laugh—except the goosed-looking woman standing at Rogers's right, Mrs. R. R. Russell, who interpreted the remark as an insinuation that her late husband had been a cattle thief. This image was snapped moments before she let him have it: A note on the back of the picture cautions that Mrs. Russell really was a popular and genial lady, and had the good manners to let Rogers finish his talk before calling him out. After some fast talking on his part, she let him off with a reprimand, and they parted friends. Rogers found a somewhat safer audience in Ma and Pa Ferguson when he visited them in the governor's mansion (*right*).

Ma also renewed the Ferguson family feud with the University of Texas, cutting its budget but softening her stand by signing the creation of a trust fund for the school's new oil royalties. As a slap at the Klan, she signed a bill outlawing the wearing of masks in public, but it was the fact of her victory, not the mask law, and the wins of other anti-Klan candidates that led to the rapid decline of the KKK in Texas after 1924. She did undermine the Canales Texas Ranger reform bill by hampering that body with patronage and frivolous "honorary" commissions again, but no real damage was done the force, even though some of the more celebrated Rangers—Frank Hamer among them—resigned in disgust.

Elected attorney general of Texas in the same contest that returned the Fergusons to Austin was a boyish-looking bachelor, only thirty-one, named Dan Moody. Like the Fergusons, he gained his reputation as an enemy of the Klan when he was district attorney in his hometown of Taylor. A vicious racial beating had left a resident "as raw as a piece of beef from the small of his back to the knees; and in many places the skin had been split and the flesh was gaping open," after which he was tarred and left chained to a tree. Moody prosecuted a prominent Klansman and won a maximum sentence of five years, after which he obtained a perjury conviction of a Baptist preacher who had testified falsely to get the culprit off. He got two years. Others involved pled guilty in return for one-year terms. Moody made the national papers, and was elected by a larger majority than Ma Ferguson.

Although he began his term as a Ferguson ally, Moody soon broke with them, partly over Pa's renewed interference in the affairs of the state highway department, which cost Texas a fortune in fraudulent contracts, and over the pardons issue: Ma had pardoned the Klansman whom Moody got convicted, after he had served two years of his sentence. Moody entered the 1926 primary for governor, his campaign doing double duty as a honeymoon with his new wife, Mildred.

The Fergusons responded to the challenge, with Pa furious at the brass of "that upstart . . . that young spud." When attacked on the issue of his law-school grades, which had been mediocre, Moody responded evenly that he was grateful that he had never been impeached and forbidden to hold office. Ma angrily threw down a challenge: If Moody led the primary by a single vote, she would resign; if she led the primary by 25,000 votes, he would resign as attorney general. He accepted, on the grounds that if he could spare Texas six more months of the Fergusons, it was worth the moral doubt of gambling away public offices. Moody beat her by 125,000, barely short of a majority, which necessitated a runoff, unless Ma resigned or withdrew. Ignoring the call of two-thirds of the county conventions that she step aside, Ma battled through the runoff, only to be buried by Moody's majority of 225,000. At thirty-three, he was the youngest governor in Texas history; the people were thoroughly enamored of him and there was talk of him making a national race one day, but the legislature passed only about half the bills he wanted, among them lengthening the school year and raising teacher salaries, and straightening out Ferguson's highway department. His failures included his efforts to establish a state civil service to eliminate patronage and corruption, constitutional amendments to ease the process of enacting taxes, and appointive state cabinet offices. Moody would have been the ideal governor to administer such a new system equitably and honorably, but Texans had grown accustomed to having a weak executive. Besides, they never knew when a Ferguson might run again, and the system Moody envisioned could, in the wrong hands, be a disaster.

In 1925, Ma Ferguson found herself upstaged briefly by another Texas woman, DOROTHY SCARBOROUGH, author of a sensational romance entitled *The Wind*. Set on the rolling plains around Sweetwater, its heroine is driven mad by the relentless blowing of the wind. Although considered a work of only regional merit by the critics, the great actress Lillian Gish was so taken with the story that she presented it to Irving Thalberg, and the result was a silent-screen classic. Exhibitors, however, refused to run the film until a happier ending was substituted for the one originally shot, which was true to Scarborough's vision. Thalberg and Gish complied, against their better judgment.

Another Texas writer of significance produced her first story two years before *The Wind* appeared. Katherine Anne Porter, born near Brownwood in 1890, had worked as a journalist in Denver and Chicago before turning to fiction. Her only novel, *Ship of Fools*, won wide respect, but it was her short stories that led her to a Guggenheim Fellowship in 1931, membership in the National Institute of Arts and Letters in 1943, and an eventual Pulitzer Prize.

A University
of the First Class

Typical of the University of Texas's physical condition was the dilapidated J Hall, which housed the Journalism Department, the Institutional History Department, and the Texas Museum of Archaeology.

THE University of Texas's feud with Governor Ferguson, and the subsequent jingo buffoonery of Governor Hobby in trying to rid it of Germanic trappings, were only symptoms of the university's real dilemma. Opened in 1883 under the mandate to develop "a university of the first class," the legislature had set aside for its support a large tract of public domain. That was good land, though, and the state later took it back, giving the university a consolation deed to some 2 million acres, mostly in the pebble desert of the trans-Pecos and the almost equally arid brush country of the border. After that, most of the school's income came from grazing leases—a piddling forty thousand dollars in 1900.

Rupert Ricker, an army veteran and university ex, came home from the Great War, distressed to find his home region—Reagan County, southwest of San Angelo— suffering from drought and the postwar recession. He determined to enter the oil business and studied geological reports of university land, which occupied vast tracts in that part of the state. He convinced himself that they contained oil—God knew, every other acre in Texas seemed to—and began taking out leases. He couldn't pay for them, and turned to an El Paso investor, Haymond Krupp, and an army buddy named Frank Pickrell, who paid Ricker a small percentage over what he had committed, and took over the operation. The leases with the university specified that drilling had to begin within a certain time, but the site chosen by their geologist was hopelessly isolated, seventy-five miles west of San Angelo. Doggedly, they had a rig hauled in from Ranger and hired a driller, Carl Cromwell, who moved into a flimsy excuse for a dwelling at the well site with his wife and daughter and also a hired tool dresser. They commenced drilling on January 8, 1921, and working slowly and expensively in the most abominable conditions—even drinking water had to be trucked in from San Angelo—they kept the bit digging for twenty-six months.

Santa Rita No. 1 only flowed a hundred barrels a day, but oil strikes on surrounding University of Texas land were in the same league as any that had gone before.

In a quest for further financing, Pickrell approached a group of New York investors, who happened to be Catholic, and they consulted with their priest about the speculative venture. He suggested they invoke the aid of Saint Rita, patroness of the impossible. Back in Texas, Pickrell clambered onto the derrick, sprinkled it with red rose petals, and christened it Santa Rita. He figured it couldn't hurt.

Arrival of the Santa Rita oil royalty somewhat eased the gloom of a campus tragedy: On New Year's Day of 1923, the university's unofficial mascot, a bowlegged bulldog named Pig, was struck by a car on the Guadalupe Street "Drag." His injuries proved mortal a few days later. He had been brought to the school as a puppy in 1914 by L. Theo Bellmont, when he arrived to assume duties as UT's first athletic director. For ten years, the dog had the run of the campus and was a great favorite with the students, who named him after "Pig" Dittner, the football center, who was also bowlegged. His favorite pastimes were chasing vultures and, by legend at least, snarling whenever someone said "A & M!"

As traffic and streetcars halted, four pallbearers carried Pig down the Drag, followed by the Longhorn band and a tide of mourners. They turned east up Twenty-first Street, stopping in a grove of live oaks near where Bellmont Hall now stands. The coffin was opened, and Pig Bellmont lay in state briefly beneath sprays of juniper boughs and lilies; a moving eulogy was delivered by Dean Thomas Taylor, founder of the College of Engineering. After "Taps" was played, the simple, dignified marker (above) was erected over the grave.

On May 28, 1923, the university's regents met to offer the school's presidency to a distinguished former faculty member, Herbert Bolton, who not only refused the post but lambasted the board for two hours on the state's having allowed the institution to slide into its present condition. On that same day, out at the lonely well shack, Mrs. Cromwell was cooking breakfast when she heard what she thought was a rattlesnake near the door. They looked outside but found instead a jet of gas and oil vapor spewing from the rig. All Carl Cromwell could say was, "Well, I'll be damned." He had suspected this the previous day; they had drilled to 3,055 feet when he and his tool dresser cleaned out the shaft with a bailer, and on the last draw beheld a bucket of oil.

In all the labor and anxiety about whether they were wasting their time, no provision had been made for storing any oil that did flow. Santa Rita was not a major well—only a hundred barrels a day—but what there was spilled onto the ground until earthen storage tanks could be graded. With pumping, the flow increased to two hundred barrels a day, but the larger story was that the Texon Oil and Land Company, with Krupp as its president and Pickrell as its manager, had proved oil on a lease of more than forty thousand acres. Santa Rita was the first tiny puncture of what became the Big Lake Field, whose vast royalties provided the University of Texas with one of the very largest endowments in the United States.

A bill was introduced to allow the oil royalties to be used to construct permanent improvements at the University of Texas. Ma Ferguson was sympathetic: "To the average man who sees the miserable-looking buildings at the University, it would appear that the state is making an effort to store up hay instead of to store up knowledge." Thus the Permanent University Fund came into being, although it was a program whose major flaw—that the money can only be used for improvements in the physical plant—haunted the institution henceforth in its chronic struggle to find money for faculty and academic programs.

Texas A & M University, which was also part of the state system, protested loudly, for the physical condition of their campus had scandalized Governor Sayers into calling it a "travesty" years before. In 1930, the Aggies began receiving one-third of the oil royalties.

The Moody Years

When DAN MOODY was born in Taylor in 1893, his father was already sixty, and the boy soon had to help his mother run the family dairy, in addition to jobs in a drugstore and as a telegraph lineman. He was admitted to the bar in 1914; after his discharge from the army after the Great War, he became a public prosecutor and held a string of posts to which he held the distinction of being the youngest person ever elected. Although his later campaign against Ma and Pa Ferguson was noted for its venom, they were united in their opposition to the Ku Klux Klan. In fact, it was Moody's successful prosecution of a KKK flogging that propelled him into the attorney general's office in the same election that brought Ma Ferguson to the governor's mansion.

After two terms as governor, Moody retired to private life, although he remained active in party politics. He died in 1966.

IN the late twenties, times in Texas, as well as in the rest of the country, were good. There had been no major news stories since Christmas of 1927, when the Santa Claus who had been greeting people in front of the bank in Cisco, in oil-booming Eastland County, calmly entered the building and, with three accomplices, held it up. Word spread through town like wildfire, and citizens armed themselves and took up positions around the bank. The robbers took hostages and shot their way out, leaving eight people dead. One bandit also died, and the rest were captured within a couple of days. Santa Claus killed somebody else while attempting an escape from jail, and was lynched.

The Santa Claus holdup was only the last of a spate of bank robberies that had plagued the state. As often happens when times are good, those who are left out want a piece of the action and sometimes resort to desperate means to get it. The Texas Bankers Association grew so exasperated at the situation that early in 1928 they publicized a reward of five thousand dollars for any dead bank robber, but "not one

When Governor Moody's new wife, the former MILDRED PAXTON, was asked whether she intended to remove Ma Ferguson's name from the mansion greenhouse once more, she replied quickly that she would not. She did not wish to provoke Mrs. Ferguson into running yet again.

Democratic continuity: Among the guests at this reception for Dan Moody was the
aged Joseph Draper Sayers, governor of Texas at the turn of the century.

cent for live ones." The effect was dramatic but wholly unexpected. Bank robberies
did not decrease, but within weeks a new cottage industry had blossomed, wherein
corrupt officials framed unsuspecting vagrants, coaxing them to the vicinity of the
bank and shooting them dead from ambush. Robbery paraphernalia was then planted
on them and the reward paid out for civic duty well done. In one particularly odious
case in Stanton, two Mexicans were offered jobs and told to wait in front of the bank.
Fortunately, perpetrators of such schemes went to the well once too often, and the
Texas Rangers quashed the setup, over the vigorous complaint of the Bankers Association. When Ranger captain Hamer was questioned whether he really wanted to
incur the enmity of such a powerful organization, he said simply, "When you go
fishing, what kind of fish do you like to catch? Big ones or little ones?"

No sooner had the hubbub over the Santa Claus robbery in Cisco died down than
the state's attention focused again on Eastland County. During the demolition of the
old courthouse, about fifteen hundred people collected to observe the opening of the
old cornerstone, because local lore had it that in 1897 county clerk Ernest Wood had
placed a horny toad in there before it was sealed, to see whether it was true that the
little lizards could enter suspended animation. Sure enough, when the stone was
opened, a mummified horned frog was discovered, which presently began to revive

and wiggle. Old Rip, as he was named (for Rip Van Winkle), was a national sensation and even merited inclusion in Ripley's *Believe It or Not*. Despite witnesses who swore that the cornerstone could not have been tampered with, a prankster stepped forward many years later when Old Rip's embalmed body was stolen from a local display.

Through much of the 1920s, baseball was ruled by Texan ROGERS HORNSBY. Born in the little town of Winter, northeast of San Angelo, in 1896, he was National League batting champion seven times, 1920 to 1925 and 1928. The "Magnificent Rajah's" best effort, a season average of .424 in 1924, remains peerless among right-handers; in a twenty-three-year career, he accumulated a lifetime batting average of .358, with 302 home runs. Even after the conclusion of his playing days, Hornsby, seen here as manager of the St. Louis Cardinals, still drew a crowd of admirers when he returned to Texas.

Texas produced other great baseball players in this era—notably, Tris Speaker of Hubbard, who was the American League's Most Valuable Player in 1912, the year his Boston Red Sox took the World Series. They repeated in 1915. Although during his twenty-two-year career the "Gray Eagle" hit 115 home runs and stole 433 bases, while earning a lifetime .344 batting average, he was even more noted in center field as one of the first great defensemen. Later came Michael Francis Higgins, who as a youngster in Red Oak once left his sickbed and played ball using his pink nightgown as underwear. As "Pinky" Higgins, he began his career with the Philadelphia Athletics in 1930, with whom he set both fielding and hitting records in both the American League and World Series.

Texas's—indeed the country's—growing business interests were aided in no small way by a rural boy from the northern Hill Country. JAMES FIELD SMATHERS entered TCU in 1904, then got a job as a typist and accountant in Missouri. Annoyed by the slowness and physical demands of existing typing machines, he began tinkering, and in 1912, at age twenty-four, obtained a patent for an electric typewriter. He perfected the invention in 1914, but World War I interfered with development until the Northeast Electric Company bought the idea in 1923. The idea was ahead of its time, however, and the company had just begun to market it successfully when it was bought out by International Business Machines Corporation in 1933. Field himself went to work for them five years later, and received various awards and fellowships for his prowess.

Other Texas inventors of note included Norman Ricker of Galveston, whose 1921 contribution of the paper-cone loudspeaker paved the way for high-fidelity sound.

Interest was also captured for a time by the news that down in the Rio Grande valley two nurserymen, A. E. Henninger and Dr. J. R. Webb, had devised a grapefruit with sweet, deep red flesh by grafting buds of the Thompson Pink variety onto Sour Orange rootstock. Their new breed, named the Ruby Red, caused a sensation and promised prosperity to times just then being made more festive by the development of *conjunto* music by Narciso Martínez. The brightly rhythmed mazurkas and polkas were given an unmistakable sound by the blending of a twelve-string Mexican guitar with an accordion's treble range. Martínez was no marketing slouch, either. *"El Huracan del Valle"* expanded the appeal of his music by marketing it himself to Cajuns as "Louisiana Pete"—or, as sometimes needed elsewhere, billing his troupe as the "Polski Quartet."

Also creating a stir was the opening of the Milam Building in San Antonio, the world's first all air-conditioned skyscraper. A chatty advertisement about the structure by one of the tenants praised the fact that "with the windows closed I can keep the wind out. If there is anything that is irritating to me it is to have my papers, telegrams, etc., distributed on my desk and then, momentarily forgetting a paperweight, have some of them blown out of order. Here I can lay the lightest papers about my desk

Billing herself as "that two-gun Texas gal," Mary Louise Cecelle Guinan put vaudeville audiences into uproars with her saucy "Hello-o-o, suckers!" and her habit of thumping tennis balls into the crowd during her act. She was a veteran of four silent features and some two hundred two-reelers before opening her New York club in 1924. She died in November 1933.

Texas produced a number of other leading vaudeville performers, including the legendary Macklyn "Fatty" Arbuckle of San Antonio.

without fear. . . ." The Milam was like a small self-contained city, with cafeteria, drugstore, barbershop, telegraph office, and cigar and stationery stores. And the size of the building and variety of tenants virtually guaranteed that one could consult with a lawyer or real estate agent, hire help from an employment agency, or visit a public stenographer, all without having to leave the comfort of the refrigerated air.

The political arena, thankfully, was mostly quiet. Moody, of course, intended a second term, but that was not the major political story in Texas in 1928. The Democratic party had not held a national convention in the South since the Civil War, and Texas's growing political clout—aided by the savvy of Houston businessman Jesse Jones—finally merited the affair. The city put up a new convention center to lure the 25,000 delegates, who converged in a very hot and muggy June.

The leading candidate for the presidential nomination was Al Smith, the "Happy Warrior," governor of New York. Legions of Texans were appalled, unsure whether to be more offended at his Catholicism or at the fact he was a wet. Franklin D. Roosevelt, also a New Yorker, put Smith's name into nomination while Houston Baptists held prayer vigils that their beloved Democratic party would come to its senses.

Texans were torn between their traditional Democratic loyalty and the prospect of voting for a New York Catholic who drank. Appraising Al Smith, they prayed loudly, agonized, beat their breasts—and went, barely, for Herbert Hoover. Moody was reelected, but the conservative Democratic backlash in Texas was such that his Republican opponent polled four times the votes—120,000—the party had received two years previously.

Sing a Song of Borger

Texas Rangers arrive in Borger to enforce martial law.

THE frontier had long since faded into history, but isolation and the phenomenon of the boomtown demonstrated that there was still one place in Texas where anarchy could rule. Oil was discovered near the Panhandle town of Borger in March of 1926; when the subsequent boom was in full roar, the town hosted some 45,000 "oilmen, prospectors, roughnecks, panhandlers, fortune seekers, cardsharks, bootleggers, whores, and dope peddlers."

The conditions were appalling even by boomtown standards, an agglomeration of "sheet-iron buildings, tents, one-by-twelve lumber shacks, people living in their automobiles and trailers." There was a whole "Ragtown" of people living in discarded carbon black tents; some men even slept in hammocks in the post office. The motor traffic was so heavy, and the town's roads so unable to cope with it, that a loaded mail truck was seen to overturn after striking a chuckhole. There was no water system at all. Dance halls were booming; one man was seen to spend thirty-two dollars at ten cents a dance. For the prostitutes, business was plentiful, but life for them had

This still near Borger was the largest ever captured in the state of Texas.

other costs, such as ostracism from decent society. "I know there was one young girl," wrote an observer. "She came in the dance hall down there one night where we were dancing. She wasn't much over sixteen years old. And she saw that crowd of youngsters. She just stood and watched 'em dance for a while. The Holloway girls were there. One of them looked around and seen this girl. Katy Holloway, she started to put on her wraps and leave, and one of the boys went out and asked the girl to leave. I've always felt sorry for that girl, because she was just left out of life."

Worst of all, the town's officials were either involved in, beholden to, or intimidated by a crime syndicate. The stench permeated the Panhandle, and an unkind ditty began making the rounds:

Let's sing a song of Borger,
   Famed for its graft and rot.
It's just a wide place in the road,
   This town that God forgot,
For this village large boasts deeper sin
   Than Sodom ever knew;
Come lend an ear kind stranger,
   And I'll whisper them to you.

Borger's remaining decent citizens appealed to Governor Moody to send Rangers, and Moody sent the best he had, Frank Hamer, who had reentered the service once the Fergusons had left office. Sneaking into town undercover in early 1927, Hamer was so sobered by what he found that he sent for reinforcements and began arresting not individual lawbreakers but the city officials and law officers. As the Rangers left town, a new prosecutor, John Holmes, was putting the former officials on trial. With the Rangers absent, however, Holmes quickly felt besieged, writing Governor Moody, "It is discouraging to a district attorney to have to fight alone and see the criminal element defy the law and run over the rights of people. I can clean up conditions here in this county if you will only help me." Moody dispatched a Ranger to assist him, but the following September Holmes was gunned down in his backyard. When Hamer returned to investigate, he found the situation even worse than before.

Borger's reputation had spread, and a dismal assortment of outlaws and wanted men had been arriving, only to disappear in the oily, violent confusion. Whiskey was being made in huge quantities at stills hidden in the Canadian River breaks. Banks were being robbed in neighboring communities, and the thieves traced back to Borger.

Despite threats on his life, Hamer opened an investigation into the Holmes murder and gathered evidence that the town's former law officers were responsible. Rather than take action immediately, he boarded a special train for Dallas and had an urgent private conference with Governor Moody, who put Borger and Hutchinson County under martial law. Hamer returned with a force of Rangers and National Guardsmen, suspended the local government and began rounding up suspects by the hundreds. Once he had filled Borger's jail, he chained more prisoners along a street. Sheriffs, constables, and ordinary policemen soon began arriving from all points distant, strolling down Hamer's "trotline," comparing prisoners against mug shots and fingerprints, and pointing out the men wanted for trial in their home jurisdictions.

Martial law lasted almost a year. When it was lifted, Borger remained a chaotic boomtown, but its modern manifestation of frontier chaos was at a thankful end.

The Troublesome Race Question

GEORGE HUGHES, in white shirt, facing camera, looked for protection from the Texas Rangers, led by CAPT. FRANK HAMER, seen behind Hughes in black hat.

LYNCHINGS were never a daily, or weekly, or even a monthly occurrence in Texas. They averaged about seven per year throughout the first third of the century (1922 was about the worst year, with sixteen). When they happened, however, they showcased white bigotry in its most cretinous and despicable guise. The great Frank Hamer might have been able to bring the wild boomtown of Borger to heel, but he was unable to save the life of one poor black wretch named George Hughes in Sherman.

In early May 1930, Governor Moody received a plea for aid from the Grayson County sheriff. Hughes, accused of raping a white woman, was safely jailed, but the courthouse was surrounded by a mob demanding his life. Governor Moody's credibility in protecting blacks from mob violence was genuine and long-standing, and at once he dispatched Hamer to Sherman to regain control of the situation. Thinking better of the "one riot, one Ranger" motto of days gone by, Hamer took three men with him. Arriving in Sherman, they found a thousand angry citizens milling and

The racial unrest and bigotry of the postwar period is quietly indicted by the life of DANIEL WEBSTER WALLACE, born into slavery near Victoria in 1860. Before he was born, his mother, Mary, was sold and separated from his father; she wet-nursed the children of her new owner, a Mrs. O'Daniel, as well as her own, and after emancipation remained in her employ. After Mary's death, her children were raised by Mrs. O'Daniel.

Disliking work as a field hand, Daniel left in 1877 to learn cow punching in the rolling plains country, and worked for such leading ranchers as John Nunn and C. C. Slaughter. He worked for Clay Mann for twenty years and took his nickname from Mann's "80" brand. He spent two winters attending a Negro school in Navarro County, and Mann withheld part of Wallace's salary in a kind of savings plan; Wallace and his new wife lived in a house on Mann's ranch. When Wallace bought cattle with six hundred dollars of his own money, Mann allowed him to turn them in with his own. Eventually, Wallace began buying land in Mitchell County; by the 1920s, he ran six hundred cattle on eight thousand acres, employed ten tenant families, and enjoyed the respect of the stock-raisers' and pioneers' societies of which he was a member. He was often called on to speak, which he did, "in language wholly lacking in Uncle Remus dialect." He died in 1939 and was buried on his ranch. A school in nearby Colorado City was later named for him.

"80 John" Wallace showed and was shown kindness all his life; he and the people around him, black and white, make the hatred and prejudice of their day seem small-minded and mean indeed.

gesticulating in front of the courthouse. Hamer deployed his men to the other entrances, and then from the front steps demanded the people go home. They defied him, and one ringleader yelled, "We're coming up to get him!"

The imposing Hamer, moon-faced and sloe-eyed as ever, drawled, "Well, if you feel lucky, come on up, but if you start up the steps there'll be a lot of funerals in Sherman tomorrow." It took the mob a while to work up their courage. But when they did move in on the courthouse, Hamer and another Ranger, deliberately aiming low, shot and wounded three of them. The crowd fell back, enraged. Hughes was inside, having made an appearance at a hearing on a change of venue. He could be protected if the Rangers got him to the jail, but getting him through the mob alive seemed impossible.

Hughes himself spied an open vault in a courthouse hallway and begged to be locked in it until things settled down. He got his wish; the heavy door was clamped shut and the tumblers spun, but Hughes had named his own death. No sooner did the mob learn of it than bricks and then bullets came crashing through the windows. Hamer responded with tear gas, which the crowd ignored, instead dousing the building with gasoline and igniting it. Most of Sherman's fire fighters had no interest in fighting the blaze, and the few who did help were hampered by goons who slit the hoses and women, some with babes in arms, who deliberately milled into their way.

Hamer set his own men at work on the fire hoses while he tore through the building to find someone, anyone, who had the combination to the vault. Every one of the officials had managed to disappear. The fire was finally put out, but by the time the vault was opened Hughes had suffocated. That night, the mob got hold of his body and cremated it in the square, then set off to Sherman's "niggertown" to loot and pillage. Governor Moody declared martial law and sent troops to snare the ringleaders, but when the latter came to trial they were acquitted by their peers of all but some minor firearms violations.

Frank Hamer himself shook the dust of Sherman from his feet as he left, and for the rest of his life he had nothing printable to say about the town or its people.

Ross Sterling and Oil Regulation

ROSS Sterling, originally of Anahuac and later of Houston, was a burly self-made man. He had bought his first oil wells in 1911 with profits he had made from selling horse feed. He then acquired a pipeline to carry petroleum from the Goose Creek Field, and in 1917 chartered and became first president of the Humble Oil and Refining Company, which eventually grew into the largest in the free world. He also owned and merged the *Houston Post* and the *Houston Dispatch*, and he used those papers to support Dan Moody's attempt to topple Ma Ferguson. Sterling was particularly indignant at the condition of the state Highway Commission; and after the election, Moody appointed Sterling its chairman. Sterling not only reorganized the department but proposed a sweeping improvement of the Texas road system, to be funded by a bond issue and gasoline taxes.

The legislature rebuffed it, of course, and with Moody's blessing Ross Sterling announced for the gubernatorial primary in 1930. Ma Ferguson put in for another try, and Moody had his doubts whether the people would vote for someone as rich as Sterling. His fear proved well founded, as Ferguson finished first in the primary, but after a vigorous runoff Sterling came out on top.

Texas had by now followed the rest of the United States into the Depression, which followed the stock market crash of October 1929. But one consolation of the state's economy having remained essentially regional in character was that, so far, Texas had suffered less than other sections of the country. Its worst effect in the state was the confusion and contention it brought to the oil business, pitting small operators, who wanted to continue producing as much as they could for what little they could get, against the big oil companies, who wanted to limit production and support a reasonable price for the product.

The industry had changed since the early days of gushers tearing the cross beams from wooden derricks. Driller James Abercrombie got fed up with having his rigs blown apart after the bits pierced high-pressure pockets of natural gas, and in 1922 he invented the blowout preventer. Steel drilling platforms now supported equipment that could punch as deep as four thousand feet. By 1925, Texas had some eighty refineries, which finally elevated the state from the colonial status of a raw-materials producer to that of an economic colossus. Since World War I, other great fields had

While it was the Fergusons who made trade on their Ma and Pa image, Ross STERLING of Anahuac, the "big business" candidate, had also been a farmer before going into business. A massive man, over six feet and weighing 250 pounds, he amassed an empire almost as daunting, parlaying two oil wells bought in 1903 into the Humble Oil and Refining Company. He divested himself of these holdings in 1925 to invest in real estate, and bought two Houston newspapers, which he combined into the *Post-Dispatch*.

Like many other businessmen, Sterling was ruined by the Great Depression, but instead of nursing his loss to Ma Ferguson in the 1932 primary he returned to private life and restored much of his fortune via a new oil company bearing his own name, the Houston National Bank and American Maid Flour Milling. He died in 1949.

been discovered and come into production—Mexia in 1920, Luling in 1922, further strikes in the Panhandle through 1926, Permian Basin in 1921 to 1929. By 1928, Texas was the largest producer of oil in the United States, and continuous new discoveries, while adding to the legend, forced the price ever lower. At Desdemona, more oil was pumped than could be stored or transported, and a small river of oil, three feet deep, flowed from the field, only to be lost in the dirt nearby. Additionally, the fact that some of the fields dribbled dry as suddenly as they had burst on the scene—Ranger and Breckenridge, as well as Desdemona—convinced some in the business of the need for conservation.

The issue was eventually forced by a titanic oil strike in east Texas in 1930. It was a seventy-year-old down-but-not-out wildcatter named Columbus Marvin Joiner who had made the discovery. Having earned and lost two separate fortunes in Oklahoma before coming to Texas in 1926, Joiner, like a few tycoons and countless bankrupts before him, was sure there was oil where the smart money said there could not be—in this case, the Piney Woods of northeast Texas. With two partners, borrowed money, old tools, and a ramshackle pine rig, he drilled in Rusk County, eight miles east of Henderson, and got nothing. A second drilling was also a dry hole.

If anything, Joiner and his geologist, "Doc" A. D. Lloyd, operated what was very close to a scam. Lloyd wasn't really even a geologist; he was an Ohio bigamist who had changed his name to keep a jump ahead of his spouses. Lloyd, the story went, drew lines connecting all the major oil fields in the country, which intersected, more or less, on the farm of a local widow named Daisy Bradford. Joiner obtained a lease, but they drilled as slowly as possible—sometimes only on Sunday when some of their growing number of shareholders drove out to inspect the works. Over a three-year period, they talked up their impending success, obtaining more credit and more investors. Probably no one was more surprised than the proprietors when their third effort, the Daisy Bradford No. 3, drilled with still more borrowed money, brought in

After Daisy Bradford #3, the rural acreages around Kilgore took on a radically different look.

The transition from village to boomtown in Kilgore was for its sheer magnitude the most chaotic of its era, but the town eventually evolved from pandemonium *(above)* to mere overcrowding *(below).*

a successful test on September 5. Marveling, Joiner arranged for all his supporters, thousands of them, to be present when the well began producing. On October 3, their automobiles lined the road for miles as they gathered to watch the "Texas tea" burst out.

Still, there was considerable worry among Joiner's creditors, who were suddenly aware of just how many of them there were, that "Dad" had sold more pieces than he had action, and there was a sudden blizzard of lawsuits. Joiner was happy to sell his interest in the well to a former cotton speculator named H. L. (for Haroldson Lafayette) Hunt and then decamp. They cut the deal on November 26, 1930; for $30,000 cash and $1.3 million in promissory notes, Hunt acquired Joiner's five thousand acres of oil leases.

Even in Kilgore's residential neighborhoods, the changes wrought by the oil boom were enormous, with swing sets and sand boxes replaced by jungle gyms of unimaginable proportions.

Thus it was that Hunt, who had the reputation for making most of his deals over poker games, acquired what Joiner had stumbled upon: the East Texas Oil Field. (In fact, Joiner later sued Hunt, claiming the latter knew from a well that came in on the day of their meeting that the Daisy Bradford was not a fluke, but had told him—Joiner—it was a dry hole. Joiner abandoned the suit as it was being tried, and dropped into obscurity.)

H. L. HUNT. Acknowledged as the father of the East Texas Oil Field, C. M. Joiner was roundly awarded the sobriquet of "Dad." Born before the Civil War started, he had, oddly enough, been a Tennessee lawyer and served in that state's legislature before he ever went west to drill for oil. Once the Daisy Bradford No. 3 tipped her oily hand, Joiner did not bring her in immediately. In debt and careful to husband every bucket, he utilized a month to complete a pipeline and storage tanks before opening the spigot. His pressing need for cash, however, prompted him to sell his interest in the East Texas field to a Dallas businessman, H.L., who parlayed the holdings into one of the world's vast fortunes. Joiner himself was just about bust at the time he died, at eighty-seven.

Although the tide of oil in East Texas began to swell in the early thirties, it did not peak until June 17, 1937, when the Bess Johnson–Adams & Hale No. 1 blew in. It sat on a one-acre tract, which soon sported some two dozen pumping wells—hence its appellation, The World's Richest Acre.

Two more wells drilled by other wildcatters blew in successfully during the winter, prompting speculation that no fewer than five counties might be underlain by one mammoth pool of petroleum—a scenario that was pooh-poohed, albeit nervously, by the professional geologists who advised the large corporations. The east Texas field was thus a paradise for the small operator; once the word got out, the rush was on. At Christmas 1930, the population of Kilgore was seven hundred; by New Year's, it was at least ten thousand. At one point, no fewer than five thousand wildcatters, traders, and assorted speculators stampeded into town in *one day*. The other statistics of east Texas development are just as shocking. By July 1931, the three original wells had mushroomed into 1,100; by the end of the year, the number was nearly 3,400, being brought in at a rate of about one per hour. Virtually none of them were dry.

Not covered by the legislation conserving petroleum was natural gas, for which there was no market, and which was commonly flared off at the wellhead in a now-almost-inconceivable waste. In 1934 in the Panhandle alone, it was estimated that a billion cubic feet of gas was burned off *every day*. Of course, the feasibility of using natural gas for light and power had been long since established—Lone Star Gas Company had been chartered in June of 1909, and in less than a year they were serving fifteen thousand customers in Dallas. Electricity, however, had so quashed the market that by then the city of Amarillo offered five years of gas free to any business that would locate there. Though it spent sixty thousand dollars on the advertising campaign, not a single firm showed up to accept. Regulation of gas flaring finally began in 1938, and producers were required to separate hydrocarbons from the raw ("wet") gas as it came from the well and recycle it back underground. Flaring, however, was not entirely ended until well after World War II.

The 1931 production was over 109 million barrels; two years later, it was nearly double that. In its first fifteen years, the east Texas field produced 2.1 billion barrels of oil, more than twice as much as any other field in the country.

The wildcatters were still dancing beneath their gushers around Kilgore when George Strake made yet another big strike near Conroe, which was the first of a dozen in that area. The combined effect of all this on prices was predictable: The bottom fell out. Oil that had been selling for over a dollar a barrel now barely commanded a dime, and the need for some form of regulation was critical. The Railroad Commission attempted to impose production limits—prorationing—but was stymied by a court decision. Governor Sterling, whose own sympathies lay on the big oil side of the dispute (and not just because their position was the economically responsible one), saw the need to act. When he received a petition imploring a production shutdown, and with the example in Oklahoma, where Governor Murray imposed martial law on that state's oil fields, Sterling also declared martial law, on August 17, 1931. He sent twelve hundred National Guardsmen to take control of the sixteen hundred wells then producing in the east Texas field and put a stop to illicit production. The small operators felt cheated, noting that Sterling was a past president of Humble and that the top two National Guard officers on the scene had close ties to Texaco and Gulf, respectively, and they sought vindication in the courts. Sterling allowed production to resume the next month, under a rigid quota of 400,000 barrels per day. The federal Supreme Court later struck down the validity of the martial-law decree, but Sterling had bought time to assert state control over oil production, which in Texas was a political milestone.

Oklahoma Invades Texas

TEXANS at their breakfast newspapers late in July 1931 were astonished to discover that units of the Oklahoma National Guard, acting on orders from that state's governor, "Alfalfa Bill" Murray, had encamped themselves in hostile array at the south end of three controversial bridges spanning the Red River, at Gainesville, Denison, and opposite Ryan, Oklahoma.

They knew he could be goofy, but this was ridiculous. Murray was a well-known eccentric and holdout populist who stood for the distribution of free seeds to farmers and who often thumbed rides to his own campaign rallies. Born in 1869 in the north Texas town of Toadsuck (reason enough for leaving the state), he had failed in Texas politics and departed for easier pickings. In Indian Territory, he took up farming, gaining his sobriquet by lecturing on the virtues of alfalfa. He had chaired the Oklahoma State Constitutional Convention at the time of its admission to the Union, and served in the state legislature and in Congress.

The bridge controversy centered over the Denison crossing and originated in a contract Texas had made with a certain bridge company granting exclusive toll rights to the existing (private) bridge. When Texas and Oklahoma jointly built a free public bridge, the company obtained a federal court injunction prohibiting it from opening. Governor Sterling obediently had barricades erected to prevent traffic from using the free bridge until the matter was settled. Oklahoma's Murray, however, claimed that the injunction did not apply to his state, and that anyway Oklahoma's half of the bridge ran the whole distance north to south, not just to the middle of the river. Thus he sent workers across the bridge to tear down the Texas barricades, to which Sterling responded by sending Rangers to see that they stayed in place. Murray responded by plowing up the roadway leading to the northern end of the toll bridge, rendering it unusable, and public demonstrations in Denison and Sherman demanded that the free bridge be opened.

Actually, what the bridge company wanted was not continuation of the tolls but only a chance to collect damages from the state of Texas for breaching its contract. It so happened the legislature was meeting in special session, and when a special provision was passed allowing the company to sue the state, the company joined the state in asking that the injunction be lifted. People south of the river thought that ended the matter. The bridge company, meanwhile, had obtained a second injunction from a federal judge in Oklahoma ordering Murray not to interfere with operation of the toll bridge. Thinking that as commander of the Oklahoma National Guard, his orders would supersede the federal court jurisdiction, Murray declared martial law around the bridge and, armed with an antique revolver, inspected the "war zone." Then, saying that he had "learned of" a plan to shut down the free bridge for good, he cited Oklahoma's border rights under the Louisiana Purchase and sent his Guardsmen across the bridge on July 27 to protect its southern end.

It was great posturing for a holdout populist, but the issue was dead by now. After the Texas injunction was dissolved, Murray withdrew his troops to martial law duty elsewhere—to enforce the shutdown of Oklahoma's oil fields.

Me for Ma, Again

Ross Sterling sought reelection in 1932, but he was a victim of the times, and his image of being a rich man unsympathetic to the problems of little people was worsened by his being compelled to repeatedly veto relief measures, funds for whose implementation the legislature could never have appropriated. Opposing him in the primary were the ubiquitous Fergusons, Ma on the ticket and Pa "picking up the chips and bringing in water for Mamma."

"Two years ago you got the best governor money could buy," taunted Ma. "This year you have an opportunity to get the best governor patriotism can give you." Virtually the entire party establishment was against her, but she finished on top in the first round. Sterling and even Moody campaigned as hard as they knew how, but in the runoff Ma Ferguson had eked out a victory by fewer than four thousand votes. Sterling was freed to return to private life to restore the fortune he had lost in the financial collapse.

Another casualty of his defeat was Jane McCallum, she who had maneuvered for the impeachment of Jim Ferguson and organized women in support of Dan Moody, who had rewarded her with the ceremonial job of secretary of state, an office in which Sterling had reappointed her. During the heat of the campaign, McCallum had made a statewide broadcast avowing that "Miriam Ferguson has never represented even a very small portion of the patriotic, intelligent womanhood of the state. . . . Mrs. Ferguson never has and never can cause them aught but shame and humiliation." The return of Ma Ferguson was the end of the line in public service for Jane McCallum but the beginning of a long and useful private life as an observer of and writer about women's affairs.

Ma's second administration proved less contentious than the first; state spending was reduced by about one-fifth, but the state's financial condition became critical as local governments defaulted on bonds, leaving the state to assume the balances. The need for relief programs was wretched, but the legislature continued to kill new tax proposals. Fortunately, the man elected President that year, whom Texans had taken a good squint at in Houston four years earlier as he touted Al Smith, was a man who rose to the occasion. Franklin Delano Roosevelt's sweeping New Deal quickly assumed nearly three-quarters of the costs of Texas's social-aid programs.

A common feature of the early days of the Depression: lines, whether to reclaim valuables from safe-deposit boxes, or to find a job at the local CWA Office.

That need seemed ever deepening. In Texas, 105,000 families were on relief in 1933; the next year, the number rose to nearly a quarter of a million. Volunteer organizations did what they could, from fishermen in Aransas Pass who sent frozen fish to feed the hungry in Dallas, to ranchers in west Texas who sent dressed rabbits to the city soup kitchens. But it was too little, and the unemployment rate for African Americans was twice what it was for whites, but they received disproportionately less assistance. As tax bases shrank, streetlights were turned off; schoolteachers who had employed husbands were let go.

Help, however, was on the horizon. The seniority system had given Texas a powerful clout in Congress; Texans chaired six powerful House committees. Among them, and this is an aspect of New Deal pie slicing that is often forgotten, there was quite a cognitive decision to exact a toll for the generations of slights Texas had suffered at Washington's hand since Reconstruction. Their fingers now controlled the fall of

JESSE JONES was already fifty-eight when Franklin Roosevelt was elected. He was so universally acknowledged as Houston's guiding patron that he was known about town as "Uncle" Jesse. His judgment was not flawless, however. He had been an initial investor in Ross Sterling's Humble Oil but sold out his shares within a year, and was happy to do so at a profit. His path to wealth would have been greatly simplified if he had kept them.

In the thirties, Texans could turn to the exploits of athlete MILDRED DIDRICKSON to forget their troubles. Born in Port Arthur in 1911, she competed effectively in basketball, baseball (on a men's team), and golf. It was at the Los Angeles Olympics in 1932, though, that the whole world took notice of "Babe." In an age when an individual could not enter more than three events, Didrickson won a silver medal in the high jump, and gold medals in eighty-meter hurdles and javelin throwing. She went on to win some eighty tournaments as a professional golfer.

coin, and they meant to look out for the home folks; over the next several years, they snagged for Texas federal appropriations more than a fourth again greater than the per capita average spent in other states.

Even happier for those home folks, sympathetic Texans were also highly placed in the executive administration. Without a doubt, the most powerful of the Texas New Dealers was Jesse H. Jones of Houston, owner of that city's most influential newspaper, the *Chronicle*, and magnate of an array of insurance, banking, and financial holdings. Although Jones was a conservative Republican whom President Hoover in 1932 had named director of the Reconstruction Finance Corporation, Roosevelt knew ability when he saw it, and he retained Jones as chairman of the same agency, which was the most important one in the allocation of federal recovery loans. FDR soon discovered the truth of Jones's reputation for humorless arrogance and took to referring to him—away from the microphones—as Jesus H. Jones.

The good news for Texas was that Jones was dedicated to his state and his city, although not in that order, and they could feel secure that Texas would fare well under the New Deal. In fact, he was known as "Mr. Houston." He owned numerous downtown buildings, where, according to his wife, "He has great sentiment about all of them. Every time he passes one, he pats and pets it." Jones's predecessor at the RFC compared him to Cecil Rhodes, with the difference that Jones preferred to build his empire where he could see it most of the time.

President Roosevelt visited Austin in 1936. Sharing the platform with him and Mrs. Roosevelt were Jesse Jones, Governor Allred, and Austin mayor Tom Miller. The sign was Miller's idea.

Jimmie Allred (*left*) was one of those people who could set goals and then work methodically to attain them. Born poor in 1899, the son of a rural mailman, he worked as a janitor and shoe-shine boy to save money for college. He had no sooner entered Rice than he left again to serve in the Great War. While serving in the navy, he had no hesitation in telling friends that upon returning to civilian life he would run for governor. He took a law degree in 1921, and in 1930 was elected attorney general, in which office he fought off legal challenges to the state school fund's oil royalties. Although the accomplishments of his gubernatorial term were formidable, Allred wrecked his political career when he opposed Pappy O'Daniel for the Senate in 1942. He was later appointed to the federal bench, on which he served until his death in 1959.

As popular as Franklin Roosevelt became in Texas, people were even more heartened that from 1935 FDR had a young soul mate in the governor's mansion. The Fergusons, bewildered by the scope and depth of the people's needs and finally confronted by their own inadequacies, stood down in 1934. They had created a Texas Relief Commission in March of 1933 to allow Texas to receive and administer federal relief funds, but they were devoid of further ideas of their own. The state attorney general, James—everyone called him Jimmie—Allred campaigned for the governorship when he was only thirty-five. He first gained attention as a populist liberal for his attacks on the Ku Klux Klan and his efforts to regulate big business. He ran for governor on a promise of no state sales tax—a position made reasonably tenable by the size of federal expenditures in Texas. He spent most of his first term tidying up after the Fergusons—revamping the Texas Rangers from hundreds of Ma's "special" commissions, and creating an independent board to govern pardons and paroles from the prison system. Allred established a planning board to coordinate relief with need, which made him an ideal partner in the federal-state sharing of responsibility for recovery, and during his administration a modest state old age–assistance pension was passed.

Another important personality began to emerge during the first FDR administration. The Texas director of the National Youth Administration was a young former schoolteacher named Lyndon Baines Johnson, a native of the Hill Country about

The thirties saw LYNDON JOHNSON as the Texas director of the National Youth Administration, and then as a congressman. His real fame still lay ahead of him.

WPA workers construct an open-air diorama at the San Antonio Zoo.

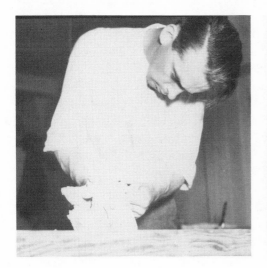

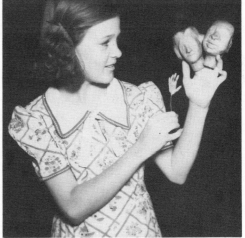

Other WPA projects covered about every subject from paleontology *(left)* to puppet making *(right)*.

This WPA mural was painted for the post office in Canyon.

halfway between Austin and Fredericksburg. Scion of the leading family of the town of Johnson City, he boasted in his family tree the Baptist preacher George Washington Baines, who had effected the conversion of the greatest of Texas rakes, Sam Houston. And in the New Deal, Lyndon Johnson found a gospel of his own. His moment came on April 10, 1937, when he bested eight other entries and was elected to Congress in a special election to fill an unexpired term.

Jimmie Allred introduced Johnson to FDR on a fishing trip in the Gulf; making the most of the opportunity, Johnson accompanied FDR back to Washington on the President's train. During his tenure at the National Youth Administration, Johnson made the acquaintance of a personable and ambitious young political brain named John Connally. They became fast friends; when Johnson was ready to sail deeper waters, he called on Connally to run his campaigns.

Once the federal money began flowing, the programs of Roosevelt's New Deal permeated virtually every aspect of life and economy. The first program on line was the Federal Emergency Relief Administration, which provided $50 million in stopgap funds, but did not approach economic recovery. Most other programs were centered around the creation of jobs—110,000 war veterans and youth in Texas employed by the Civilian Conservation Corps. Of far greater moment was the Work Projects Administration, which employed under its various banners more than 600,000 Texans, as many as 120,000 at one time. Although mostly remembered for the massive number of construction projects such as dams, bridges, and stadiums, the WPA also provided employment, sometimes useful and sometimes make-work, in art, music, literature, and even child care and housekeeping. Although not phased out entirely until 1943, the need for the WPA began to decline after February of 1936.

Agriculture was also affected. Corn prices had fallen to only a dime a bushel, and the market for cotton had collapsed—that price fell all the way to five cents a pound, and no one had money for clothes, anyway—so the administration initiated a program of crop reduction: subsidizing farmers who did *not* plant. Its theory may not have been universally understood by Texas farmers, but in July of 1933 William Morris, a cotton farmer who lived near Corpus Christi, received the first federal crop-reduction check for plowing under forty-seven acres.

The Chicken Ranch

THE world's oldest profession, which had profited so much in the oil boomtowns, did not shut down with the advent of the Great Depression. At this time, Galveston was still the vice capital of Texas, with perhaps the highest per capita ratio of prostitutes—one hooker for every sixty-two citizens—of any city in the world. The most distinguished single brothel in Texas, however, was about three miles south and east of the town of LaGrange, an ideal location both in geography—about equally distant from Austin, Houston, and San Antonio—and in temperament. The region had originally been settled by Bavarian and Bohemian immigrants who prospered on their ethics of work hard, mind your own business, and tolerate your neighbor. Being Bohemians, they also enjoyed their pleasures.

According to tradition, the establishment had been in continuous operation at one address or another since 1844; by the very nature of the business, of course, documentation is impossible, but, if true, it would have been the oldest bawdy house in the United States. Since 1905, it had been the enterprise of Faye Stewart of Waco, who under her *nom de nuit*, Jessie Williams, gained wide acclaim and the acquaintance of probably more Texas politicians than any other person in the state. Formidable but kindhearted, she built her business downtown for ten years before moving it out to a farmhouse, its prosperity underwritten by informal accords with both the city marshal and county sheriff, who were two brothers named Loessin. Miss Jessie, for her part, allowed no drinking, no Negroes, and no breaches of the peace, and she supported local charities generously. During the Great War, she and her girls even shipped cookies to doughboys overseas. The Loessin brothers recognized the economic benefit to their otherwise-backwatered town, and so they tolerated her. (Not that the Loessins were corrupt. Among Texas law officers, they were in the lead in crushing the local Ku Klux Klan.) The sheriff and marshal also presented semiannual reports to the grand jury, who took action only to mandate that the girls get weekly checkups from the county medical examiner. When it was pointed out that Fayette County had no medical examiner, one was hired. (The grand jury may also have been aware that Miss Jessie faithfully informed the Loessins when a customer tried to impress one of the girls by bragging about some criminal act or other.)

Miss Jessie also tolerated no kinkiness. When the boys sailed home with exotic appetites acquired from French tarts, she could get positively biblical about it. One patron tried to coach a girl in one particularly felicitous new skill; unfortunately, she was the employee known as Deaf Eddie, and his exhortations were necessarily rather loud. "Miss Jessie heard me," he recalled, "and come acrashin' inta there hittin' me with a big iron rod and hollerin'. . . . She throwed me out an' wouldna let me back fer a month." And he had been a thrice-a-week customer.

With the advent of the Depression, Miss Jessie became an ardent New Dealer. While moralizing Republicans were allowed to come in and spend their money, badmouthing FDR was strictly taboo under her roof. As her business was the most stable in town, she made certain to spread her purchases of supplies and services evenly among the other merchants, and she reduced her rates. A lady's favor could now be had for $1.50, about half the previous rate for a basic four-get (get up, get on, get off, get out). Even at that price, however, many of the would-be patrons simply couldn't come up with the money. Thus Mme. Williams instituted the policy of accepting a chicken as payment for relief, and another Texas legend was born; the ladies' growing flock quickly led to the establishment's famous sobriquet. Over the years, business expanded gradually and rooms were added on until it grew like a wood-frame domino game into the elaborate complex seen on page 188.

The Story of the Decade: Bonnie and Clyde

MA Ferguson's wholesale pardons and Pat Neff's reforms of the penal system had neither emptied the prisons nor turned them into vacation resorts. Doing time in Texas was still a life of brutality and hard labor. Work on road gangs and agriculture was notorious, and acts of self-mutilation to escape the field were not altogether rare. That was the case with a small-time thief and loser named Clyde Barrow, who, early in 1932, persuaded a fellow inmate to lop off two of Barrow's toes with an ax. His friend obliged—days before Barrow's pardon was issued—and he was freed to gimp home on crutches. It was the story of his life.

Clyde Barrow was almost twenty-two, from Teleco, a fifth-grade dropout, one of eight children and in trouble with the law since he was seventeen. He was short, skinny, sallow-chested, and mean. Shortly before his first incarceration in 1930, he had met and fallen for a loudmouthed Dallas redhead named Bonnie Parker. Friends said his main attraction to her was that she was so small—four feet ten inches and weighing eighty-five pounds—that she made him look hefty by comparison. She was six months younger than he, a former honor student but with a self-destructive wild streak. She drank much harder than he did, though she couldn't hold it, dyed her hair even redder than her natural color, painted her toenails, and wrapped her ample figure in bright red outfits. She had earlier married a man sentenced to life, and remembered him with a tattoo on her inner thigh.

She had known Clyde a month when he went to jail the first time; she managed to get a gun to him, and he broke free. He was inexperienced as a real criminal, however, and was recaptured days later and sent to Huntsville, where he was serving time when the incident with the ax occurred. Once he had recovered, Barrow and Parker began pulling a string of small-time heists around the Dallas area, and they took in an accomplice named Raymond Hamilton. Their operation hit a snag in March of 1932, when Bonnie was captured and jailed in Kaufman after an attempted robbery. The grand jury no-billed her, but not until June, so it was ironic that the first sensational Bonnie and Clyde murder hit the national headlines with, apparently, another woman in her place.

In the little town of Hillsboro, about halfway between Waco and Dallas, Barrow convinced local store owner J. W. Bucher to buy some knives from him. The sixty-year-old Bucher and his wife, Martha, lived above the store, and Barrow went back

several nights later—after closing—and got Bucher to open up the store and sell him some guitar strings. Barrow paid for the strings with a large bill; Bucher couldn't see to open the safe because he had left his glasses upstairs. Martha came down and opened the safe; when she turned around to make change, she saw Barrow holding a gun on her. A young woman then entered the store and held a pistol on Bucher. Stupidly, he tried to wrest it from her, and Barrow shot him through the head. It was April 30, 1932; Clyde Barrow was now a fugitive in earnest, and he responded by declaring war on the law-enforcement establishment.

BONNIE PARKER *(left)* and CLYDE BARROW *(right)*, as depicted in the photographs
seized in the Joplin bungalow.

When Bonnie was freed in June, she went home to Dallas to her mother and told
her she was through with Clyde Barrow. But within weeks of her release, the pair,
along with Ray Hamilton, were laired in Wichita Falls. They visited Mrs. Parker again
on the first of August, then drove to Atoka, Oklahoma, and killed a sheriff and deputy
who tried to break up a fight between Ray and Clyde at a dance. After robbing the
Neuhoff Packing Company in Dallas, they ranged from east Texas to New Mexico
before heading to Michigan to visit Ray Hamilton's father. There, Hamilton split from
them. A girlfriend soon turned him in, and after extradition to Texas he got a term
of 263 years.

By October, Bonnie and Clyde were back in Texas, where they murdered a grocer
in Sherman (they let another one live to identify them). Then in Temple, in December,
they killed a local lumber salesman as he tried to prevent them from stealing his car.
But Texas was now becoming too hot for them to stick around, as they discovered in

January 1933. Ray Hamilton had been transferred to the Hillsboro jail. Bonnie and Clyde were trying to arrange his escape when they approached the West Dallas residence of an acquaintance, but were met by a deputy sheriff who was waiting in the bushes and demanded their surrender. Barrow, by now continually vigilant, already had his gun drawn and shot him dead before leaping onto the running board of his car as Bonnie sped away. They kept going until they got to South Joplin, Missouri, where they rented a cottage and were joined by Buck and Blanche Barrow, Clyde's brother and sister-in-law.

The four lived together for several weeks, until neighbors finally complained to the authorities of the group's odd habits—the men would leave for days, but the women almost never left the house; the group was loud and often drunk. When one of the neighbors reported seeing a whole collection of license plates in the garage, the Joplin police and state highway patrol had a suspicion who the mystery couples were. On the evening of April 13, an automobile with four officers inside drove up to the house. Constable J. W. Harryman approached it but was shotgunned to death without warning ten feet from the garage. The other three officers began shooting in reply, and were startled to see a second-story window open. A woman yelled, "Pour it in 'em, Clyde. We're coming right down. Keep 'em out of the garage!" Detective Harry McGrath was killed trying to reach the downed Harryman. Clyde was firing and Buck was starting the car; both were cursing at the women, stumbling under a weight of luggage, to hurry. Barrow braved the bullets long enough to push Harryman's body out of the driveway, and with a machine gun blazing from the squealing car, the four made good an escape.

Reporters prowling the bungalow found an unfinished poem on which Bonnie had been working and a roll of camera film. The photos, taken during a picnic, made national headlines for their playful, mocking poses. Near Wellington, Oklahoma, in June, Parker and Barrow were injured when they ploughed their car into the Salt Fork of the Red River. The nearby farmers who helped them wound up being held prisoner during the pair's convalescence. One of them eventually escaped and brought the law, but the two officers were later found, handcuffed together and tied with barbed wire to trees. Despite the treachery, Bonnie and Clyde let the farmers live, though they shot in the hand the woman who had nursed Bonnie's burns.

Back in Missouri at the end of July, near Platte City, police closed in on a motel where the pair, reunited with Buck and Blanche, were holed up. They were almost successful; in a furious gun battle, all the fugitives but Blanche were badly wounded. They escaped, but the authorities this time were prepared to pursue, and they overtook Blanche and Buck. Blanche, twisting and shrieking, was taken into custody as Buck, whose wounds proved mortal shortly after, lay on the ground. Bonnie and Clyde retired to parts unknown, and did not surface again until early in 1934.

This photograph is of the first capture, in which a hysterical Blanche Barrow is restrained from reaching her mortally wounded husband, Buck, who is sitting on the ground in his bloody undershirt.

On the morning of January 16, Barrow sprung Raymond Hamilton from the Eastham prison unit near Huntsville. The morning had dawned foggy, and as a work crew began their day's labor, an accomplice named Palmer pulled from under a log a .45 that Barrow had left there. Hamilton joined him and held up a second .45 as Clyde and Bonnie arrived in an automobile. Hamilton, Palmer, and two others made a break for freedom as gunfire erupted, killing one of the guards. The car sped away as the fugitives piled into the back and rumble seats.

The early thirties was a heyday throughout the United States for premier criminals, but even figures of the Chicago underworld had to share headlines with, and sometimes give way entirely to, Bonnie and Clyde. The Eastham break was the last straw, however, for Lee Simmons, the shrewd, angular director of the Texas prison system. "I lay awake nights," he wrote later, mulling and brooding over a scheme to get the infamous pair. He began by nabbing one James Mullin, a recently released multiple loser who had served time in eight different pens. Simmons had a hunch that Mullin knew the details of the break, and he bargained successfully to get them. He then had the state prison board create a new position, special investigator, to which he could hire a full-time Barrow hunter. Not even the board was to know who he was; utter secrecy was imperative, but Simmons made up his mind to approach Frank Hamer, the now retired Ranger captain.

Simmons was then politic enough to visit Ma Ferguson for her approval. Hamer detested the Fergusons, and had resigned his commission before she took office the second time. "Frank is all right with us," she said. "We don't hold anything against him." Simmons also asked permission to grant clemency to any of Bonnie and Clyde's accomplices who turned on them. This was also agreed to. It was about two weeks after the Eastham break that Simmons approached Hamer, who was reluctant. He was doing better for himself, making five hundred dollars a month as a security agent for an oil company, than he ever had by the state of Texas. Chasing Bonnie and Clyde would be dangerous, time-consuming, and, with the Fergusons involved, political interfering of some kind was always possible. Simmons appealed, successfully, to Hamer's public spirit, and the fifty-year-old ex-Ranger took up the chase.

Hamer deduced, correctly, that however far they might roam, their base was in Louisiana, the one state in the region where they were not wanted. His cunning use of informants and stool pigeons led him to locate their hideout in only a week; upon concluding that they might be protected by the local authorities, he manipulated a change in their lair to Bienville Parish, where he could better control events. Without ever laying eyes on them, Hamer shadowed them. "I learned the kind of whiskey they drank, what they ate, and the color, size, and texture of their clothes. . . . Barrow traveled farther in one day than any fugitive that I have ever followed. He thought nothing of driving a thousand miles at a stretch. He was also a master of side roads, which made his movements irregular. Around Dallas, Joplin, and in Louisiana, he seemed to know them all." Ray Hamilton had split from the gang on unfriendly terms, and his place was assumed by Henry Methvin, who had been one of the Eastham escapees. Hamer was always on their tail, or else sifting through their Louisiana camp, to which he knew they would eventually return.

His intention was to surprise them in their sleep, then disarm and handcuff them before they knew what had happened. He was almost ready to strike, when a federal raid in nearby Ruston caused them to quit the area and make one more tour of destruction. Bonnie and Clyde did not kill every time they struck; indeed, they enhanced their press with the quirky habit of, every few months, kidnapping one or two "laws" for long, taunting joyrides before letting them go. When they did kill, however, their brutality was stupefying. The killing that most aroused the hatred of Texas authorities occurred during this jaunt, Easter Sunday of 1934, on the highway between Dallas and Grapevine. Driving a new Ford, Clyde and Bonnie stopped on the shoulder of the road—they intended to meet Bonnie's mother to give her a rabbit for Easter; an old farmer named William Schieffer, who lived within sight, saw a whiskey bottle sail out of the window. Two motorcycle patrolmen stopped behind the Ford and approached, perhaps thinking to offer assistance. Schieffer watched in horror as gun muzzles emerged from the car's windows and the officers were cut down in a short fusillade. Schieffer crawled, keeping out of sight, to the fence. A light-haired young woman—he didn't know it was Bonnie Parker, but it was her fingerprints on the whiskey bottle—got out of the car, hefting a sawed-off double-barreled shotgun. With her foot, she pushed one of the laws over onto his back, and, seeing he was still alive, she lowered the gun to his face and pulled both triggers. "Why, look-a-there," she said, laughing. "His head bounced just like a rubber ball." She hopped back into the car and it careened away.

They went into Oklahoma, where they killed an elderly constable who offered to help pull their car from the mud. At the same time, they wounded a policeman named Percy Boyd, whom they forced to pull them from the mud, and then they took him on a fourteen-hour joyride. Bonnie decided she liked him, and released him with expense money to get home—with a message. "Tell them I don't smoke cigars,"

The key to Hamer's success in finding Bonnie and Clyde lay in exploiting the necessity of gang members to communicate with one another via secluded "mail-boxes," and in his gaining the cooperation of another gang member's family with a pledge of clemency. He also excluded local authorities, whom he believed corrupt.

The death car was mobbed and stripped after it was towed into the town of Arcadia.

she told Boyd. Although Mrs. Parker was perfectly aware of the mayhem her daughter was spreading, she took feisty issue with her smoking, and Bonnie had troubled to write home, denying newspaper reports that she smoked cigars. The photograph, she said, had been a gag, but she lied. Back in Louisiana, Hamer was waiting for them, sifting through their garbage, discovering that Clyde smoked Bull Durhams; Bonnie smoked Camels.

Hamer had also found Clyde's mail drop, under a board near a big pine stump, on the west side of a narrow road about eight miles from the town of Plain Dealing. By now, he had taken a few local officers into his confidence, after making them swear personal loyalty over official orders. Hamer used a promise of clemency for Henry Methvin to extract the cooperation of Methvin's father, and with this aid Hamer and his five men set up an ambush on the east side of the road, opposite the mail drop. They were in place, under cover, by 3:30 A.M. on May 23, 1934. Hamer's order was to take them alive if possible. They waited nearly six hours before a gray Ford approached at a high rate of speed, then slowed and stopped at the predicted spot.

Both occupants peered intently out the passenger side, toward the pine stump, as Hamer stepped from the blind of pine boughs.

He knew them from their photographs, but this was the first time Frank Hamer had laid eyes on Bonnie and Clyde. Covering them with a .35 Remington autoloader with a twenty-round magazine, Hamer barked, "Stick 'em up!" Clyde and Bonnie both raised shotguns instead—Hamer said it was like looking down the Holland Tunnel—and, with Hamer in the lead, a deafening fusillade erupted from the concealed lawmen. Bonnie, they said, "screamed like a panther" when she was hit; Clyde's foot slid off the clutch and the gray Ford rolled a short distance before heading into weeds at the side. Clyde fell out when Hamer opened the door; Bonnie's head was slumped between her knees, blood and brains dripping onto her stockings. Hamer, who had seen plenty of gore in his time, almost got sick. Inside, they found one revolver, nine automatic pistols, three Browning automatic rifles and two sawed-off shotguns, and five thousand rounds of ammunition.

News of the ambush spread like wildfire; hundreds of cars parked along the dirt road impeded the wrecker that towed the gray Ford into Arcadia, where in a short

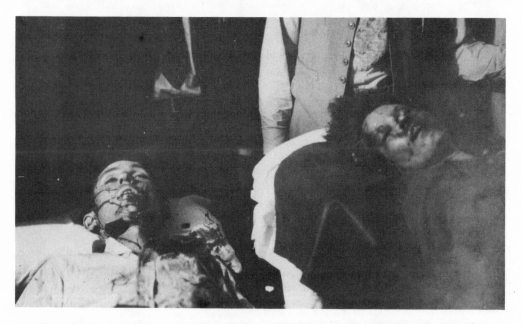

Beset by hordes of the morbidly curious, the bodies were wheeled into Arcadia's combination furniture store and undertaker's parlor for a brief inquest and then preparation for burial. Several women who elbowed into the tiny embalming room for a glimpse of the corpses had to be carried out when they fainted.

In the garage of his Austin home, FRANK HAMER (*left*) displays a Browning automatic and a sawed-off shotgun he removed from Bonnie and Clyde's car. Two months after the fray, Hamer received a letter from Clyde Barrow's aged mother, crudely written in pencil on ruled tablet paper: "Mr. Hamer, we have been told here by Sheriff Smoot Shmid in Dallas that you have in your possession some guns that were in the car at the time you and the officers killed my boy Clyde. Now Mr. Hamer, I do hope you will be kindly enough to give me those guns as you know you have no right to try and keep those guns. I feel you should think you have caused me enough grief and hardships without trying to cause me more trouble now. . . . You don't never want to forget my boy was never tried in no court for murder and no one is guilty until proven guilty by some court so I hope you will answer this letter and also return the guns I am asking for." Bonnie Parker's mother also tried to recover the weapons, referring the matter through her attorney, but both attempts were futile. Hamer kept them until he died. The man standing at *right* is Hamer's longtime deputy Manny Gault, who took part in the ambush.

time a crowd of several thousand tore the windows from their fittings and ripped blood-soaked souvenirs from the interior. The door of the undertaker's parlor was ripped from its hinges by the mob trying to get into the eight-by-ten embalming room to get a look at the bodies. Bonnie Parker's brother Buster arrived, distraught, insisting to the crowd that "no ten laws would have faced them" in a fair fight.

Frank Hamer attended Clyde Barrow's funeral in Dallas two days later, and Bonnie Parker's the day after that. She had written once that she wished to be buried with Clyde, but her mother refused. The story ended with a twist that was curious, but typical for Hamer. With justice having been done, he saw to it that vengeance did not extend further. He testified in defense of Bonnie Parker's sister and Ray Hamilton's brother, even then on trial in Fort Worth for the Grapevine murders. Bonnie and Clyde, he said "talked to people about the killing and described it. Just because [they are] related is no reason to fasten this on them. I know they did not do it." They were acquitted. Nor did he forget his agreement with Henry Methvin's family for their part in setting up the ambush. In August, Hamer and Lee Simmons convinced Ma Ferguson to issue a pardon, and, the times still being what they were, Hamer even found Methvin a job.

The Dust Bowl

THE Depression that followed the stock market crash of 1929 coincided, on the southern Great Plains, with a drought of apocalyptic proportions. In a sense, Texas's share of the Dust Bowl began even before the arrival of the farmers. It began with cattlemen's nonsensically shortsighted insistence on overgrazing the range. And it wasn't as if they were never warned: The federal Department of Agriculture had tried to educate them as early as 1897 on the carrying capacity of the native grasses. In response, the ranchers passed a resolution—unanimously—that "none of us know, or care to know, anything about grasses, native or otherwise, outside the fact that for the present there are lots of them, the best on record, and we are after getting the most out of them while they last."

What the cattle began, the sodbusters finished, their furrows curling asunder millions of acres of prairie grass into bare, exposed dirt. When the rains stopped and the winds began, the result was horrifying. And curiously, it was the discovery of water under the vast plains in 1910 that sealed the region's doom in the thirties, for

While the western part of Texas choked in the Dust Bowl, Austin and the surrounding Hill Country were repeatedly devastated by cataclysmic floods. By a freak of geography and weather patterns, this region—the foot of "Tornado Alley"—is subject to horrendous deluges. The record for the heaviest rain event in the United States belonged to the little town of Thrall, where, in 1921, thirty-six inches of rain fell in eighteen hours. On May 6, 1930, tornadoes flattened sections of nineteen Texas cities and towns, including Abilene, Austin, and San Antonio; eighty-two people died. The flood shown *above* on the Colorado River roared through Austin in 1935. It was the last straw, and spurred construction of a complicated series of flood-control dams; shown *opposite* is the dedication of Mansfield Dam, which created twenty-thousand-acre Lake Travis, whose storage capacity of 1,144,000 acre-feet finally put a stop to the rampages.

the possibilities of irrigation set off a round of land speculation, and more land was plowed than could ever be watered.

The savagery of such dust storms as the one pictured on page 201 was almost beyond comprehension to Easterners who had no experience with them. When one of them blew east as far as Washington and darkened the sky over the capitol during a key committee hearing, however, it proved very helpful in getting aid legislation passed. The automobile in the foreground of the photo brings to mind another car which, in driving through just such a gritty maelstrom, was sandblasted through both paint and primer, and emerged a vehicle of shiny steel.

A number of Texas plains families were unable to keep their farms and ranches going in the face of such terrors, and they sought refuge in California with the hordes of Okies and Arkies also en route. The sad parade inspired an eccentric balladeer from Pampa, Woody Guthrie, to write one of his most poignant songs, "So Long, It's Been Good to Know You."

A National Park

TEXAS'S first, and still largest and most celebrated, national park almost didn't happen. At that time, wildlands were not strictly preserved for their own sake; to qualify for national park status a tract had to exhibit some quantifiable superlative—contain the highest mountain, deepest canyon, or the like, and, in short, the Big Bend of the Rio Grande's place as most remote desert was not on the list of national priorities. A congressional resolution was passed in 1931 ordering a study to see whether Big Bend was suitable, and it took the National Park Service less than two years to conclude that it was not.

The region's seductive loneliness, romantic history, and bizarre natural features had many backers within Texas, however, and the legislature, without actually purchasing land not already owned by the state, created a state park covering much of the intended national park acreage as bait for the feds. In 1934, the National Park Service reconsidered and, after a little well-placed pressure by the Texas delegation in Congress, found Big Bend suitable. The park legislation became law in June 1935.

The Park Service was still not entirely convinced, however, and the law establishing the park also placed on the state the burden of procuring the land. While the state anted up 250,000 acres of its own, 1935 was no year for any expenditures short of the crucially needed, and Governor Allred vetoed an appropriation of $750,000 to buy the balance of the land. Over the next several years, acreage was purchased through two separate fund-raising subscriptions, a hefty donation by Fort Worth philanthropist Amon Carter and, finally, a $1.5 million legislative appropriation. It was not until 1943 that the National Park Service, still a bit reluctantly, accepted without cost title to nearly 800,000 acres, making Big Bend at the time the fifth-largest park in the system. Only with later study of the area's unique geology and life-forms was a general agreement reached that Big Bend was an irreplaceable treasure of the park system.

Centennial! Texas Turns 100

Chief designer for the Centennial Exposition was Donald Nelson, who had a hand in the Chicago World's Fair of 1933. Working under technical director and architect George Dahl, they devised a style of building that was part classical, part southwestern, and thoroughly Art Deco. Dahl christened it "Texanic." In this night view *(above)*, the Hall of State at the head of the esplanade is reflected in a seven-hundred-foot pool of water. The display of colored floodlights and searchlights dazzled nighttime visitors.

Even after the close of the exposition, Dallas reaped a harvest of new public buildings and museums, including an aquarium *(opposite)* located on a crescent of museums in Fair Park. The whole orgy of Art Deco cost some $25 million.

AFTER the popular, if not financial, success of the world's fair in Chicago, there seemed no other way to celebrate Texas's one hundredth anniversary of independence than with an exposition of truly colossal proportions. Actually the idea dated back to Governor Hogg at the turn of the century, and business boosters such as the Advertising Clubs of Texas had held meetings since 1923, but the official wheels turned much more slowly. It was not until 1932 that a Texas Centennial Commission was authorized by an amendment to the state constitution. By the time its members were appointed in June of 1934, there was less than two years to pick a site, plan, and build the equivalent of a major world's fair.

That Dallas was chosen to host the expo surprised no one, as the Centennial Corporation was anchored by Big D's three biggest bankers, who saw to it that the city sweetened its offer with an impressive $10 million package of cash, bonds, land, and perks. The choice was probably also the best one from a practical standpoint— the state fairgrounds already possessed an impressive physical plant—but it was not universally acclaimed. With so much money and so many jobs at stake, competition for the bonanza had been fierce. Houston boosters were so crabbed at losing the centennial deal that they published a booklet listing Dallas's contributions to the revolution. Its pages, of course, were blank. The city of Fort Worth even staged a rival exposition called the Frontier Centennial Celebration, and as the official expo opened, Dallas found itself papered with billboards and fliers proclaiming, "Dallas for Culture—Fort Worth for Fun." (The latter claim was a bit unfair, as Dallas officials had gone to extraordinary lengths to ensure a carnival atmosphere in Fair Park, including dismissal of a rock-ribbed city manager in favor of one who could wink at a little gambling and nudity. As a result, visitors on the midway eventually got a chance to catch the acts of Paris Peggy, Lady Godiva, and Corinne the Apple Dancer.)

Still, it was not an easy project to get off the ground. The planning started late, and then ideas had to pass through a labyrinth of commissions, committees, and boards. The city of Dallas purchased an additional twenty-six acres right next to downtown to enlarge the fairgrounds, and surrendered all control of the existing buildings for renovation. The exposition's team of architects leveled and remodeled in wide swaths, creating an intimidating esplanade of titanic buildings in a kind of Art Deco–neo-Egyptian style, reflected in a seven-hundred-foot-long pool. The Hall of State alone, which housed pertinent historical exhibits, was funded by the Texas legislature to the tune of $1.2 million. Among the more oddball structures were an entertainment strip shaped like a luxury liner, a six-story cash register to house the exhibits of the National Cash Register Company, and a marionette theater shaped like a mushroom.

The latter-day Luxor was built by an army of eight thousand in less than a year, at a cost of some $25 million. The whole affair opened on June 16, 1936, some three months after the actual centennial date, with a parade through downtown Dallas reviewed by 150,000 people. Most of them later passed through the gate opened by Governor Allred with a fifty-thousand-dollar jeweled key. President Roosevelt visited the fair the following week.

The panoply that waited inside was calculated to dazzle. Historical re-creations ranged from a mock-up of Judge Roy Bean's Jersey Lilly saloon to a reproduction of London's Globe Theatre, complete with an Elizabethan dance troupe and perform-

Visitors to the centennial bash could spend a night in the amphitheater *(right)* listening to a wide variety of music, after having spent the day inspecting the Cubist-looking pillars of the midway *(left)*. One of the main attractions there was "Ripley's Believe It or Not," a museum exhibit of wares from the famous syndicated cartoon feature. Souvenir hunters could purchase a packet of twenty miniature photographs for a quarter—one of which furnished the views seen here.

Displays of the new automobile models were a great hit at the centennial, and have remained a staple of the state fair ever since. Of two of the first exhibitors, Ford *(above)* chose a modernistic setting, and General Motors *(below)* opted for the southwestern look.

Done out of hosting the centennial party, Houston put its effort instead into construction of a suitable monument at the site of the Battle of San Jacinto, where Texas won its independence in 1836. Jesse Jones won federal aid to help with the $1.5 million cost by pointing out that it was not as tall as the Washington Monument. He didn't lie, really; he merely failed to include the height of the two-story museum at its base. The overall structure towers 570 feet, including the 34-foot three-dimensional Lone Star at the summit. It is built of reinforced concrete but faced with buff-colored fossilized native limestone; the tower is forty-eight feet square at the base, tapering to thirty feet at the top, which contains an observation room.

The University of Texas's own salute to the centennial of independence was to construct a twenty-seven-story tower of white limestone and red roofing tile, in a sort of southwestern variant of the Art Deco style. Dedicated in 1937, for many years it housed the main library, although the storage of so few books on each of so many floors made it a nightmare to use.

J. FRANK DOBIE, a folklorist and perhaps Texas's premier writer of the time, was dismissed from the UT faculty for his vocal opposition to building the tower. Even though the constitution limited Permanent Fund money to the construction of buildings, Dobie, who gained national prominence with the publication of his *Coronado's Children* in 1931, was scandalized that such an extravagance should be raised when the funds might better be used for programs and faculty. Wags had it that the immediate cause of his firing was his reference to the 309-foot tower as the final erection of an impotent administration.

ances of Shakespeare. The heart of the expo's entertainment, however, was the "Cavalcade of Texas" production, featuring more than three hundred actors, singers, longhorn cattle, horses, covered wagons, and a stagecoach. It was seen by more than a million during the course of the fair.

Exhibitors were allowed wide latitude on the nature of their presentations. The federal government displayed a rather staid exhibit of a weather map, a census board, ethnic trinkets from America's exotic possessions of Hawaii and the Philippine Islands, a model of Boulder Dam, and a show of rare postage stamps worth some $4 million. The greatest reverence was reserved for the glass case containing a copy of the Constitution. Sinclair Oil wowed visitors with two life-sized dinosaurs, while Gulf Oil ensconced themselves in a modern radio-broadcasting station and let fairgoers see all phases of its workings. It was a good training ground for the station manager, a young fellow named Art Linkletter, who had never worked in radio before. There was also a wide scope of occasional events, such as a beauty pageant, whose queen was crowned by movie star Ginger Rogers, performances by the U. S. Marine Corps Band, Duke Ellington, the choir of Salt Lake City's Mormon Tabernacle, and western-style singing by a troupe called the Sons of the Pioneers, who featured a baby-faced singer named Len Slye, who was in his Dick Weston phase and had not yet changed his name to Roy Rogers.

Also in western wear were the fair's hostesses, the Rangerettes (named after the state police), young lovelies decked out in boots, chaps, bandannas, and cowboy hats. Eateries varied from the Chuckwagon, which served western fare in a building shaped like an oversized covered wagon, to a Bavarian fantasy called the Black Forest Village, where diners were entertained by exhibitions of ice-skating on an outdoor rink.

During its six-month run, the Centennial Exposition expended the services of four managing directors—two resigned under fire and one dropped dead, as did the first financial director. It hosted well over 6 million visitors, and left a phalanx of George Dahl's "Texanic" structures to enthrall and cow future generations. Like most world's fairs, it lost money, but, to recoup some of the expenditure, the grounds reopened the following year as the Greater Texas and Pan-American Exposition and attracted even more visitors than during the centennial itself.

The New London School Disaster

THE town of London had existed peacefully in between Kilgore and Henderson since 1890. Dad Joiner's oil strike, however, spurred the area into the now-familiar boomtown tizzy. New villages sprang up overnight, among them New London, which appeared on the map in 1930, with six hundred people and seventy businesses. One aspect of the east Texas oil boom was that the public schools there became among the best-heeled in the world; when the towns and hamlets of western Rusk County combined their resources into a single school district, they endowed it with a physical plant worth about a million dollars.

Its showpiece in 1937 was the New London Consolidated School, with some two thousand students—about equal to the population of the rest of the town that year. It was an elaborate medieval-looking structure of castellated brick, set in a complex of other buildings that included a gymnasium and administrative offices. The school cost some $300,000, and took no little pride, with its seven oil wells located right on the campus, in being one of the richest, if not the richest, public school on earth.

At 3:20 P.M. on Monday, March 18, the intermediate grades had already been dismissed for the day, so there would have been about fifteen hundred students and teachers still inside the building. The rest were to be dismissed in ten minutes. Raymond Bonner, standing on his porch nearby, heard a thudding rumble in the direction of the school. Looking over, he saw the massive tile roof seem to lift slightly into the air, then walls and windows blew out in a shattering roar, with bricks blown high in the air, some to rain down a quarter of a mile away. The roof hung as if suspended for a second, then crashed heavily into the smoke and debris. Automobiles parked outside the school were crushed like egg cartons.

From the neighboring gymnasium, where the local PTA had been meeting, stunned members streamed outside and ran toward the school. Some survivors were quickly rounded up—one boy blown two hundred feet clear of the school could not remember his name. One classroom and the second-story study hall were all that remained of the structure, and some seventy-five students dropped from the latter's windows to save themselves. As word spread, townspeople flooded to the site, both to learn word of their children and to join the effort to free survivors from the rubble. The carnage that they found was hideous. Dead and injured alike were mostly naked, their clothes blown from their bodies; pieces of human anatomy were strewn thickly

among the brick and lumber and tile. Initial estimates of the death toll—perhaps 650 dead—were inflated because bodies were blown into so many pieces that they were counted twice. The only way to reach survivors was to dig.

By nightfall, about a thousand people were on the scene, passing peach baskets full of bricks hand to hand to two dump sites. Rescuers slurped coffee from community buckets to keep them going; oil-field workers rigged electric lights overhead to work through the night. Worst of all, a driving rain had begun. Trucks found no purchase in the mud; cables snapped, sending heavy beams crashing back into the wreckage. Eighty-five of the injured were sent to hospitals in Tyler; several hundred to Overton. In the confusion, many were sent to makeshift aid stations where there were no doctors, and parents wandered distracted from morgue to morgue, never knowing whether the next mangled body they viewed would be that of their child.

When the search for survivors was over, the New London School was reduced to three huge middens, a shallow hole in the ground, and two blown-out shells of rooms not leveled in the blast.

The following day, thirty doctors, fifty nurses, and twenty-five embalmers arrived from Dallas. Some organization finally developed, and lists of dead and alive took on some definition. The emotional toll on the medical volunteers was also grievous. One doctor, accosted by a parent who described his missing boy in detail, knew he had seen the child's remains in one of the morgues, but he shook his head. "I simply cannot tell another parent his child is dead," he told a reporter. "He will have to go to the morgue to find out."

School officials had been warned of the smell of gas but had not acted. Dr. E. P. Schoch, an explosives expert and chemistry professor at the University of Texas, examined the remains of the heating system. The school had had no central boiler; each of the seventy-two radiators had functioned on its own. Of the remaining six, only one was fitted with a functioning vent. In the others, the vents emptied into the walls, which had no flues. Thus, once gas began leaking, it accumulated not only in the crawl space beneath the floor but inside the walls themselves, accounting for the totality of the blast. "It's the old story," Schoch concluded sadly, "of saving a few dollars and endangering a thousand lives."

As more injured began showing up in hospitals and doctors' offices from the variety of makeshift aid stations, the death toll was eventually reduced to 293—still the worst school disaster in American history.

Pass the Biscuits, Pappy

W. Lee O'Daniel is seen here utilizing the medium that made his election and continued popularity possible. Learning from Franklin D. Roosevelt the advantages to be gained from mass media was perhaps his shrewdest judgment, and belies the fact that his administration was a failure.

JUST when Texans were sure they had seen it all in their politics, along came a yodeling hillbilly Kansas flour salesman named W. Lee O'Daniel, and they fell for him hook, line, and sinker. He had gotten his start in the flour business at eighteen, in 1908, as a stenographer, then went into sales, and arrived in Fort Worth in 1925 as the sales manager of the Burrus Mill and Elevator Company. To promote his product, O'Daniel formed a singing troupe, the Light-Crust Doughboys. He didn't like their music, but when they let him stand up to the microphone to hawk his flour, O'Daniel had a revelation. He began using the opportunity to broadcast homespun philosophy, and just barely before the 1938 primary season, he urged his listeners to send a penny postcard if they wanted him to run for governor. There was nowhere to store the stacks of sacks of postcards, 54,499 of them, all but four swearing to support "Pappy"—the nickname derived from his flour pitch, "Pass the biscuits, Pappy."

O'Daniel toured the state in a beat-up old bus with his family and band, drawing crowds that were vast in proportion to the size of the towns he visited—eight thousand came to hear him in San Angelo; three thousand in Colorado City waited three hours for him when his bus broke down. At a typical rally he would open with music, then sheepishly tell the audience that the singing was over and if anyone wished to leave, they could do so. His biggest campaign promise, which he had no prayer of delivering on, was thirty dollars a month state pension for the elderly. Lacking a legislative platform beyond that, O'Daniel ran literally upon the Golden Rule and the Ten Commandments, took as his slogan, "less Johnsongrass and politicians, and more smokestacks and business men," and fiddled and sang for all he was worth. He would send his children into the crowd to pass the hat, warning, "We have not one dollar in our campaign fund. . . . If you want me to run the race on a bicycle, while the other candidates have high-powered racing cars, that is up to you. . . . I say to you in all sincerity, you had better take that old rocking chair down and mortgage it and spend the money in the manner you think best to get your pension."

Among the tunes that propelled him to victory were such showstoppers as "Beautiful Texas," "Your Own Sweet Darling Wife," and "The Boy Who Never Gets Too Big to Comb His Mother's Hair." His chances also seemed enhanced by the fact that there were twelve other candidates in the primary. This factor proved not to be decisive, as O'Daniel got more than half the tally, anyway, and escaped a runoff. It gave him no pause whatever that he himself could not vote, having never paid the poll tax. In the general election he garnered 473,000 votes; his Republican opponent nearly 11,000.

Once in office, O'Daniel discovered that his rhetoric had so alienated the legislature that he was virtually a lame duck from the moment of his tumultuous inauguration. The state pension was so popular, however, that lawmakers dared not defeat it; they did get even, by voting a small—nowhere near thirty dollars a month—pension, but turned down all the revenue bills that would have supported it, thus putting Texas into an operating deficit. O'Daniel realized that President Roosevelt had hit upon a winning gimmick with his Fireside Chats, and O'Daniel imitated them in Texas as a platform to reassure the voters that, whatever his problems with the legislature, he was still a right guy with a good heart. When controversy threatened, he merely took his band—including family members—on the road, and he continued to draw mobs to hear him twang his tunes and abuse the political establishment.

In 1940 he was reelected in a sweep. The best-known of his half-dozen opponents in the primary was Ma Ferguson, who told Texans they had elected a singer and shouldn't be surprised that they got a song and dance. She finished fourth. With

One thing that Pappy did do for Texas was launch the career of a country singer named BOB WILLS, *(facing page, top),* who had been playing clubs in Fort Worth for a couple of years. Then unemployed, Wills approached O'Daniel with a request that Burrus Mills sponsor him, Harry Arnspiger, and Milton Brown in a radio show. O'Daniel agreed; after two weeks of performances on Fort Worth's low-power KFJZ, however, O'Daniel so disliked their music that he canceled the agreement. It took Wills a good two days of constant pestering to get O'Daniel to reconsider, which he did, but with the proviso that each of the musicians work a full day's labor in the mill in addition to maintaining their performances. "Our hands were so sore and stiff," complained Arnspiger, "you couldn't note a guitar or play a fiddle." The program was so successful, however, and sold so much Light Crust Flour, that O'Daniel doubled their pay to fifteen dollars a week each and excused them from manual labor, but he still insisted they practice forty hours a week. He still didn't like their music, but, when Wills suggested that O'Daniel take the microphone himself to do the promotional spots, O'Daniel recognized radio as a gold mine. He gave them another raise—to twenty-five dollars a week—and switched from KFJZ to the much more powerful WBAP.

Wills had developed a unique style that combined folk elements from black work songs to Appalachian fiddle tunes. It became known as Texas (or western) swing, replete with hollered falsetto "a-a-a-a-ha!"'s and "Lord, Lord!"'s that scandalized Bible Belt prudes—of whom O'Daniel was one. He fired Wills again in August of 1933 over Wills's drinking and his insistence on playing at dances. Wills moved to Waco, where he organized the Texas Playboys, whom he then removed to Oklahoma. The former boss hounded the band and managed to get them fired from a station in Oklahoma City before KVOO in Tulsa told him to get lost. O'Daniel filed a lawsuit to force Wills to stop billing his troupe as "formerly the Light Crust Doughboys." Wills defeated the suit in the United State Supreme Court, and, not to put too fine a point on it, struck a deal with General Mills to distribute a "Play Boy Flour." Their recording of "New San Antonio Rose" in 1940, sung by Wills's lead vocalist, Tommy Duncan, sold over a million copies.

Wills's success paved the way for entertainers of similar talent, most notably a cowboy singer from Tioga—a little town near Sherman—named Gene Autry. Will Rogers had heard Autry singing on his job as a railroad telegraph operator and encouraged him to try performing. His recording of "That Silver-Haired Daddy of Mine" sold 5 million copies, which he then parlayed into a second career starring in "singing cowboy" Westerns, beginning with *Tumblin' Tumbleweeds* in 1935. Woodward Maurice Ritter of Panola County took the nickname "Tex" and made his radio debut in 1934; Ernest Tubb and his Texas Troubadours played the Grand Ole Opry for the first time in 1942.

economic recovery well under way, it was a safe enough time to have Pappy O'Daniel running the show. This was due in great part to the amount of defense-contract money that was pouring into Texas under FDR's preparedness program, and state political shenanigans were rather a sideshow as far as most people were concerned.

Pappy O'Daniel shattered Texas's tradition of quiet, dignified capitol inaugurals by hosting 75,000 people in the University of Texas stadium, where they were serenaded by over a hundred different bands. Mesmerized by the show, the electorate returned him to office two years later as the first Texas governor to receive a million votes.

Pappy O'Daniel's inaugural featured a barbecued buffalo, with the slaughtering honors done by the governor-elect himself.

As the decade waned, Texans had acquired an evolving sense of self and undertook to refine their culture. They still enjoyed their chili, to be sure, but in 1936 the San Antonio Health Department shut down the last of the street vendors who had been part of the local plaza color for as long as people could remember.

They even gained some grasp of the larger culture. A state Institute of Letters was organized in 1936, and a truly major triumph was scored in 1939. After nine years of badgering by Dallas merchant Arthur Kramer, the New York Metropolitan Opera agreed to put Dallas on its tour itinerary. Dallas did not even have a professional symphony orchestra, although a music teacher at Southern Methodist conducted locals in performances that were more sincere and energetic than accomplished. (However, the Met's hot, newly debuted baritone Mack Harrell was a Texan, from Celeste.) Kramer landed the Met by pledging $65,000 to cover their expenses, and then began putting the touch on Dallas's cultural pretenders to ante up. He produced $136,800. The Met was impressed, and in its turn dazzled the town with performances of *Manon*, *Otello*, *Tannhäuser*, and *La Bohème*, and put Dallas on their permanent tour list.

The business leaders in Dallas had finally realized that if you want something done, forget the politicians: Talk to the moneybags. The leading banker, R. L. Thornton, organized the Dallas Citizens' Council in 1936, a cabal of wealthy community pillars who could rule the city without ever having to stand for election. As Thornton philosophized, "We didn't have time for no proxy people. . . . We had to have people who could underwrite." Thus when Dallas money developed a fixation on something, be it Centennial Exposition or Verdi, not much stood in their way.

Opera, of course, wasn't for everyone. Most people were more interested in the football exploits of Texas Christian University of Forth Worth. In 1938, they brought home the national championship, thanks to the weird side-arm aerials of quarterback "Slingin' Sammy" Baugh, who went on to fifteen years with the Washington Redskins. The following year the trophy went to the Aggies, and the back-to-back championships cemented Texas as a football powerhouse.

The close of the thirties also marked an important change in the complexion of the state Democratic party: Conservatives, headed by the very wealthy oil and business tycoons, had been growing increasingly restive over the New Deal. John Nance Garner, whom they looked to as their man, was a natural to succeed Roosevelt, and they looked forward to the day when Cactus Jack would turn national policy more their way. FDR's decision to run for a third term cost Garner an almost sure lease on the White House. Garner retired in a snit, and Texas conservatives were in a mood to prowl the state looking for liberal prey.

Their first victim was the mayor of San Antonio, Maury Maverick, a descendant of that city's frontier leader. Maverick was a loyal New Dealer, an enemy of Garner's, and even worse, a one-time attorney for the American Civil Liberties Union. Reluctantly he had granted a request from Emma Tenayuca, organizer of the pecan shellers' union, to use the city auditorium for a meeting of the Communist party. An anti-Communist mob of five thousand crashed the meeting, trashed the building, and forced Tenayuca and her hundred or so "pinkos" to flee. Maverick was defeated for reelection, as he knew he would be, and ever afterward in Texas liberal enlightenment was equated with communism in the minds of the simple. Maverick, for his part, was later accosted after a church service by an important society lady, who observed, "I hear talk all over town that you're a Communist. But if you come to church, well, you can't be a Communist." Unimpressed, Maverick shot back, "I hear all over town that you're a whore, but I don't believe that, either."

Some liberals other than Maverick were learning how to fight back. The University of Texas's radical economics teacher, Robert Montgomery, put a decidedly nationalistic (in the Texas sense) stamp on his condemnation of northern business interests, which, he claimed, had turned Texas into "the largest—and incomparably the richest—

Nineteen thirty-nine also saw the debut of a ladies' precision drill team from Kilgore Junior College. They called themselves the Rangerettes. Perhaps it was the thought of so much cheesecake kicking in formation that inspired the Texas Aggies to take the 1939 National Football Championship, winning it away from a powerful TCU program that brought Texas its first Heisman Trophy in the hands of Davey O'Brien.

foreign colony owned by Manhattan." Among the disciples of "Professor Brimstone" was his former student and boarder, Lyndon Johnson, who henceforth preferred giving business, whether personal or governmental, to locally owned concerns.

Some people followed events in Europe, thanks in part to a Texas newspaperman from Yoakum named Hubert Knickerbocker, who had been expelled from Germany in 1933 for writing unadmiring articles about Adolf Hitler. He wrote a book called *Will War Come to Europe?* Once the question was answered in the affirmative, he covered the conflict for the wire services until he returned home to add his voice to FDR's call for preparedness. Among those who did read his dispatches, though, Germany still seemed far away, and Japan even farther.

The census taken in 1940 was the last in which rural Texans still outnumbered the city people. In the peaceful months of the autumn of 1941, probably the most prominent story was that the state treasurer, a forty-five-inch dwarf named Charlie Lockhart, was resigning after ten years in office.

Back to War

Whitler finally invaded Poland and Europe blew up, the United States was neutral for the first two years and more. But it was an official neutrality only; both nationally and in Texas, there was no mistaking where sympathies lay, and German Texans in the Hill Country braced themselves for another going-over. Frank Hamer, now fifty-five and semiretired from his reputed fifty-two gunfights (with fatal results to twenty-three opponents, "not counting Mexicans"), offered his services to King George VI in rounding up fifty former Texas Rangers for sabotage detection and coast watching. The king accepted, and Hamer began organizing, but federal officials, fearful of compromising U.S. neutrality, quashed the scheme.

During the two years and three months between the start of the war and America getting into it, the place of Texas in the national power structure evolved considerably, for both good and ill. Throughout Franklin Roosevelt's second term, his relationship with his crusty Vice President deteriorated. As FDR became more liberal, John Nance Garner became more conservative, and the President's decision to run for a third term chapped Cactus Jack so badly that he retired from politics—he was seventy-two after all—and returned to Uvalde. Garner had once wielded real power as Speaker of the House; had Roosevelt gone willingly, Garner would have been a formidable contender as his successor, but he had no heart for four more years in a job that, as he confided to young Lyndon Johnson, "isn't worth a pitcher of warm spit."

Elsewhere in Washington, Jesse Jones, FDR's brilliant but stuffy financial whiz, was made secretary of commerce, and Texas gained a powerful new voice when Sam Rayburn of Bonham, a member of Congress since the election of 1912 and majority leader since 1937, was elected Speaker of the House in 1940. He was a loyal enough New Dealer, but he had an independent streak that made his selection palatable to congressional conservatives as well. He was a master parliamentarian, which, combined with the respect he commanded from the Republicans for his candid even-handedness, made him a peerlessly effective legislator.

An equally powerful voice was silenced. Morris Sheppard had served Texas as a senator since 1913, and had risen to chairman of the powerful Military Affairs Committee. His death in April 1941 gave Governor O'Daniel the opportunity to fill the vacancy by appointment until a special election could be held, and he responded in typical Pappy fashion. Of all the able politicans Texas held at the ready, O'Daniel named to the post Andrew Jackson Houston, the tottering eighty-seven-year-old

With so much general feeling that U.S. entry into the war was inevitable, some Texas pilots did not wait on their government's go-ahead. They joined the Royal Canadian Air Force and were flying missions in Europe long before Pearl Harbor. In this photograph, the prime minister of Canada, Mackenzie King, congratulates a Texas pilot on a successful return.

Many other Texas airmen joined in China's war against Japan. Texas native Claire Lee Chennault, who since 1937 had been a military adviser to Chiang Kai-shek, organized a mercenary air force known as the American Volunteer Group, or, more popularly, the Flying Tigers. After the United States entered the war, they remained in China, incorporated into the U.S. service as the Fourteenth Air Force.

second son of Big Sam himself. There was no chance he would run for reelection—in fact, he got to Washington and died three weeks into the job. O'Daniel, however, resigned the governorship and announced for the Senate seat himself. It seemed the governor's mansion was no longer large enough to contain him. Thinking that surely the people must be fed up with him by now, a whole gaggle of aspiring politicos, including Representative Johnson, lined up to oppose him, but Pappy O'Daniel roared by them and went to Washington as a senator.

In a curious way, that was the beginning of his undoing: At home, he was local color; in the Senate, where the whole country could see him, he was an embarrassment. This special election had to be confirmed in the regular election the following year, when O'Daniel won a full term. It is not difficult to assess O'Daniel's senatorial accomplishments. There aren't any; in fact, it was said that during his seven years there, no bill he proposed received more than four votes.

After Roosevelt asked Congress for a declaration of war, it was Texas's other senator, Tom Connally, as chairman of the Foreign Relations Committee, who introduced the war resolution.

The consolation prize for having to endure Pappy O'Daniel as a senator was, at least he was out of Texas. Indeed, the party powers who supported him hardly bothered to deny that such was their object. He was an ignorant, ineffective showboat, but within Texas's borders he had been unstoppable; the people adored him. When

Pappy O'Daniel congratulates ANDREW JACKSON HOUSTON on his appointment to the United States Senate. At eighty-seven, this must have made Houston the most senior junior senator in history.

If these marine recruits from Texas had any idea of the grim, bloody struggle ahead of them, they showed no sign of it as they boarded their train.

he resigned, though, he had left the governorship to an entirely different kind of man. Coke Stevenson was a self-made pioneer rancher-businessman from the sparsely populated northern fringe of the Hill Country. He had pulled himself up by his own bootstraps, and saw no reason why anybody else could not do the same. He was shrewd, silent, and fiercely devoted to hard work and a hard conservative philosophy. Stevenson had been on the job four months when the Japanese bombed Pearl Harbor, and Texans almost overnight steeled themselves to the wartime regimen of rationing, wage and price controls, blackouts, air-raid drills, and victory gardens. They bought war bonds and took Red Cross training, remained alert to the threat of the Fifth Column, and bore the oversight of the War Manpower Commission to make sure all were effectively employed.

The Tough 'Ombres Return

WITH the advent of hostilities, both the Texas Division and the Tough 'Ombres of the Alamo Division of World War I were reactivated for further service in the army.

The Tough 'Ombres were called up at Camp Barkeley, a huge new military post near Abilene, in March 1942. Briefly designated a motorized division, the Ninetieth soon reverted to infantry status and sailed to England at the end of March 1944. Their first action was on D day at Normandy, from where they fought across northern France, the Ardennes, and crossed the Rhine into Germany, suffering some eighteen thousand casualties, including nearly four thousand dead. They remained in Germany for occupation duty until November 1945, and were then brought back for deactivation.

The Thirty-sixth (Texas) Division of National Guard had been brought into service even earlier, mobilized again in November of 1940 under the Selective Service Act. After training extensively before sailing, they took part in the invasion of Oran, North Africa, in April 1943. The following September they were the first ashore at Salerno, thus becoming the first American troops to strike on the Continent. After several months in Italy, the Texas Division was pulled out, and their experience was relied upon in the invasion of southern France. By war's end they had fought their way through France, Germany, and into Austria, had taken 175,000 prisoners, and had suffered the third highest casualty rate in the army: nearly 4,000 dead, more than 4,300 missing, and over 19,000 wounded. After six months' occupation duty, they were brought home and returned to the control of the state executive, having purchased a glorious record at a terrible price.

One of the Texas Division's units, the Second Battalion of the 131st Field Artillery Regiment, gained even wider fame for being in and out of the fight before the rest. After spending virtually all of 1941 in training, first near Brownwood and then in Louisiana, they sailed on November 21 from San Francisco aboard the steamer *Republic*. They didn't know their destination, only its code name: Plum. They docked in Pearl Harbor but were there only a few hours before resuming their voyage westward. When they were a week out, in convoy with ten other ships, they received news of

President Roosevelt was a former assistant secretary of the navy, and the twelve-year-old heavy cruiser USS *Houston* (CA-30) *(facing page)* was reputedly one of his favorite vessels. He had taken two long cruises on her, in 1934 and 1935, and she had served stints as both the Asiatic Station flagship and U.S. Fleet flagship, and late in 1940 assumed the duties of Asiatic Fleet flagship. Displacing 9,300 tons, *Houston* packed as much capability in her six-hundred-foot length as the limitations of the Washington Treaty would allow. Her main armament of nine eight-inch guns in three triple-mounted turrets became the standard for U.S. heavy crusiers.

Japan's sudden barrage of attacks on and after December 7, 1941, so extended the frontiers of her empire that many Allied ships were caught behind the perimeter. In only a month, Japan was ready to assault South Asia's richest prize, the Dutch East Indies, a colony wallowing in oil, tin, rubber, food—everything needed to sustain the war effort. The best the Allies could do to oppose them was to hastily assemble under Dutch command an international force of cruisers—two heavies, the American *Houston* and the British *Exeter*, and three lights, the Australian *Perth* and the Dutch *Java* and *De Ruyter*—and several destroyers. In six weeks of constant fighting, the Allies lost island after island, while, on February 4, *Houston* took a bomb that killed fifty-five men and gutted the aft eight-inch turret.

The fall of Bali on February 19 cleared the way for a Japanese invasion of Java, which was the last Dutch hold on the colony. The Allied task force sortied against more than forty Japanese transports headed for eastern Java at the end of February, but were instead engaged by a Japanese screen of four cruisers and fourteen destroyers. It was an even match on paper, but the Allies were hampered by language difficulties, the improved Japanese torpedoes, and the lack of any air presence for either support or fire spotting behind Japanese smoke screens. Only *Houston, Perth,* and six destroyers survived the bloodbath.

After taking on fuel at Jakarta, *Houston* and *Perth* were ordered to attempt an unescorted escape around the west end of Java, through the Sunda Strait, to reach Australia. They proceeded as far as Banten Bay, where they stumbled upon more Japanese transports, the western invasion force, busily unloading. The enemy troops were already ashore, Java was doomed, and *Houston* and *Perth* were under orders to retire. Instead, they attacked furiously, sinking one transport and one minesweeper while heavily damaging and forcing aground three destroyers and three more transports. The action was suicidal, however, for they were pounced upon by the Japanese cruisers *Natori, Mikuma,* and *Mogami,* along with some dozen destroyers. *Perth* sank just after midnight of March 1. *Houston,* her two good eight-inch turrets trained one to port and one to starboard, fought savagely but went down in an hour and a half. Of her complement of 982, there were only 260 survivors, who were held as prisoners of war. *Houston*'s fate was a mystery until after the war, at which time her captain, A. H. Rooks, was awarded a posthumous Medal of Honor, and the ship was accorded a Presidential Unit Citation, one of only three cruisers so honored in the war.

the bombing. With the Philippines also under attack, the *Republic* took on supplies at Suva, in the Fiji Islands, and thence proceeded to Australia, where the men spent Christmas in Brisbane. Three days later they sailed on a Dutch ship, the *Bloemfontein*, and finally docked at Soerabaja, on the island of Java.

These were the weeks during which the British, Australian, Dutch, and American navies were mounting their furious but futile defense of the Dutch East Indies, and the Second Battalion was taken inland to defend the Malang Airfield. Because the Allied warships—including the heavy cruiser *Houston*—were unable to prevent the Japanese from invading Java from both the east and west, the land forces were doomed. The Texans fought the Japanese on February 28 and March 10, before surrendering on that day, along with the rest of the Allied forces on the island. For the duration of the war, the men of the Second Battalion 131st Field Artillery of the Texas Division

Soldiers of the Thirty-sixth (Texas) Division wade ashore at Salerno, making them the first U.S. troops to strike European soil. As often happened when the news cameras were present at such landings, they were reenacted in several "takes," during which some T-Patchers could not resist a grin for the home folks.

Engineers of the Thirty-sixth (Texas) Division defend a perimeter by laying barbed wire by hand (*left*) and using a mechanical "weasel" (*right*), which barely had to slow in crossing rugged terrain or streams, to string telephone wire.

Texas was not slow to honor its home divisions—even the sphinxlike Governor Stevenson was pleased to be photographed with the brass.

performed forced labor under the most brutish conditions, from the jungles of Singapore to northern China. Most notably, they were compelled to work on the Burma-Thailand Railroad, made famous in the Pierre Boulle book and David Lean film: *The Bridge on the River Kwai.*

Throughout the war, the U.S. government remained doggedly silent on their fate, despite repeated calls for an accounting, which led to this unit's common appellation, the Lost Battalion.

Oveta Culp Hobby

PRESIDENT Roosevelt signed the bill creating the Women's Army Auxiliary Corps in May of 1942. Sworn in as its director, with the rank of colonel, was Oveta Culp Hobby of Houston, a "pretty and soft-spoken" thirty-six-year-old mother of two, wife of the Texas governor who had encouraged and presided over women's suffrage in Texas.

Born in Killeen in 1905, Oveta Culp had never been a shrinking violet. Even in sixth grade, when a Bible was to be given as a prize to the best speller in the class at the end of the year, she did not merely resolve to compete for it. She told the teacher, "You might as well write my name in it now." She won. It was determination inherited from her suffragette mother, Emma Culp, who left her daughters to can the peaches and departed to campaign for Will Hobby in 1918. Oveta herself went to Austin the following year as a protégée of her father, State Representative Isaac Culp, but lost no time in making her own way. She graduated first in her high school class, entered and deserted Mary Hardin–Baylor College before auditing courses at the University of Texas Law School. In 1925, she was appointed parliamentarian of the state house, served for six years, and wrote a book on parliamentary procedure.

She enjoyed moving in political circles. She attended the 1928 Democratic National Convention in Houston, having roomed with Ross Sterling's sister, and went to work for the *Houston Post-Dispatch*, which Sterling had established. President of the paper was former governor Hobby, who had fallen on hard times. Recently widowed and nearly bankrupt from bad insurance investments, Hobby married her in February of 1931, and they worked in full partnership at establishing a communications empire. Eventually, they owned both radio station KPRC and the *Post* in which, as a matter of note, Oveta Hobby made certain to cover news of interest to the black community in Houston.

Like many Texans, the Hobbys fell out of step with the New Deal once recovery was under way, and, in fact, supported Wendell Willkie against Roosevelt in 1940. In regard to war preparedness, however, they supported the administration, and Oveta donated her time for one dollar a year to head the War Department's Bureau of Public Relations' Women's Interest Section. En route home to Texas when news came of Pearl Harbor, she aborted the trip and returned to Washington to organize the Women's Auxiliary Army Corps.

Although she had always maintained an avid interest in politics, OVETA CULP HOBBY made only one try for elective office—a run for the state house in 1929. Her ridicule and defeat by a Ku Klux Klan candidate soured her on the process, and she chose to serve her state and country in appointive positions, at which she excelled.

Perhaps reflecting some residual suspicion whether the military would really take women seriously, Hobby told War Secretary Henry Stimson in her acceptance remarks, "You have said the army needs this corps. This is enough for me, and I assure you it is enough for the women of the United States. I will give it all the devotion, all the strength, and whatever ability I possess." American women responded. While the bill authorized an initial recruitment of 25,000 volunteers of an envisioned 150,000-women corps, applications within a few days of the WAAC creation numbered over 100,000. They were to be organized into twenty-seven units, including two companies of black women.

Once installed, her no-nonsense administration earned her a good deal of respect. Slinky lingerie was banned from the corps's uniforms and replaced by khaki; the military-looking suits were topped by trim, billed, sensible "Hobby hats," which became the identifying mark of the uniform. Sadly, her suspicion that old career army officers would patronize their women's auxiliary began to materialize, but she would have none of it. "This is a serious job for serious women," she had told the congresswoman who had sponsored the legislation. Determined that women in the service should do more than prepare coffee for the men, Hobby insisted on a listing of jobs for which women were certified, and got them—239 of them, including by war's end the major part of the aircraft warning service. There were times when she felt she must be fighting her mother's battles all over again. Brass decreed that Waacs who became "pregnant without permission" would receive dishonorable discharges; when Hobby pressed the issue that the servicemen who got them pregnant be treated equally, pregnant Waacs were discharged with honor, without loss of benefits. Eventually, Colonel Hobby had the satisfaction of seeing the word *auxiliary* dropped from the corps's name when it was incorporated into the regular army, and of seeing similar women's corps organized for the other branches of service.

Exhausted from overwork, she resigned her command in 1945, a holder of the Distinguished Service Medal. "Democracy is a wonderful thing," she said. "All of us ought to bear military service."

The *Texas* Finally Fights

After fourteen years as a flagship serving in three different capacities, USS *Texas* was now a gracefully aging but still deadly dowager. In the Atlantic, she ran convoy duty, once narrowly careening past a torpedo fired by the German submarine *U-201*, until the Allies were ready for their first major counterstroke of the war, the invasion of North Africa. With the Pacific Fleet still under repair and most of the third-generation battleships not yet delivered, the fourteen-inch guns of the "Mighty T" were fired in conflict for the first time in support of that operation. She is depicted here in her North Africa camouflage.

TEXAS'S naval namesake escaped the carnage of Pearl Harbor. When war broke out, she was steaming patrols in the Atlantic.

Between the wars, *Texas* had gone back to the yard for a two-year renovation. Her coal-fired boilers were modified to accommodate fuel oil, which reduced her number of boilers from fourteen to six and, hence, her stacks from two to one. The fourteen-inch rifles of her main battery were refitted to allow high-angle fire. As the threats presented by modern war changed, *Texas* changed with them in two modifications: a bristling antiaircraft defense and long, sweeping antitorpedo blisters that thickened her beam at the waterline some eleven feet, paralleled within the hull by a web of strong of new bulkheads. Most noticeably, her lattice-cage masts, once the hallmark of the U.S. battleship, were replaced with massive steel tripods. It was in this new configuration that she rejoined the navy in 1927, as flagship of the U.S. fleet commander, and had the honor of conveying President Hoover on a visit to Cuba.

By the opening of World War II, though, she was an old, slow battlewagon; times had changed, and naval technology had left *Texas* and her "second generation" behind. Battleships now were as fast as the battle cruisers of her own day, and most of the world's major powers mounted bigger guns on their "third generation" ships— fifteen-inch in the German navy, sixteen-inch in the American, and Japan's two new battleships trumped them all with eighteen-inch main batteries. With the loss of the U.S. Pacific battle fleet at Pearl Harbor, however, every remaining capital ship doubled in importance.

After convoy duty in the Atlantic and supporting the invasion of North Africa, *Texas* entered the Mediterranean. During the campaign up the Italian peninsula, *Texas*, operating in tandem with the smaller and older *Arkansas* with her twelve-inch guns,

Years of scrutiny as a flagship pressured *Texas*'s gunners into maintaining a formidable reputation for accuracy. This rubble was a fortified German gun emplacement until it was shattered by a *Texas* fourteen-inch shell.

This view shows battle damage incurred by *Texas* in the gun duel with Nazi shore batteries near Cherbourg, June 25, 1944.

aided stymied infantry units with well-placed salvos of fourteen-inch gunfire. Some in the army still entertained considerable suspicion—aided by the usual interservice rivalries—about the value of naval ordnance fired in close support of troops on the ground. They simply would not believe that guns so large could shoot accurately enough to miss their own troops. Aided by spotter planes, however, *Texas* laid round after round of fourteen-hundred-pound "haymakers" squarely on German fortifications and gun emplacements, to the gratitude of the infantry.

On June 6, 1944, she stood off Omaha Beach and her fifty-two-foot-long rifles were fired again. Soldiers waiting on a troopship three-quarters of a mile away felt the deck jerk under their feet from the concussion. After D day, *Texas* ranged down the Normandy coast, pulverizing entrenchments of Hitler's "Fortress Europe." On June 25, she suffered her only casualty. Utilizing a common tactic, the Germans had implanted heavy naval guns along the shore, where their range and accuracy could strike Allied ships far beyond the reach of land-based artillery. The accuracy especially of German eleven-inch ordnance had been proven repeatedly during World War I. Near Cherbourg, *Texas* stood in to duel just such a shore battery, and in a furious three-hour slugfest was repeatedly straddled despite skillful evasion. At length, one of her crew looked up and saw an eleven-inch shell arcing toward the superstructure. He had time to remark only that this one was for them before the shell penetrated the conning tower and blew the wheelhouse apart. With one dead and thirteen injured, *Texas* quickly regained steerage and continued the fight. A second, nine-inch shell also struck her, but it failed to explode. After repairs, she provided fire support for the invasion of southern France on August 15.

Audie Murphy

At the time he enlisted in the army, AUDIE MURPHY stood only five feet seven inches
and weighed 130 pounds. His childhood friends remembered that he had always
been small but couldn't be pushed around. The wartime heroics that earned him
so many decorations also left him ravaged with battle-related emotional difficulties;
he developed the insistence of sleeping with a light on, and had trouble with
alcohol.

WHEN the "Mighty T" opened up in support of the landings on southern France
in August of 1944, one of the sons she sent ashore was Audie Murphy of Farmersville,
who had just turned twenty. Born into the grinding poverty of a tenant farming
family, he found it difficult not to be bitter and ashamed of his background. One of
twelve children (nine survived), he once said, "Every time my old man couldn't feed
the kids he had, he got him another one." Audie joined in picking cotton at the age
of five, the family living in and around Hunt County in a succession of rental shacks
and even a boxcar or two. Stung by having to take charity from churches and even
his schoolteachers—Murphy was a good student when he got to go to school—he
grew up irascible. He perfected his marksmanship shooting rabbits and squirrels with
a .22; he could also handle a shotgun, and once shot a black man in the backside for
kicking his dog, though the range was far enough that the pellets only stung him.

Murphy had tried to join the marines right after Pearl Harbor but was denied on
account of his age, so he enlisted in the army on his eighteenth birthday and was

assigned to the Third Infantry Division, which saw some of the most hellish fighting of the war.

The action for which Murphy won the Congressional Medal of Honor occurred near Holtzwihr, France, on January 26, 1945. By now, he had earned a battlefield commission as a lieutenant, and after a three-day fight he was the only officer left in his company, which had fewer than thirty men left. The previous day's advance had netted only six hundred yards, and Murphy was ordered to hold a forest position until a reinforcement arrived; they were already late, and ultimately never showed at all. At two in the afternoon, some two hundred German infantry attacked, supported by a half-dozen tanks. To oppose them, Murphy had only his couple of dozen men and two tank destroyers, one of which ran into a ditch and had to be abandoned; the other quickly took a hit from a German 88-mm shell and was left a burning hulk. He did have artillery support available, but someone had to direct the fire. After ordering his men into forest cover, Murphy took his telephone, jumped on the burning tank destroyer, swept the dead gunner from the turret, and opened up its .50-caliber machine gun on the advancing enemy. He spotted artillery fire homing in at him. After inquiries from the fire control about how far the Germans were from his position, Murphy finally blurted into his radio, "Hold the phone; I'll let you talk to one of the bastards!"

A forward artillery observer who witnessed the action wrote one of the letters that won Murphy the CMO decoration. "With the Germans 100 yards away . . . he was completely exposed to the enemy fire and there was a blaze under him that threatened to blow the destroyer to bits. Machine gun, machine pistol, and 88-shell fire was all around him. Twice the tank destroyer was hit by direct shell fire and Lieutenant Murphy was engulfed in clouds of smoke and spurts of flame. His clothing was riddled by flying fragments of shells and bits of rocks. I saw that his trouser leg was soaked with blood. He swung the machine gun to where 12 Germans were sneaking up a ditch in an attempt to flank his position, and he killed all of them at 50 yards."

Over a period of perhaps thirty minutes, Murphy killed or wounded fifty German soldiers, some as close as ten yards away. When the enemy pulled back, Murphy refused medical aid (but did take time to excoriate the inadequacy of the artillery) and led a pursuit toward the retreating Germans. Far from feeling himself a hero, Murphy later wrote that his existence had taken on the quality of a dream—clear, detached, and in slow motion. He was in camp near Salzburg, Austria, when on May 24 he was notified of the Congressional Medal. To him, as he wrote his sister, it meant five more points accrued toward getting to come home. After the striking of the usual postwar medals, Murphy's chest bore thirty-seven decorations, eleven of them for valor. The most honored soldier in American history, he personally accounted for about 240 enemy dead.

The Home Front

GOVERNOR Stevenson used the war to give his conservative legislative program a patriotic tint, which allowed him to ram home a retrenchment budget that squeezed the corsets of state agencies and universities alike. Despite the lack of achievement during Pappy O'Daniel's administration, Texas finances were left a mess. The state debt had reached $25 million, and the federal government was threatening to suspend its contributions to the pension fund if the state did not keep up its end of the finances. The legislature was also behind in its commitments to the teacher retirement fund, and to child-care and eleemosynary institutions. Proposals were floated for both state sales and income taxes, which went nowhere, but right at the end of Pappy O'Daniel's administration an array of minor taxes were hiked, about half of which went into the pension fund.

Stevenson's austerity program cut state spending to the bone. Special sessions of the legislature were virtually unheard of during his tenure, regardless of what issues pressed. Even state judges, when they proposed a salary increase from five thousand to six thousand dollars per year, got nowhere. Stevenson not only denied the raise, he managed not to fill vacancies on the bench, thus adding the work load onto the remaining judges. He also jawboned a no-strike pledge from Texas labor, while the attorney general announced he would not enforce antitrust laws against businesses engaged in war production. Stevenson, or "Calculatin' Coke" as the press called him, then waited for the war effort to turn to Texas for gas and oil, of which Texas held nearly half the nation's entire supply, as well as food, cotton, and production of war material.

He was banking on the fact that Texas would win at least its share of defense contracts (even during the prewar preparedness year of 1941 such contracts had amounted to nearly $600 million) and the power of the Texas delegation in Washington did not let him down. Dallas and Fort Worth became preeminent centers of airplane manufacture. Mammoth plants of North American Aviation in Dallas and Convair in Fort Worth turned out assembly-line B-24 and then B-36 bombers. Between them, they employed some sixty thousand workers. Houston, which some people once considered a frivolous candidate even for a ship channel, became a powerhouse of naval construction. Brown Shipbuilding on Green's Bayou lacked the space to build deep-water capital ships but turned out some three hundred smaller vessels—landing craft, destroyer escorts, and submarine chasers. For want of harbor space to send them down the ways traditionally, Brown's ships were christened and launched Great

Lakes–style: sideways. Even more remarkably, Todd Shipyards, on the ship channel itself, took a contract from the U. S. Maritime Commission for the mass production of the freighters known as Liberty Ships. In only four months, Todd quintupled its

Texas's wartime governor remained Coke Stevenson, elected twice in his own right after Pappy O'Daniel bequeathed him the office. He was the last Texas chief executive to come from self-made pioneer stock. Born in a log cabin near Mason in 1888, and named for the burly Texas governor who had overthrown the Reconstruction government in 1874, he obtained only a rudimentary education before going to work as a ranch hand at fourteen. He managed to save enough money to buy six horses and a freight wagon, and took a correspondence course, which he studied while hauling cargo through lonely stretches of the Hill Country, often reading by the light of a camp fire. At a bank in Junction, he started as janitor, but in two years he became a cashier. In his spare time, Stevenson built a house out of salvaged lumber. He passed the bar in 1913.

Stevenson acquired various business and financial interests, and in politics rose from county attorney to county judge, made it to the state house, and was speaker two terms. He was then lieutenant governor. As governor, his hard-bitten, self-reliant success gave him attitudes strange in a state that had benefited so much from the New Deal: He was certain that Texas, like himself, would prosper if left to its own hard work and thrift. Stevenson cooked his own breakfast, drove himself to the capitol in a Ford—getting there by six in the morning—and made sure the lights were out when he left. He seldom spoke out on controversial issues, citing his own beatitude: Blessed is he who sayeth nothing: for he shall not be misquoted.

He did enjoy his pipes, however, and during six years in the mansion was given about 150 of them.

As part of the attack on Pearl Harbor, five Japanese two-man midget submarines penetrated the American naval base. The captured HA-19 *(above)*, only seventy-eight feet long, then toured the country to raise money for the war effort; purchase of stamps or bonds allowed one to look inside the hull at Japanese-uniformed mannequins at their stations. HA-19's stop in the Hill Country town of Fredericksburg was no accident; the hotel in the background was founded in 1847 and still run by the family of the commander in chief of the Pacific Fleet. The Nimitzes had always been one of Fredericksburg's leading families; the fleet admiral himself was born just up the street.

A scrap-metal drive in Lubbock *(right)* gave citizens a chance to line up at a cardboard cutout of the Führer, with a bull's-eye on his bottom, and assault him with skillets, saucepans, washtubs, and even a coffeepot or two.

work force, from four thousand to twenty thousand. Only three in every one hundred of the new people knew anything about naval architecture. Nevertheless, construction time was slashed from 254 days to only 53, and in the course of the war Todd produced 222 of the tough, stocky, dependable Liberty freighters.

San Jacinto Shipbuilding Corporation held the contract to produce barges made of concrete, an unlikely-sounding substance for ship construction, but actually they were quite serviceable and even became stronger with use. San Jacinto was poorly managed and went under, but, as the war effort geared up, some forty-five firms in Houston held major defense contracts.

Stevenson's planning paid off; the state deficit began to shrink, and family incomes rose by about 30 percent. Defense contracts led to unprecedented urban growth—Dallas, Forth Worth, Houston, Austin, and San Antonio all grew to about half again larger than their prewar size.

Coke Stevenson was not cozy with the federal wartime administration, however, and a particularly serious quarrel erupted over gasoline rationing. He knew very well,

As countless Victory Gardens sprouted across Texas, not all of them were individual backyard projects. The city of Austin utilized vacant acreage along the Colorado River for a major effort; in this view, volunteers harvest bushels of sweet potatoes.

With so much manpower diverted overseas, American women stepped in and assumed jobs that were at one time unthinkable, doing it with élan and humor. Said one of the women rebuilding this bomber engine at Kelly Field, "No nail polish needed here."

as the Washington bureaucrats did not, that Texas's vast geography created special needs. A gasoline allotment suitable for Connecticut—three gallons per week was the national guideline for a nonfarm household automobile—would not begin to cover the distances in Texas. Gasoline, said Stevenson, had taken its indispensable place in the progression of Texas history, alongside "the saddle, the rifle, the ax, and the Bible that won Texas for the society we now have."

When Stevenson and the lieutenant governor, John Lee Smith, joined forces in pooh-poohing both gas rationing and its intended side effect on relieving the rubber shortage, Interior Secretary Harold Ickes (who was even then stealing doormats from the White House for the rubber pool) blew up. "As you go vociferously forth," Ickes complained bitterly, "draped in the outer garments of patriotism and the underwear of self-interest, please remember that our tanks and trucks and jeeps cannot burn as fuel the crocodile tears you shed." When the feds took umbrage at the sight of Texans driving cars to football games, Stevenson resurrected the specter of the Texas Rangers and hinted darkly that, in a real contest, the federal gumshoes would come off second-best. The problem was solved in two ways. First a winking sort of compromise was reached, which allowed local ration boards to certify higher-priority cards to rural families. And second, families who needed more regulated goods than they were allowed began buying ration tickets from blacks and Hispanics who either did not need their full ration or couldn't afford it if they did.

What Coke Stevenson wanted most from Washington was for them to do business when necessary, do it fairly, and otherwise just leave Texas the hell alone. It was a hugely popular stance, for more reasons than merely conflicts over war administration. While Texans were united in the war effort, they had become increasingly disenchanted with the liberalism of Roosevelt's New Deal—how quickly they had forgotten how much they benefited from it—and they most particularly resented the fact that FDR's decision to run for a third term had done Cactus Jack Garner out of an almost sure lease on the White House.

There was also a significant racial factor involved. Motivated partly by traditional prejudice and partly with memories of the Houston race riots during World War I, Texas conservatives complained about the stationing of too many black troops in the

This view of the race riot in Beaumont shows members of the white mob straining for a glimpse of their quarry, black laborers who had taken refuge inside the building.

In addition to a basic regimen of calisthenics, students at the U.S. Navy Flight Preparatory School at the University of Texas in Austin were given "expert instruction in four important strokes," as well as in wrestling and military track. The training provided background for a number of daring at-sea rescues.

state. (Houston defused its own situation by establishing a military-civilian committee intended to end the mistreatment of black servicemen.) Texas blacks themselves were understandably frustrated that the return to prosperity did not, by and large, include them. Whites stayed worried, and tensions boiled over in Beaumont, in a twenty-hour race riot in June of 1943 that had to be quelled by National Guard troops in addition to police and rangers. The spark had been a rumor, which proved to be untrue, that a white woman had been raped by a black. This set some two thousand white shipyard workers rampaging through—as it was called and every city had one—niggertown. Three people died and hundreds were injured on both sides.

Stevenson had already caused consternation among federal officials over the race issue the previous year, when a Texarkana black was lynched on the accusation that he had raped a white woman. Nazi propagandists had a field day with the affair, and the attorney general of the United States asked the Texas governor to see to it that those responsible for the lynching were prosecuted. Stevenson answered loftily that "certain members of the Negro race from time to time furnish the setting for mob violence by the outrageous crimes which they commit." This particular offense was so heinous, he went on, that even a white man would have been lynched for it; therefore, it was not a race issue.

The federal Supreme Court complicated the situation enormously and even caused a split in the state Democratic party in 1944, when in the case of *Smith* v. *Allwright* it declared that Texas's white-only primaries were unconstitutional. Conservatives who controlled the state convention tried to strong-arm delegates into pledging their opposition to the decision, which caused the convention to disintegrate. The conservatives reformed into the Texas Regulars and campaigned, with formidable organization and money, against the Roosevelt-Truman ticket. It was a sign of changing times that they failed, their candidates sometimes faring even worse than the Republicans.

Stevenson managed to float statesmanlike above the fratricidal mayhem, but his conservatism and ambivalence toward the federal government carried him to easy reelection in 1942 and 1944. In the latter primary, he won nearly 700,000 votes; his eight opponents split about 125,000. The Republican party, by the way, was still not making much of a showing. In 1942 Stevenson beat his GOP opponent by 281,000 to 9,000.

As victory for the Allies became ever more certain, growing numbers of enemy captives swelled prisoner of war camps in Texas, such as this one *(above)* near the town of Brady. At first, emphasis was on preventing escape, but before the end of the war some 27,000 POWs were used in agricultural labor. With twenty-one permanent prison camps and twenty temporary camps, Texas had more than twice as many POW installations as any other state. More than 45,000 Germans, Italians, and Japanese passed through them.

As Japanese bombs began falling on Pearl Harbor, a Texan became one of the first heroes of the struggle. Twenty-two-year-old mess attendant DORIS MILLER *(left)* of Waco was serving breakfast on board the battleship *West Virginia;* like all blacks in a white man's navy, his duties were limited to the galley. The vessel was struck by two bombs and six torpedo hits, and then was swamped with burning oil and wreckage when her neighbor on battleship row, *Arizona,* blew up. Miller helped carry *West Virginia*'s mortally wounded captain to a place of safety and then seized a machine gun, which he had never been trained to use, and was credited with downing two of the attacking planes. "It wasn't hard," he was quoted as saying. "I just pulled the trigger, and she worked fine." The navy awarded him its highest decoration, the Navy Cross, and Miller went on to duty for a year and a half on the cruiser *Indianapolis.* He was still a galley attendant when he was killed in action aboard the escort carrier *Liscombe Bay* in 1943—the year that a race riot in Beaumont killed two, and the year before the Democratic primaries were reopened to black voters.

The military made good trade on Miller's heroism, perhaps hoping that black servicemen would pay less notice to the fact that they were entertained in segregated facilities. Pictured above is the hall operated in Austin by the Negro War Recreation Council. Named for Doris Miller, it attracted some fifteen hundred servicemen of color each week.

Relations with Hispanics fared somewhat better under the Stevenson administration. As early as 1941, pacification of Latin America had become a priority in the face of a European war, and the legislature in that year passed acts allowing the teaching of Spanish in elementary schools, and, more importantly, one allowing state-supported colleges to accept on scholarship five students from each of the Latin American countries. There was a low point in 1943, when the government of Mexico, citing insufferable discrimination suffered by its nationals in Texas, suspended its "bracero" program of providing cross-border laborers. With wartime agricultural production at risk, Stevenson approved the Caucasian Race Resolution, which outlawed discrimination against any white (and putatively brown) persons. He also cooperated when the State Department's Office of Inter-American Affairs asked him to create a Good Neighbor Commission to improve relations with Latin America. Still, other bills to attach criminal penalties to discrimination against Hispanics failed in the legislature.

The inactivity of the Coke Stevenson administration on matters of racial justice is a judgment sharpened by hindsight and modern sensibilities. In the context of the

University of Texas students protested vigorously against the firing of HOMER RAINEY. The effort was futile, but the academic cloud that the incident left over the university lasted almost a decade.

day, his term, which was the longest of any Texas governor up to that time, was a success. Once there were means to pay for it—and by 1945 the legislature had a cash surplus from which to make appropriations—he raised teachers' salaries, put the fund for state highway construction on a sound footing, improved soil-conservation laws, and expanded university building programs.

Stevenson did get into seriously hot water with academia once, in what was probably the hottest ongoing battle of his administration, but which in the history books has been overshadowed by the war. That was the firing of Homer Rainey, longtime president of the University of Texas, by the board of regents. Rainey had been appointed under a liberal governor—Jimmie Allred—with a liberal board. Both O'Daniel and Stevenson, however, had appointed to the regency almost exclusively wealthy, archconservative businessmen, whom Rainey had been stiff-arming for years in their attempts to force the university to reflect their political views by getting liberal, leftist, or otherwise-inconvenient faculty members fired. When they finally dismissed him in November of 1944, the excuse was so trivial that the firing became not just an academic but a political tar baby that would not be flung away. As the regents made ever wilder charges against Rainey to justify his sacking, the legislature held hearings, at which one of the regents even accused Rainey of allowing the university to become a "nest of homosexuals." (A subsequent Department of Public Safety investigation found no such thing.) At the conclusion of the regent's testimony, one state representative asked tiredly, "Any other dirty thing about the university you want to volunteer?" The firing stuck, but the University of Texas was blacklisted by the American Association of University Professors, and remained under sanctions for nine years.

Texas Aviation: More Important Than Ever

The preparedness buildup in Texas began with Randolph Field, whose elegant white administration building became known as the Taj Mahal.

Texas's long history as a leader in American aviation, and its unchanged advantages in climate and geography, made it inevitable that once war came, Texas's importance to the war in the air would be all but impossible to overstate. Preparedness began quietly enough, with the realization that Texas held a population far above the per capita average of capable civilian pilots. Beginning in July of 1939, Randolph Field in San Antonio began the Civilian Pilot Training Program, to ensure that if the need arose, qualified flight instructors could be quickly pulled out of the civilian population. Once the war started, actual flight instruction was pulled out of Randolph, which became the major school for teachers, of whom some fifteen thousand graduated during the course of the conflict.

When the Army Air Force Training Command was created in June of 1941 with headquarters in Fort Worth, its most important centers for primary flight training did stay in San Antonio, at Brooks and Kelly fields. From an initial training goal of 30,000 pilots per year, a year into the war this was revised to an unprecedented—almost unthinkable—102,000 per year. This required the establishment of scores of air bases in Texas to serve every conceivable function from a Marine glider base in Fort Worth to a bomber school at Sheppard Air Force Base in Wichita Falls. In the two and a quarter years from January 1942 to May 1944, Texas alone turned out 44,958 pilots, 12,534 bombardiers, and 12,706 navigators.

With the advent of the aircraft carrier in replacing the battleship as capital fleet vessels, naval aviation also took up residence in Texas for their pilot training. Hensley Field near Dallas was appropriated as the Dallas Naval Air Station, with duties as disparate as parts storage and the training of Free French cadets. The real story, however, took shape along the coast. As early as December of 1938, a recommendation was made for the establishment of a Naval Air Station near Corpus Christi. Land was flat and cheap, population was sparse, and the weather close to ideal. By the time the contracts were approved in June of 1940, war preparedness was well under way and the 2,050-acre base was finished in only nine months. Not only that, before it was even half finished, three more satellite naval airfields were begun around it, at a total expend-

This panoramic view of the CORPUS CHRISTI NAVAL AIR STATION gives some idea of the size of the facility.

Among the airmen who won their wings in Texas was Elliott Roosevelt, the President's son.

iture of more than $40 million. Corpus Christi Naval Air Station welcomed its first class of fifty-two cadets only a week after its commissioning, and by the time the Japanese bombed Pearl Harbor the school was graduating some three hundred navy pilots every month. After the war, this was more than doubled, which necessitated the bringing on line of no fewer than twenty-two more subsidiary fields, as far away as Kingsville Auxiliary Air Station and Chase Field in Beeville, which made it the largest naval air center in the world. By the end of the conflict, about 35,000 naval airmen had trained in the Corpus Christi complex.

The unquestioned need for such extravagant numbers of military pilots created a critical shortage of qualified pilots for noncombat duty, which led, inevitably, to the suggestion that women be trained to fill the gap. The need only barely overcame the resistance, and the program began with a squeak: The Ferry Command was authorized to recruit women who were under thirty-five, were already trained pilots rated to fly planes of two hundred horsepower or more, and had at least five hundred hours in the air. Twenty-three such women were signed up, as the Women's Auxiliary Ferrying Squadron. Under the leadership of Jacqueline Cochran, the program was then expanded to produce Women's Air Service pilots, after an intensive 210-hour training course. Shop was set up at the Houston Municipal Airport, which unfortunately was far removed from the location of the classrooms, to and from which transportation was spotty and undependable. In addition to a curriculum never having been developed for training women pilots, their housing was awful and sometimes there was no food at all.

Hope for a smoother program was offered by transferring the operation to the newly available Avenger Field in Sweetwater, on the rolling plains near Abilene. The site was not perfect—the county was dry, which meant no alcohol, and accommodations were often shared with scorpions and rattlesnakes. After the first eighty-seven trainees showed up in February of 1943, however, the kinks were ironed out, and Avenger Field began turning out qualified female pilots for both the Ferry Command and the Air Transport Command. They trained in a hodgepodge of PT-19s, BT-13s, AT-17s, and ubiquitous AT-6 Texans, but by the end of the war they had been rated in and flown every type of wartime aircraft.

Whereas Dorothy Scarborough was inspired by Sweetwater to pen her novel of prairie madness, *The Wind*, female cadets at Avenger Field were more mindful of its crawling vermin. Some 40 percent left before graduating.

Texas in the Pacific

Number Three Turret Firing.

Texas's reciprocating engines made it difficult to keep up with the modern fleet. However, her broadside "throw weight" of seven tons—ten fourteen-hundred-pound shells—and the legendary marksmanship of her crew made her an incomparable fire-support vessel for amphibious landings. By war's end, she had participated in five invasions—a record.

AFTER supporting the landings in France, the venerable *Texas* sailed to New York for a month-long overhaul. With heavy guns no longer needed in that theater, she was refitted for Pacific duty, loaded with still more antiaircraft guns and her mottled camouflage repainted a dark Pacific blue. The expenditure of more than a thousand rounds of fourteen-inch shell had worn out her thirty-year-old gun liners, which were replaced.

Analysts studying the effectiveness of heavy-caliber naval gunfire to "soften up" landing beaches in Europe had discovered as many enemy killed in their positions by sheer blast as by shrapnel, and concluded to lengthen preinvasion bombardments from maybe half an hour to, in some cases, days. Thus *Texas* broke in her new gun liners by firing a stunning 923 rounds into Japanese positions at Iwo Jima on and after March 7, 1945. She ended her wartime career three weeks later in a blaze, thundering out more than two hundred broadsides in support of the landing on Okinawa.

Texas was now the oldest ship in the fleet, and, hobbled as she was with her antique reciprocating steam engines, she was excused further duty in harm's way. She patrolled in the Philippines but was not present at the last battleship surface action ever fought, in the nearby Surigao Strait. Had she been called, she would have answered, but that final eighteen-minute orgy of vengeance was reserved for her sisters raised from the mud at Pearl Harbor. After three shuttles bringing servicemen home in Operation Magic Carpet, *Texas* returned to Norfolk and was mothballed.

To honor the cruiser *Houston*, sunk at the beginning of the war, the navy redesignated the light cruiser *Vicksburg*, then being built in Newport News, as a new *Houston* (CL-81). Citizens of the namesake city underwrote the $40 million for construction and then provided a thousand volunteers to man her—although four hundred of the new complement were survivors of the recently lost USS *Helena*. Precious training time was saved by importing crews already used to fighting together.

As a light cruiser, she was less heavily limited by the Washington Treaty, she was larger (608 feet by 13,000 tons full load) and faster (33 knots) than her namesake, and still mounted a withering battery of twelve six-inch and twelve five-inch guns.

Commissioned in December 1943, she joined the fleet in time to support her big sister *Texas* at the invasion of Iwo Jima. The new *Houston* also made her presence felt at Saipan, Guam, Tinian, the Philippines, and Peleliu before being holed and crippled by a Japanese torpedo bomber off Formosa in October 1944. She lost fifty-five sailors but refused to sink, despite a second torpedo hit while under tow. Repairs in New York took until after war's end. After goodwill cruises, she was mothballed in 1947 and scrapped in 1959.

Sam Dealey and the USS *Harder*

Graduated from Annapolis in 1930, COMDR. SAMUEL DAVID DEALEY pulled duty
on the battleship *Nevada* and the destroyer *Reuben James* before settling in submarine
duty to command the experimental trainer S-20. As the United States entered the
war, *Nevada* sank in Pearl Harbor, and Dealey's best friend went down with the
Reuben James off the coast of Iceland. Dealey's repeated requests for combat duty
were not heeded until he was given command of the USS *Harder* at her commis-
sioning in April 1943. In this first four cruises, before the sortie into Sibutu Passage,
Dealey sank eleven Japanese ships totalling fifty thousand tons.

ON June 6, 1944, a day when the *Texas* was earning one of her five battle stars off
the coast of Normandy, another Texan, Cmdr. Sam Dealey of the submarine *Harder*,
was about to make a name for himself in the Pacific.

Three different subs had tried and failed to rescue a team of British and Australian
commandos from the north coast of Japanese-occupied Borneo, where they had been
operating for some two years. Now it was Dealey's turn. To get there he had to make
it through the Sibutu Passage, right under the nose of a major Japanese fleet anchorage

at Tawi Tawi, at the southwest tip of the Philippine Islands. Dealey entered the narrow strait at night, submerged, but when contact was made with a six-ship convoy Dealey decided the commandos would have to wait, and he ordered a battle-surface. It was a short-lived idea, however, as a sudden gust of wind cleared the overcast. *Harder* was seen instantly and a Japanese destroyer heeled over to attack. Destroyers are designed and built specifically to attack and destroy submarines, and in World War II subs rarely took one on deliberately. Sam Dealey's philosophy differed, however. The Japanese navy was top-heavy in capital battleships and carriers but suffered a well-known shortage of destroyers. To Dealey's mind, if the destroyers could be sunk, the rest of the navy would be at the mercy of U.S. subs. Under attack, Dealey merely turned ninety degrees to port and awaited a firing solution for the after tubes. Of three torpedoes fired, only one missed, and the destroyer *Minatsuki* blew up and sank. A second destroyer attacked, more warily; six more torpedoes from *Harder* all missed, and Dealey and his crew endured a fearsome four-hour depth charging.

Early the next morning, Dealey stalked another target, a smudgy silhouette that proved to be a small island—a common enough gaffe in those waters—and then continued toward the rendezvous. A second target proved to be another destroyer, and this time Dealey left his periscope up to draw him in. He held his torpedoes until 650 yards, fired three, and the destroyer *Hayanami* sank seconds after her magazine detonated. Dealey was now himself surprised by another ship, and was depth-charged for two hours before sneaking away to meet the commandos.

Off the north coast of Borneo, Dealey awaited the safety of night before sending in a rubber boat and plucking the weary Brits and Aussies off the beach. Cruising on the moonlit surface, Dealey retraced his route through the Sibutu Passage, intending to complete his assignment by scouting the Japanese base at Tawi Tawi, when the sudden sight of two destroyer pickets sent him crashing below. It was a situation in which even a brave submariner would have lain low and plotted an escape. Dealey, however, figured the destroyers' course for a firing solution, and sank them both with one salvo of four torpedoes; in undersea warfare it was a feat without parallel. Dealey surfaced and nosed his way through the steam and flotsam to give his allies a look, but he was soon chased below by bombs from Japanese planes.

Faced with the loss of four precious destroyers in four days, Admiral Soemu Toyoda at Tawi Tawi frowned over his maps and sent a message to Tokyo that his fleet had been discovered. "The Tawi Tawi anchorage is surrounded by a great force of submarines. I do not have the destroyers to cope with the situation, and am therefore moving the fleet." Toyoda's force, three battleships, four cruisers, and a screen of his remaining eight destroyers, blew out of Tawi Tawi the next day like quail out of a mesquite thicket, right before Dealey's wide eyes. As he drooled over his periscope, the crew exchanged worried glances; surely he wouldn't. Just then

Three hundred and twelve feet long, *Harder* was a state-of-the-art vessel at the time she went to sea, carrying twenty-four torpedoes to be fired through six bow tubes and four stern ones. Four diesel engines generated nineteen knots on the surface, with four electric motors for submerged cruising. When he was offered the traditional commander's prerogative in the placement of the three-inch deck gun—forward or abaft the conning tower—Dealey, the most decorated American sailor of the war, was said to have replied, "Forward, of course. . . . Whom are we running away from?"

Harder was rocked by the near-miss of an aerial bomb—the Japanese air cover had spotted them in the crystal water. Worse, one of the destroyers swung out to attack, at whom Dealey fired a desperate "down the throat" salvo before going deep right under her hull; the concussion of the destroyer blowing up very nearly accomplished what four other tin cans had been unable to do.

Harder then took a hammering from they didn't know how many of Toyoda's remaining seven destroyers. Dealey pulled every evasive maneuver in the book, but, as the explosions rolled them in the water, gear shook loose, valves popped open—at one point in the three-hour ordeal an Aussie commando came up to Dealey as he stood at his periscope: "I say, old man, would you mind taking us back to Borneo?"

By the time they were able to surface again, Toyoda's fleet had fled—straight into a blistering defeat at the Battle of the Philippine Sea. The gallant *Harder* went down with all hands two months later; Dealey's Congressional Medal of Honor was awarded posthumously.

Chester Nimitz

WHEN the Society for the Protection of German Immigrants bought Henry Fisher's 4 million acres of Hill Country in the 1840s, they did so upon Fisher's fraudulent assertion that the region was ideal for coastal commerce. The irony turned sweet, however, when the region produced one of the great naval commanders of the war. Chester Nimitz was born in 1885 in Fredericksburg, where the family had owned a hotel since the early days of settlement; when he was six, his widowed mother married his uncle and relocated to Kerrville. When at sixteen he received an appointment to the U.S. Naval Academy, his math teacher lamented the fact he had not finished school; Nimitz assured her that one day he would return as an admiral.

At Annapolis, he studied voraciously but still had time to serve as stroke oar on the rowing team, and he graduated seventh in a class that produced several other brilliant officers. Nimitz admitted to having two heroes—Lord Nelson and Heihachiro Togo, the brilliant admiral who broke the Russian Baltic Fleet at Tsushima in 1905. In fact, as a young officer serving aboard the predreadnought battleship *Ohio*, on port call in Tokyo in 1907, Nimitz attended an Imperial garden party held in Togo's honor, and met the great seaman.

The navy nearly lost Nimitz several times. As a young commander, he was court-martialed for running his destroyer aground, but he stayed in the service. In one port he leaped overboard to rescue one of his sailors who, oddly enough, could not swim, and the two were swept out to sea together; that they were found at all was miraculous. Shortly before World War I, he was assigned to Germany to study diesel engines, and he inspected one so closely that moving gears caught his sleeve and sucked his arm into the machinery. His Annapolis class ring jammed a wheel—he lost half the finger but was spared a mangling that could have ended his career. Instead, Nimitz oversaw the outfitting of the first diesel engines in a U.S. ship. He became such an expert that he was offered a lavish contract to enter private business, but he turned it down.

On board the heavy cruiser *Baltimore*, Pearl Harbor, July 26, 1944, President Roosevelt confers with General MacArthur and Admiral Nimitz.

During and after World War I his resume became even more varied. After different submarine commands, he gained administrative experience as chief of staff to a flag officer. He became ranking member of the Board of Submarine Design, studied at the Naval War College, and created a pioneer naval ROTC program before taking command of the heavy cruiser USS *Augusta*, and became a rear admiral in 1938.

Immediately after Pearl Harbor, when Roosevelt named a new commander in chief for the Pacific, he promoted Nimitz over twenty-eight other flag officers who ranked him. It was a choice typical of FDR's shrewdness. Nimitz had predicted fifteen years earlier that the next war, when it came, would be with Germany and Japan. He had seen the broadest possible sea duty—in gunboats, destroyers, cruisers, battleships, and submarines, and understood the potential for the new aircraft carriers. Nimitz was an innovative thinker—it was he who designed the modern fleet formation to replace the battle line that had dominated naval theory since the days of Nelson. And he was an adroit leader of men and women, able to pitch horseshoes with common seamen and order gallant ships into harm's way. He was firm but compassionate, an indispensable quality in a command of nearly 2.25 million.

At a level of service where politics can outweigh merit, Nimitz justified every confidence placed in him. After the war, he was given a thunderous ticker-tape parade in New York City, and served a term as Chief of Naval Operations. He returned briefly to Fredericksburg, and to his immense pleasure accepted a high school diploma from the math teacher whom he had promised to return an admiral.

In an interview given shortly before his death in 1966—which he insisted not be published while he lived—Nimitz predicted a third world war, which would begin not over ideology but from the pressure of rampant overpopulation. He is buried in San Francisco.

The Dead and the Decorated

Texas had a much smaller claim to its other high-ranking native son. Supreme Allied Commander Dwight David Eisenhower was born in Denison in 1890, but the family moved to Kansas soon after. After graduating from West Point in 1915 he was assigned to duty in San Antonio, a second lieutenant in the Nineteenth Infantry; there he courted and married Mamie Doud. Eisenhower's career developed mostly as an administrator—in the Panama Canal Zone, France, and the Philippines—but he also trained the men of one of the first tank corps in the army and developed the Philippine air force.

His handling of war maneuvers in Louisiana in the fall of 1941 finally revealed him to be a battle planner of uncommon talent; thereafter, Eisenhower rose rapidly, until he was named General of the Army in December 1944.

BY the close of the war, Texans discovered that they had given birth or long residence to 12 naval admirals and more than 150 general officers, including the General of the Army and the Fleet Admiral of the Pacific. They could look upon their contribution to the war effort with a mixture of pride and grief; 728,000 of their men and 12,000 women had served—a greater proportion of Texas's population than that offered by any other state. They mourned the 23,000 who had died, but Texans took some consolation in the knowledge that their people had acquitted themselves in a manner worthy of their history. Six Texas sailors and no fewer than thirty Texas soldiers won Congressional Medals of Honor, including the war's single most heavily decorated individuals in two branches of service. The Aggies certainly had done their part— twenty thousand of them fought, 70 percent as officers, including one admiral and thirty-nine generals. Six Aggies won Congressional Medals of Honor.

The survivors returned home to a Texas that was grateful. Although the federal GI Bill was already on the books, in Texas state laws granted even more benefits, from free attendance at state colleges to poll-tax exemptions to the renewal of old driver's licenses without examination. And, in a peculiarly Texan gesture that hearkened right back to the days of the Republic, the electorate passed an amendment to the state constitution, authorizing the issuance of bonds with which the state purchased land for resale at low interest to veterans.

The survivors also returned home to a Texas that had changed irrevocably: It had become modern, and urbanized, and more than a little confused. When the Forty-ninth Legislature convened in January of 1945, no fewer than eighty-four proposed constitutional amendments were submitted to try to come to grips with the question, What now? War had always given Texans a certainty in their place and their duty, and now—no less than in the peaceful paranoia that followed World War I—Texans faced a new era of unforeseen trial, unexpected promise, and change to which they scarcely knew how to adapt.

In Texas no less than the rest of the country, people poured into the streets to celebrate the surrender of Japan. This was the scene on Congress Avenue in Austin.

Notes on the Text

THE 1900s

A fuller glimpse of Ned Green is found in the biography of his more famous mother, Hetty; see Arthur Lewis, *The Day They Shook the Plum Tree*. The photo of the Swedish family is from *Svenskarne i Texas: Ord Och Bild*, a privately printed double-volume that speaks eloquently of the identity maintained by European colonists—for in many ways that is what they remained—in Texas. Thomas Munson's story is told in Terry Curry, "The Man Who Saved France's Wine Industry."

Seth McKay provides good analysis of the gubernatorial campaigns in *Texas Politics 1906–1944*. Other more general discussions are not lacking. See Alwyn Barr, *Reconstruction to Reform: Texas Politics 1876–1906*, and V. O. Key, Jr., *Southern Politics in State and Nation*. For a Joe Bailey biography, see Sam Acheson, *Joe Bailey: The Last Democrat*. Colonel House's impact in these early years is examined in Rupert Richardson, "Edward M. House and the Governors."

The chapter of social history is gleaned from the general sources. One should see C. Richard King, "Sarah Bernhardt in Texas." The history of Reverend Bloys and his gatherings is told in Joe Evans, *Bloys Cowboy Camp Meeting*. At the opposite end of the pew from the mild-mannered Bloys, read Allyn Russell, "J. Frank Norris: Violent Fundamentalist."

City histories include *Galveston: A History*, and *Houston: A History*, both by David G. McComb, and John Waler and Gwendolyn Wingate, *Beaumont: A Pictorial History*. Mary Sibley, *The Port of Houston*, has more on the ship channel and its intended choking of Galveston. The brief quotes describing life in the early boomtowns are from the outstanding record of oral history compiled by Roger M. Olien and Diana Davids Olien, *Life in the Oil Fields*. Going into greater depth, from a single source, see Charlie Jeffries, "Reminiscences of Sour Lake." And of course one should also see Walter Rundell, *Early Texas Oil: A Photographic History*. For a boomtown history located in the interior, try Abby Wheelis Cooper, "Electra: A Texas Oil Town."

The lumber industry and John Henry Kirby are treated in many sources: Baker and Maxwell, *Sawdust Empire*; Ruth Allen, *East Texas Lumber Workers*; Lawrence Walker, *Axes, Oxen and Men*; and Mary Lasswell, *John Henry Kirby, Prince of the Pines*. For a somewhat more modern view of the latter, see George T. Morgan, "The Gospel of Wealth Goes South."

One aspect of the loss of public domain is covered in R. D. Holt, "School Land Rushes in West Texas." Lawrence Graves covers the *History of Lubbock* in three volumes; information used here on Molly Abernathy is from the supplement to the *Handbook of Texas*. Background on the pastoral development of the Hill Country will be found in Douglas Barnett, "Angora Goats in Texas." Schreiner's preeminence in development of the region will be understood from Gene Hollon, "Captain Charles Schreiner: Father of the Hill Country."

The story of the rise of Anglo patrons in the Rio Grande valley is told in Evan Anders, *Boss Rule in South Texas: The Progressive Years*, and in his article, "The Origins of the Parr Machine in Duval County." See more generally J. Lee Stambaugh, *The Lower Rio Grande Valley of Texas*. The principal source on the Gregorio Cortez story is still Americo Paredes, *With a Pistol in His Hand*, which, while factually valid, is so bitter and sarcastic as to remind one that its author is better known as a folklorist than historian.

A more detailed account of the squabble over how to preserve the Alamo is L. Robert Ables's article, "The Second Battle of the Alamo," and both principals' stories are told in separate segments of Crawford and Ragsdale, *Women in Texas*. The dedication of the Confederate Memorial provides a final glimpse of the great John Reagan, portrayed more fully in Ben Proctor, *Not Without Honor*.

More information on the building of Post is contained in Charles Dudley Eaves and C. R. Hutchinson, *Post City, Texas*. The "Forest of Windmills" is detailed in T. Lindsay Baker, "The Windmill Waterworks of Post City." An article on the waterworks is contained in the same author's *Building the Lone Star*, which is a highly interesting compendium of major engineering feats in both nineteenth- and twentieth-century Texas. A more general understanding of the plight of the tenant farmers can be gleaned from Graham Adams, "Agrarian Discontent in Progressive Texas."

THE 1910s

Early Texas aviation is summarized nicely in Roger Bilstein and Jay Miller, *Aviation in Texas*. Early military development is given there and in greater detail in Ben Foulois's own memoir, *From the Wright Brothers to the Astronauts*. One should also see Barney Giles, "Early Military Aviation in Texas."

Jack Johnson tells of his own rise in his own fashion in his autobiography, *Jack Johnson Is a Dandy*. See also Randy Roberts, "Galveston's Jack Johnson: Flourishing in the Dark." June Rayfield Welch includes a vignette of Albert Lasker in *All Hail the Mighty State*. University of Texas athletics are discussed in James Pohls, "The Bible Decade and the Origins of National Athletic Prominence."

Woodrow Wilson's ascent in Texas is traced in Arthur Link, "The Wilson Movement in Texas, 1910–1912." See also C. Richard King, "Woodrow Wilson's Visit to Texas in 1911." More on the elusive and fascinating Colonel E. M. House is found in Arthur Smith, *Mr. House of Texas*, and Rupert Richardson, *Colonel Edward M. House, the Texas Years*. For an interesting look at another high-ranking Texan, see Adrian Anderson, "Mr. Wilson's Politician: Albert Sidney Burleson of Texas." A good encapsulation of the political milieu is Lewis Gould, "Progressives and Prohibitionists: Texas Democratic Politics, 1911–1921." See also the more general Dewey Grantham, "Texas Congressional Leaders and the New Freedom, 1913–1917."

The principal source used for this brief account of Georgia O'Keeffe was Laurie Lisle, *Portrait of an Artist*, fleshed out with O'Keeffe's own notes in *One Hundred Flowers*; Jan Castro, *The Art & Life of Georgia O'Keeffe*; and Daniel Rich, *Georgia O'Keeffe*. For a narrower focus one can see John Matthews, "The Influence of the Texas Panhandle on Georgia O'Keeffe."

Walter Webb's *The Texas Rangers: A Century of Frontier Defense* has been superseded in some ways, but to my thinking is one of the most instructive accounts of the border troubles, not least because it can now be seen as sharing the limitations of social consciousness that was so often exhibited by Rangers on the scene. One should also see Charles Cumberland, "Border

Raids in the Lower Rio Grande Valley—1915," and Carole Christian, "Joining the American Mainstream: Texas's Mexican-Americans during World War I."

James Green, "Tenant Farmer Discontent and Socialist Protest in Texas, 1901–1917," will give a good idea why Ferguson's promised land reform played so well in the rural areas. A summary of Ferguson's feud with the University of Texas is contained in Lewis L. Gould's "The University Becomes Politicized: The War with Jim Ferguson, 1915–1918." A very able biography of Governor Hobby is James Clark, *The Tactful Texan*. Crawford and Ragsdale, *Women in Texas*, contains chapters on both Jane McCallum and Annie Webb Blanton.

A good summary of the buildup of air power in Texas is Bilstein and Miller, *Aviation in Texas*. See also William Pool, "Military Aviation in Texas, 1913–1917."

A detailed study of the Houston race riot is Robert V. Haynes, *A Night of Violence: The Houston Riot of 1917*, containing a very useful critical essay of previous sources. Texas Ranger operations in the Big Bend are amplified in Walter Webb, *The Texas Rangers: A Century of Frontier Defense*.

THE 1920s

The contribution of Hackberry Jones to conservation in Texas is outlined in Robert S. Maxwell, "One Man's Legacy: W. Goodrich Jones and Texas Conservation." A fine multifaceted book on the history and ecology of the Big Thicket is Pete Gunter, *The Big Thicket*. Pat Neff left his own autobiography, *The Battles of Peace*. Charles Culberson's dignified career is covered in the James William Madden biography, *Charles Allen Culberson, His Life, Character, and Public Services*.

For more on the development of the helium industry, see L. W. Brendt, "Helium."

Frank Hamer's memoir, *I'm Frank Hamer*, contains his recollection of the Mexia Raid. See also Kyle Shoemaker, "How Mexia Was Made a Clean City."

The Fergusons' daughter, Ouida Nalle, left a memoir of life in this colorful family, *The Fergusons of Texas, or "Two Governors for the Price of One."*

Drilling of Santa Rita is recounted in Carl Coke Rister, *Oil! Titan of the Southwest*, and M. W. Schwettmann, *Santa Rita No. 1*, among other sources. The political journey of the money from wellhead to U.T. accounting is David F. Prindle, "Oil and the Permanent University Fund: The Early Years." The sidebar on Pig Bellmont comes from *The Perip*, the U.T. campus walking tour guide pamphlet. A glimpse of U.T. life in those days can be seen in T. U. Taylor, *Fifty Years on Forty Acres*.

The incidents cited in Eastland County are summarized in June Rayfield Welch, *All Hail the Mighty State*, and fleshed out in Edwin T. Cox, *History of Eastland County*.

Captain Hamer's memoir, *I'm Frank Hamer*, gives his account of the doings in Borger. A contemporary appraisal is H. O. Jennings, "Texas Rangers Praised." For a broader social history, Olien and Olien, *Life in the Oil Fields*, contains telling vignettes of life in the later boomtowns, as well as those of the post-Spindletop era.

THE 1930s

Frost and Jenkins, *I'm Frank Hamer*, contains a chapter on the Sherman race riot. Daniel Webster Wallace's principal biographer was Hetty Branch, and her work *The Story of "80 John."*

For a recounting of the East Texas petroleum discoveries, see James Clark and Michael Halbouty, *The Last Boom*. The craziness of it is well recalled in Robert Boyle, "Chaos in the East

Texas Oil Field, 1930–1935." The early years of the Great Depression in Texas are recounted in Donald Whisenhunt, *The Depression in Texas: The Hoover Years*. For setting the stage for the Dust Bowl, see Tkhadis Box, "Range Deterioration in West Texas."

An interesting look at the early career of Lyndon Johnson is found in Christie Bourgeois, "Stepping Over Lives: Lyndon Johnson, Black Texans, and the National Youth Administration." For a different close-up, see Clayton Brown, "Sam Rayburn and the Development of Public Power in the Southwest."

By far the most accessible, and most readable, history of the Chicken Ranch is Al Reinert, "Closing Down LaGrange." This account was supplemented with vertical files from the Fayette County Heritage Society.

Two vastly different interpretations of Bonnie and Clyde can be found in, on the one hand, Jan Fortune, *The Fugitives*, and on the other hand, Lee Simmons, *Assignment Huntsville*; Frank Hamer's chase of them is detailed in Frost and Jenkins, *I'm Frank Hamer*.

A concise history of the Big Bend National Park and the effort to get it established is John R. Jameson, *Big Bend on the Rio Grande: Biography of a National Park*; and one should see also Ronnie Tyler, *The Big Bend: A History of the Last Texas Frontier*.

Kenneth B. Ragsdale, *The Year America Discovered Texas: Centennial '36*, is a fine overview of what went into the centennial celebration. Nancy Wiley, *The Great State Fair of Texas*, has good coverage of the Dallas Centennial Exposition.

This account of the New London school explosion is pieced together from contemporary news accounts. A more detailed look at how W. Lee O'Daniel turned Texas politics on its ear is Seth McKay, *W. Lee O'Daniel and Texas Politics, 1938–1942*.

THE 1940s

An account of the Lost Battalion is found in Hollis G. Allen, *The Lost Battalion*. The histories of both cruisers U.S.S. *Houston* is Steve Ewing, *American Cruisers of World War II: A Pictorial History*, and were supplemented by articles from the *Handbook of Texas*. The same reference works contain sketches of the World War II activities of the Tough 'Ombres and T Patchers— the latter is much fleshed out in Fred L. Walker, "The 36th Was a Great Fighting Division."

Sources on Oveta Culp Hobby include Crawford and Ragsdale, *Women in Texas*. See also Clarice Pollard, "WAACs in Texas During the Second World War."

Principal sources used for this sketch of Audie Murphy are the Don Graham biography, *No Name on the Bullet*, and Murphy's own autobiography, *To Hell and Back*. Those interested in Murphy should also read the Harold Simpson biography, *Audie Murphy, American Soldier*.

For an account of one of the more articulate critics of the Roosevelt administration, see Irvin May, "Peter Molyneaux and the New Deal." Coke Stevenson and his administration are covered in greater detail in two biographies, Booth Mooney's *Mister Texas*, and Fredeorica Wyatt and Shelton Hooper's *Coke R. Stevenson, A Texas Legend*. Darlene Clark Hine, "The Elusive Ballot: The Black Struggle Against the Texas Democratic White Primary, 1932–1945," is self-explanatory, as is Johnny McCain, "Texas and the Mexican Labor Question, 1942–1947." A glimpse of POW camps is found in Arnold Krammer, "When the *Afrika Korps* Came to Texas."

The exploits of Lieutenant Commander Dealey are recounted in greater detail in Fred Warshofsky, *War Under the Waves*. Most of the information used about Admiral Nimitz was taken from the many excellent exhibits at the Nimitz State Historic Park, located in the old Nimitz Hotel building in Fredericksburg.

Bibliography and Further Reading

MANUSCRIPTS

Dooley, Deanna D. "The Decision to Drink: An Explanation of the Wet/Dry Boundary in Texas." M.A. thesis, Department of Geography, Ohio University, Athens, 1974.

Hoffman, Katherine A. "A Study of the Art of Georgia O'Keeffe from 1916–1974." Ph.D. diss., New York University, 1975.

Holmes, William M. "An Historical Geography of Dry Farming in the Northern High Plains of Texas." Ph.D. diss., Department of Geography, University of Texas, Austin, 1975.

Madla, Frank L. "The Political Impact of Latin Americans and Negroes in Texas Politics." M.A. thesis, St. Mary's University, San Antonio, 1964.

Spillman, Robert C. "A Historical Geography of Mexican American Population Patterns in the South Texas Hispanic Borderland: 1850–1970." M.A. thesis, Department of Geography, University of Southern Mississippi, Hattiesburg, 1977.

BOOKS

Abernethy, Francis Edward. *Legendary Ladies of Texas*. Dallas: E-Heart, 1981.

Acheson, Sam Hanna. *Joe Bailey: The Last Democrat*. New York: Macmillan, 1932.

———. *35,000 Days in Texas: A History of the Dallas News and Its Forebears*. New York: Macmillan, 1938.

Allen, Hollis G. *The Lost Battalion*. Jacksboro, Texas: L. McGee, 1963.

Allen, Ruth A. *Chapters in the History of Organized Labor in Texas*. Austin: The University, 1941.

———. *East Texas Lumber Workers, An Economic and Social Picture. 1870–1950*. Austin: University of Texas Press, 1961.

———. *The Great Southwest Strike*. Austin: The University, 1942.

Anders, Evan. *Boss Rule in South Texas: The Progressive Era*. Austin: University of Texas Press, 1979.

Baker, Robert, and Robert S. Maxwell. *Sawdust Empire*. College Station: Texas A & M University Press, 1963.

Baker, T. Lindsay. *Building the Lone Star: An Illustrated Guide to Historic Sites*. College Station: Texas A & M University Press, 1986.

Barr, Alwyn. *Reconstruction to Reform: Texas Politics, 1876–1906*. Austin: University of Texas Press, 1971.

Bilstein, Roger, and Jay Miller. *Aviation in Texas*. Austin: Texas Monthly Press, 1985.

Branch, Hetty. *The Story of "80 John": A Biography of One of the Most Respected Negro Ranchmen in the Old West*. New York: Greenwich Book Publishers, 1960.

Brown, Norman D. *Hood, Bonnet, and Little Brown Jug: Texas Politics, 1921–1928*. College Station: Texas A & M University Press, 1984.

Carver, Charles. *Brann the Iconoclast*. Austin: University of Texas Press, 1957.

Castro, Jan Garden. *The Art & Life of Georgia O'Keeffe*. New York: Crown Publishers, Inc., 1985.

Clark, James A. *The Tactful Texan: A Biography of Governor Will Hobby*. New York: Random House, 1958.

Clark, James, and Michael T. Halbouty. *The Last Boom*: New York: Random House, 1972.

Cox, Edwin T. *History of Eastland County*. San Antonio: The Naylor Company, 1950.

Crawford, Ann Fears, and Crystal Sasse Ragsdale. *Women in Texas: Their Lives, Their Experiences, Their Accomplishments*. Burnet, Texas: Eakin Press, 1982.

Eaves, Charles Dudley, and C. A. Hutchinson. *Post City, Texas: C. W. Post's Colonizing Activities in West Texas*. Austin: Texas State Historical Association, 1952.

Evans, Joe. *Bloys Cowboy Camp Meeting*. El Paso, Guynes Printing Company, 1959.

Everett, Donald E. *San Antonio: The Flavor of Its Past*. San Antonio: Trinity University Press, 1975.

Ewing, Steve. *American Cruisers of World War II: A Pictorial History*. Missoula, Montana: Pictorial Histories Publishing Co., 1984.

Fehrenbach, T. R. *Lone Star: A History of Texas and the Texans*. New York: Macmillan, 1968.

Fischer, John. *From the High Plains*. New York: Harper & Row, 1978.

Fortune, Jan. *The Fugitives: The Story of Clyde Barrow and Bonnie Parker, as Told by the Mother of Bonnie and the Sister of Clyde*. Dallas: The Ranger Press, 1934.

Foulois, Benjamin D. *From the Wright Brothers to the Astronauts: The Memoirs of Benjamin D. Foulois*. Edited by Carroll V. Gaines. New York: McGraw-Hill, 1968.

Frantz, Joe B. *Texas: A History*. New York: W. W. Norton & Co., 1976. Reprint, 1984. Unnumbered volume of The States and the Nation Series, general editor, James Morton Smith.

Frost, H. Gordon, and John H. Jenkins. *"I'm Frank Hamer": The Life of a Texas Peace Officer*. Austin and New York: The Pemberton Press, 1968.

Gracy, D. B. *Littlefield Lands: Colonization on the Texas Plains, 1912–1920*. Austin: University of Texas Press, 1968.

Graves, Lawrence, ed. 3 vols. *History of Lubbock*. Lubbock: West Texas Museum Association, 1959–1962.

Green, James R. *Grass-roots Socialism: Radical Movements in the Southwest, 1895–1943*. Baton Rouge: Louisiana State University Press, 1978.

Green, A. C. *A Place Called Dallas: The Pioneering Years of a Continuing Metropolis*. Dallas: Dallas County Heritage Society, 1975.

Gunter, Dr. Pete. *The Big Thicket: A Challenge for Conservation*. Austin: Jenkins Publishing Company, 1972.

Handy, Mary Olivia. *History of Fort Sam Houston*. San Antonio: The Naylor Company, 1951.

Hart, Katherine, et al. *Austin and Travis County: A Pictorial History*. Austin: Encino Press, 1975.

Haynes, Robert V. *A Night of Violence: The Houston Riot of 1917*. Baton Rouge: Louisiana State University Press, 1976.

Holmes, Jon. *Texas: A Self-Portrait*. New York: Harry N. Abrams, Inc., 1983.

Howard, James. *Big D Is for Dallas: Chapters in the Twentieth Century History of Dallas*. Dallas: n.p., 1957.

Jameson, John R. *Big Bend on the Rio Grande: Biography of a National Park*. New York: Peter Lang, 1987. Volume 18 of Series IX, "History," of American University Studies.

Johnson, John Arthur. *Jack Johnson Is a Dandy: An Autobiography*. New York: Chelsea House, 1969.

Jones, Billy Mac. *Search for Maturity*. Austin: Steck-Vaughn Co., 1965.

Jordon, Terry G., et al., *Texas: A Geography*. Boulder, Colorado, and London: Westview Press, 1984.

Key, V. O., Jr. *Southern Politics in State and Nation*. Knoxville: University of Tennessee Press, 1984.

King, John O. *Joseph Stephen Cullinan: A Study of Leadership in the Texas Petroleum Industry, 1897–1937*. Nashville: Vanderbilt University Press, 1970.

Lang, Aldon Socrates. *Financial History of the Public Lands in Texas*. New York: Arno Press, 1979.

Lasswell, Mary. *John Henry Kirby, Prince of the Pines*. Austin: Encino Press, 1967.

Lea, Tom. *The King Ranch*. Boston: Little, Brown & Co., 1957.

Lewis, Arthur H. *The Day They Shook the Plum Tree*. New York: Harcourt, Brace & World, Inc., 1963. Reprint. New York: Bantam Books, 1969.

Lich, Glen E. *The German Texans*. San Antonio: The University of Texas Institute of Texan Cultures, 1981.

Lisle, Laurie. *Portrait of an Artist: A Biography of Georgia O'Keeffe*. New York: Seaview Books, 1980.

Madden, James William. *Charles Allen Culberson, His Life, Character and Public Services*. Austin: Gammel's Book Store, 1929.

Martin, Robert L. *The City Moves West: Economic and Industrial Growth in Central West Texas*. Austin: University of Texas Press, 1969.

McComb, David G. *Galveston: A History*. Austin: University of Texas Press, 1986.

———. *Houston: A History*. Austin: University of Texas Press, 1969.

———. *Texas: A Modern History*. Austin: University of Texas Press, 1989.

McKay, Seth S. *Texas Politics, 1906–1944, with Special Reference to the German Counties*. Lubbock: Texas Tech Press, 1952.

———. *W. Lee O'Daniel and Texas Politics, 1938–1942*. Lubbock: Texas Tech Press, 1944.

McKay, Seth S., and Odie Faulk. *Texas After Spindletop*. Austin: The Steck Co., 1965.

Meinig, Donald W. *Imperial Texas: An Interpretive Essay in Cultural Geography*. Austin: University of Texas Press, 1969.

Miller, Edmund Thornton. *A Financial History of Texas*. Austin: The University, 1916.

Mooney, Booth. *Mister Texas: The Story of Coke Stevenson*. Dallas: Texas Printing House, 1947.

Nackman, Mark E. *A Nation Within a Nation: The Rise of Texas Nationalism*. Port Washington, N.Y.: Kinnikat Press, 1976.

Nalle, Ouida Ferguson. *The Fergusons of Texas, or "Two Governors for the Price of One."* San Antonio: The Naylor Co., 1946.

Neff, Pat Morris. *The Battles of Peace, An Autobiography.* Fort Worth: Pioneer, 1925.

Newton, Lewis W., and Herbert P. Gambrell. *Texas Yesterday & Today, with the Constitution of the State of Texas.* Dallas: Turner Co., 1949.

O'Keeffe, Georgia (ed. by Nicholas Callaway). *One Hundred Flowers.* New York: Knopf, 1987.

Olien, Roger M. and Diana Davids. *Life in the Oil Fields.* Austin: Texas Monthly Press, 1986.

Paredes, Americo. *With a Pistol in His Hand: A Border Ballad and Its Hero.* Austin: University of Texas Press, 1958.

The Perip: A Self-Guided Walking Tour of the University of Texas at Austin. Austin: University of Texas Office of Admissions, 1989.

Proctor, Ben H. *Not Without Honor: The Life of John H. Reagan.* Austin: University of Texas Press, 1962.

Ragsdale, Kenneth B. *Quicksilver: Terlingua and the Chisos Mining Company.* College Station: Texas A & M University Press, 1976.

———. *The Year America Discovered Texas: Centennial '36.* College Station: Texas A & M University Press, 1987.

Reed, S. G. *A History of the Texas Railroads.* Houston: St. Clair Publishing Co., 1941.

Rich, Daniel Catton. *Georgia O'Keeffe.* Chicago: The Art Institute of Chicago, 1943.

Richardson, Rupert N. *Colonel Edward M. House: The Texas Years, 1858–1912.* Abilene: n.p., 1964.

———. *Texas: The Lone Star State.* Englewood Cliffs, N.J.: Prentice-Hall, 1943. 4th ed., 1981.

Rister, Carl Coke. *Oil! Titan of the Southwest.* Norman: University of Oklahoma Press, 1949.

Rundell, Walter, Jr. *Early Texas Oil: A Photographic History, 1866–1936.* College Station: Texas A & M University Press, 1977.

Sandweiss, Martha A., gen. ed. *Historic Texas: A Photographic Portrait.* Austin: Texas Monthly Press, 1986.

Scarborough, Dorothy. *The Wind.* New York: Grosset & Dunlap, 1925.

Schwettmann, Martin W. *Santa Rita No. 1: The University of Texas Oil Discovery.* Austin: Texas State Historical Association, 1958.

Shelton, Edgar G., Jr. *Political Conditions Among the Texas Mexicans Along the Rio Grande.* San Francisco: R & E Research Associates, 1974.

Shockley, John S. *Chicano Revolt in a Texas Town.* Notre Dame, Ind.: Notre Dame University Press, 1974.

Sibley, Marilyn. *The Port of Houston.* Austin: University of Texas Press, 1968.

Simmons, Lee. *Assignment Huntsville: Memoirs of a Texas Prison Official.* Austin: University of Texas Press, 1957.

Smith, Arthur. *Mr. House of Texas.* New York: Funk & Wagnalls Co., 1940.

Sopher, David E. *Geography of Religions.* Englewood Cliffs, N.J.: Prentice-Hall, 1967.

Stambaugh, J. Lee. *The Lower Rio Grande Valley of Texas.* San Antonio: The Naylor Co., 1954.

Steen, Ralph W. *History of Texas.* Austin: The Steck Company Publishers, 1939.

———. *The Texas Story.* Austin: Steck-Vaughn Co., 1948. Revised Edition, 1960.

———. *Twentieth Century Texas: An Economic and Social History.* Austin: The Steck Co., 1942.

Stone, Ron. *Book of Texas Days.* Fredericksburg, Tex.: Shearer Publishing Co., 1984.

Taylor, Thomas V. *Fifty Years on Forty Acres.* Austin: Alec Book Co., 1938.

Texas Historic Crop Statistics 1866–1975. Austin: Texas Crop & Livestock Reporting Service, 1977.

Texas Monthly. *Texas, Our Texas: 150 Moments That Made Us the Way We Are.* Austin: Texas Monthly Press, 1986.

Tolbert, Frank H. *Tolbert's Texas:* Garden City, New York: Doubleday & Co., Inc., 1983.

Tyler, Ronnie C. *The Big Bend: A History of the Last Texas Frontier.* Washington, D.C.: U.S. Department of the Interior, 1975.

Walker, John H., and Gwendolyn Wingate. *Beaumont: A Pictorial History.* Norfolk; Virginia: Donning Publishing Company, 1983.

Walker, Lawrence, *Axes, Oxen & Men: A Pictorial History of the Southern Pine Lumber Company.* Diboll, Texas: Angelina Free Press, 1975.

Warshofsky, Fred. *War Under the Waves.* New York: Pyramid Books, 1962.

Webb, Walter Prescott. *The Texas Rangers: A Century of Frontier Defense.* Boston: Houghton Mifflin Co., 1935.

Webb, Walter Prescott, H. Bailey Carroll, and Eldon S. Branda, eds. *The Handbook of Texas.* Austin: Texas State Historical Association, 1952–76 (3 vols).

Welch, June Rayfield. *All Hail the Mighty State.* Waco, Texas: Texian Press, 1979.

———. *Going Great in the Lone Star State.* Dallas: G.L.A. Press, 1976.

———. *The Texas Governor.* Dallas: G.L.A. Press, 1977.

———. *The Texas Senator.* Dallas: G.L.A. Press, 1978.

Whisenhunt, Donald W. *The Depression in Texas: The Hoover Years.* New York: Garland, 1983.

Winkler, Ernest W. *Platforms of Political Parties in Texas.* Austin: The University, 1916.

Wyatt, Fredeorica, and Shelton Hooper. *Coke R. Stevenson, A Texas Legend.* Junction: Shelton Press, 1976.

Wylie, Nancy. *The Great State Fair of Texas: An Illustrated History.* Dallas: Taylor Publishing Co., 1985.

Zavala, Adina De. *History and Legends of the Alamo and Other Missions in and Around San Antonio.* San Antonio: n.p., 1917.

ARTICLES

Ables, L. Robert. "The Second Battle of the Alamo." *Southwestern Historical Quarterly* 70 (January 1967).

Adams, Graham, Jr. "Agrarian Discontent in Progressive Texas." *East Texas Historical Journal* 8 (March 1970).

Albert, Marvin H. "Killer in Skirts." *Argosy Magazine* (March 1956).

Allen, Lee N. "The Democratic Presidential Primary of 1924 in Texas." *Southwestern Historical Quarterly* 61 (April 1958).

Anders, Evan. "Boss Rule and Constitutent Interests: South Texas Politics During the Progressive Era." *Southwestern Historical Quarterly* 84 (January 1981).

———. "The Origins of the Parr Machine in Duval County." *Southwestern Historical Quarterly* 85 (October 1981).

———. "Thomas Watt Gregory and the Survival of His Progressive Faith." *Southwestern Historical Quarterly* 93 (July 1989).

Anderson, Adrian. "President Wilson's Politician: Albert Sidney Burleson of Texas." *Southwestern Historical Quarterly* 77 (January 1974).

Ashburn, Karl E. "The Texas Cotton Acreage Control Law of 1931–1932." *Southwestern Historical Quarterly* 61 (July 1957).

Baker, T. Lindsay, "Houston Waterworks: Its Early Development." *Water: Southwest Water Works Journal* 56 (July 1974).

———. "The Windmill Waterworks of Post City." *Water: Southwest Water Works Journal* 55 (March 1974).

Barnett, Douglas E. "Angora Goats in Texas: Agricultural Innovation on the Edwards Plateau, 1858–1900." *Southwestern Historical Quarterly* 90 (April 1987).

Bourgeois, Christie L. "Stepping Over Lives: Lyndon Johnson, Black Texans, and the National Youth Administration, 1935–1937." *Southwestern Historical Quarterly* 91 (October 1987).

Box, Tkhadis W. "Range Deterioration in West Texas." *Southwestern Historical Quarterly* 71 (July 1967).

Boyle, Robert D. "Chaos in the East Texas Oil Field, 1930–1935." *Southwestern Historical Quarterly* 69 (January 1966).

Brendt, L. W. "Helium." Article in *Encyclopedia of the Chemical Elements*. New York: Reinhold Book Corp., 1968.

Brown, D. Clayton. "Sam Rayburn and the Development of Public Power in the Southwest." *Southwestern Historical Quarterly* 78 (October 1974).

Caldwell, Edwin N. "Highlights of the Development of Manufacturing in Texas, 1900–1960." *Southwestern Historical Quarterly* 68 (April 1965).

Cardoso, Lawrence A. "Labor Emigration to the Southwest, 1916–1920: Mexican Attitudes and Policy." *Southwestern Historical Quarterly* 79 (April 1976).

Carleton, Don E., and Katherine J. Adams. "A Work Peculiarly Our Own: Origins of the Barker Texas History Center, 1883–1950." *Southwestern Historical Quarterly* 86 (October 1982).

Champagne, Anthony. "Sam Rayburn: Achieving Party Leadership." *Southwestern Historical Quarterly* (April 1987).

Christian, Carole E. "Joining the American Mainstream: Texas's Mexican Americans during World War I." *Southwestern Historical Quarterly* 92 (April 1989).

Cooper, Abby Wheelis. "Electra: A Texas Oil Town." *Southwestern Historical Quarterly* 50 (July 1946).

Cumberland, Charles C. "Border Raids in the Lower Rio Grande Valley—1915." *Southwestern Historical Quarterly* 57 (January 1954).

Curry, Terry. "The Man Who Saved France's Wine Industry." *Texas Historian* (November 1974).

Davies, Christopher. "Life at the Edge: Urban and Industrial Evolution of Texas, Frontier Wilderness-Frontier Space." *Southwestern Historical Quarterly* 89 (April 1986).

Doughty, Robin W. "Sea Turtles in Texas: A Forgotten Commerce." *Southwestern Historical Quarterly* 88 (July 1984).

Fickle, James E. "The S.P.A. and the N.R.A.: A Case Study of the Blue Eagle in the South." *Southwestern Historical Quarterly* 79 (January 1976).

Giles, Barney M. "Early Military Aviation in Texas." *Southwestern Historical Quarterly* 54 (October 1950).

Gould, Lewis L. "Progressives and Prohibitionists: Texas Democratic Politics, 1911–1921." *Southwestern Historical Quarterly* 75 (July 1971).

———. "A Texan in London: A British Editor Lunches with Colonel Edward M. House, February 15, 1916." *Southwestern Historical Quarterly* 84 (April 1981).

———. "Theodore Roosevelt, William Howard Taft, and the Disputed Delegates in 1912: Texas as a Test Case." *Southwestern Historical Quarterly* 80 (July 1976).

———. "The University Becomes Politicized: The War with Jim Ferguson, 1915–1918." *Southwestern Historical Quarterly* 86 (October 1982).

Grant, H. Roger. "'Interurbans Are the Wave of the Future: Electric Railway Promotion in Texas." *Southwestern Historical Quarterly* 84 (July 1980).

Grantham, Dewey W., Jr. "Texas Congressional Leaders and the New Freedom, 1913–1917." *Southwestern Historical Quarterly* 53 (July 1949).

Grider, Sylvia Ann. "The Shotgun House in Oil Boomtowns of the Texas Panhandle." *Pioneer America* 7 (July 1975).

Green, James R. "Tenant Farmer Discontent and Socialist Protest in Texas, 1901–1917." *Southwestern Historical Quarterly* 81 (October 1977).

Harris, Charles H., and Louis R. Sadler. "The 1911 Reyes Conspiracy: The Texas Side." *Southwestern Historical Quarterly* 83 (April 1980).

Haynes, Robert V. "The Houston Mutiny and Riot of 1917." *Southwestern Historical Quarterly* 76 (April 1973).

Hine, Darlene Clark. "The Elusive Ballot: The Black Struggle Against the Texas Democratic White Primary, 1932–1945." *Southwestern Historical Quarterly* 81 (April 1978).

Hollon, Gene. "Captain Charles Schreiner: Father of the Hill Country." *Southwestern Historical Quarterly* 48 (October 1944).

Holt, R. D. "School Land Rushes in West Texas." *West Texas Historical Association Yearbook* 10 (1934).

House, Boyce. "Spindletop." *Southwestern Historical Quarterly* 50 (July 1946).

Hughes, Pollyanna B., and Elizabeth B. Harrison. "Charles A. Culberson: Not a Shadow of Hogg." *East Texas Historical Journal* 11 (Fall 1973).

Humphrey, David C. "Prostitution and Public Policy in Austin, Texas, 1870–1915." *Southwestern Historical Quarterly* 86 (April 1983).

Isaac, Paul E. "Municipal Reform in Beaumont, Texas 1902–1909." *Southwestern Historical Quarterly* 78 (April 1975).

Jeffries, Charlie. "Reminiscences of Sour Lake." *Southwestern Historical Quarterly* 50 (July 1946).

Jennings, O. H. "Texas Rangers Praised: Make Short Work of Cleaning Up Oil Boom Town, Borger." *The State Trooper* (September 1927).

Johnson, Elmer H. "A Sketch of the Historical Development and Outlook of Manufacturing in Texas." *Texas Business Review* 12 (1938).

Johnson, William R. "Rural Rehabilitation in the New Deal: The Roperville Project." *Southwestern Historical Quarterly* 79 (January 1976).

Jordan, Terry G. "A Century and a Half of Ethnic Change in Texas, 1836–1986. *Southwestern Historical Quarterly* 89 (April 1986).

———. "Forest Folk, Prairie Folk: Rural Religious Cultures in North Texas." *Southwestern Historical Quarterly* 80 (October 1976).

King, C. Richard. "Sarah Bernhardt in Texas." *Southwestern Historical Quarterly* 68 (October 1965).

———. "Woodrow Wilson's Visit to Texas in 1911." *Southwestern Historical Quarterly* 65 (October 1961).

Kinney, Harrison. "Frank Hamer, Texas Ranger." *The American Gun* (1961): pp. 1–2.

Krammer, Arnold P. "When the *Afrika Korps* Came to Texas." *Southwestern Historical Quarterly* 80 (January 1977).

Link, Arthur. "The Wilson Movement in Texas, 1910–1912." *Southwestern Historical Quarterly* 48 (October 1944).

Machado, Manuel A., Jr. "The United States and the de la Huerta Rebellion." *Southwestern Historical Quarterly* 75 (January 1972).

Machado, Manuel A., Jr., and James T. Judge. "Tempest in a Teapot? The Mexican–United States Intervention Crisis of 1919." *Southwestern Historical Quarterly* 74 (July 1970).

Matthews, John F. "The Influence of the Texas Panhandle on Georgia O'Keeffe." *Panhandle-Plains Historical Review* 57 (1984).

Maxwell, Robert S. "One Man's Legacy: W. Goodrich Jones and Texas Conservation." *Southwestern Historical Quarterly* 77 (January 1974).

May, Irvin M., Jr. "Peter Molyneaux and the New Deal." *Southwestern Historical Quarterly* 73 (January 1970).

McCain, Johnny M. "Texas and the Mexican Labor Question, 1942–1947." *Southwestern Historical Quarterly* 85 (July 1981).

McClesky, Clifton, and Bruce Merrill. "Mexican-American Political Behavior in Texas." *Social Science Quarterly* 53 (March 1973).

Morgan, George T., Jr. "The Gospel of Wealth Goes South: John Henry Kirby and Labor's Struggle for Self-Determination, 1901–1916." *Southwestern Historical Quarterly* 75 (October 1971).

Neu, Charles E. "In Search of Colonel Edward M. House: The Texas Years 1858–1912." *Southwestern Historical Quarterly* 93 (July 1989).

Niemeyer, V. L. "Frustrated Invasion: The Revolutionary Attempt of General Bernardo Reyes from San Antonio in 1911." *Southwestern Historical Quarterly* 67 (October 1963).

Palmer, Pamela Lynn. "Dorothy Scarborough and Karle Wilson Baker: A Literary Friendship." *Southwestern Historical Quarterly* 91 (July 1987).

Pohls, James W. "The Bible Decade and the Origins of National Athletic Prominence." *Southwestern Historical Quarterly* 86 (October 1982).

Pollard, Clarice. "WAACs in Texas during the Second World War." *Southwestern Historical Quarterly* 93 (July 1989).

Pool, William C. "Military Aviation in Texas, 1913–1917." *Southwestern Historical Quarterly* 59 (April 1956).

Prindle, David F. "Oil and the Permanent University Fund: The Early Years." *Southwestern Historical Quarterly* 86 (October 1982).

———. "The Texas Railroad Commission and the Elimination of the Flaring of Natural Gas, 1930–1949." *Southwestern Historical Quarterly* 84 (January 1981).

Reese, James V. "The Evolution of an Early Texas Union: The Screwmen's Benevolent Association of Galveston." *Southwestern Historical Quarterly* 75 (October 1971).

Reinert, Al. "Closing Down LaGrange." *Texas Monthly* (October 1973).

Rhoads, Edward J. M. "The Chinese in Texas." *Southwestern Historical Quarterly* 81 (July 1977).

Rice, Bradley R. "The Galveston Plan of City Government by Commission: The Birth of a Progressive Idea." *Southwestern Historical Quarterly* 78 (April 1975).

Richardson, Rupert N. "Edward M. House and the Governors." *Southwestern Historical Quarterly* 61 (July 1957).

Roberts, Randy. "Galveston's Jack Johnson: Flourishing in the Dark." *Southwestern Historical Quarterly* 87 (July 1983).

Rundell, Walter, Jr. "Texas Petroleum History: A Selective Annotated Bibliography." *Southwestern Historical Quarterly* 67 (October 1963).

Russell, C. Allyn. "J. Frank Norris: Violent Fundamentalist." *Southwestern Historical Quarterly* 75 (January 1972).

Schmelzer, Janet. "Thomas M. Campbell: Progressive Governor of Texas." *Red River Valley Historical Review* 3 (fall 1978).

Shoemaker, Kyle W. "How Mexia Was Made a Clean City." *Owenwood Magazine* (May 1922).

SoRelle, James M. "The Waco Horror: The Lynching of Jesse Washington." *Southwestern Historical Quarterly* 86 (April 1983).

Walker, Fred L. "The 36th Was a Great Fighting Division." *Southwestern Historical Quarterly* 72 (October 1968).

Warner, C. A. "Texas and the Oil Industry." *Southwestern Historical Quarterly* 50 (July 1946).

Weeks, O. Douglas. "The Texas Direct Primary System." *Southwestern Social Science Quarterly* 13 (September 1932).

———. "The Texas-Mexican and the Politics of South Texas." *American Political Science Review* 24 (August 1930).

Woolford, Sam. "Carry Nation in Texas." *Southwestern Historical Quarterly* 63 (April 1960).

Wright, Carl C. "A University Reminiscence, 1928–1946." *Southwestern Historical Quarterly* 88 (January 1985).

Photographic Credits

Guide to Abbreviations

ABB—Courtesy Archives of the Big Bend, Fort Davis

AHC—Courtesy the Austin History Center, Austin Public Library, Austin, Texas

ANM—Courtesy the Admiral Nimitz Museum State Historic Park, Fredericksburg

BLAC—Courtesy the Nettie Lee Benson Latin American Collection, University of Texas, Austin

BTHC—Courtesy the Eugene C. Barker Texas History Center, University of Texas, Austin

BUTC—Courtesy the Texas Collection, Baylor University, Waco

DPL—Courtesy Texas/Dallas History and Archives Division, Dallas Public Library

DRT—Courtesy the Daughters of the Republic of Texas Research Library, the Alamo, San Antonio

FHMA—Courtesy the Fayette Heritage Museum and Archive, LaGrange

HP—Courtesy the *Houston Post*, Houston

HRC—Courtesy Harry Ransom Humanities Research Center, University of Texas, Austin

ITC—Courtesy the University of Texas Institute of Texan Cultures, San Antonio

KCRM—Courtesy the Kilgore College Rangerette Museum, Kilgore

MTRM—Courtesy Moody Texas Ranger Museum, Waco

NA—Courtesy the National Archives, Washington, D.C.

PPHM—Courtesy the Panhandle-Plains Historical Museum, West Texas State University, Canyon

RL—Courtesy the Rosenberg Library, Galveston

RRHM—Courtesy Red River Historical Museum, Sherman

SL—Courtesy the Ralph W. Steen Library Special Collections, Stephen F. Austin State University, Nacogdoches

SM—Courtesy the Spindletop Museum, Beaumont

SWC—Courtesy the Southwest Collection, Texas Tech University, Lubbock

TA & M—Courtesy University Archives, Texas A & M University College Station

TCU—Courtesy Texas Christian University Library Special Collections, Forth Worth

TPWD—Courtesy the Texas Parks and Wildlife Department, Austin

TSL—Courtesy the Archives Division, Texas State Library, Austin

USNI—Courtesy the United States Naval Institute, Annapolis, Maryland

UTA—Courtesy the University of Texas at Arlington Library, Special Collections, Fort Worth *Star-Telegram* Photograph Collection

Index